PRAISE FOR *OF BLOOD AND BONES*

"Witchcraft is not tame. We do a disservice to our craft in thinking so. *Of Blood and Bones* is an excellent introductory guide to exploring the depths of witchcraft and finding value in its darker side. Freuler leads readers through difficult topics in an approachable and authentic way. A good resource for anyone working with this side of magickal practice."

—Stephanie Woodfield, author of *Dark Goddess Craft*

"Witches are light, dark, and everything in between. This impressive piece of work both guides and encourages modern witches to reach into the deeper wisdom of their sacred hearts to uncover genuine healing and self-awareness. The book's original recipes, brilliant insights, and damn potent spells can be utilized by occultists of all varieties. This is the real deal. Written with intelligence, integrity, and sincerity, *Of Blood and Bones* is a brave exploration into the beautiful shadowscape of magickal work and personal development."

—Raven Digitalis, author of *Esoteric Empathy*

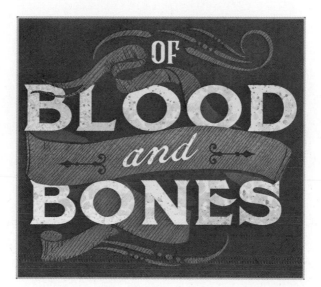

© Steve Knox

ABOUT THE AUTHOR

Kate Freuler lives in Ontario, Canada. She has owned and operated the witch-craft shop White Moon Witchcraft (whitemoonwitchcraft.com) since 2010. When she's not writing or crafting items for clients, she is busy being creative with art or reading a huge stack of books.

TO WRITE TO THE AUTHOR

If you wish to contact the author or would like more information about this book, please write to the author in care of Llewellyn Worldwide Ltd. and we will forward your request. Both the author and publisher appreciate hearing from you and learning of your enjoyment of this book and how it has helped you. Llewellyn Worldwide Ltd. cannot guarantee that every letter written to the author can be answered, but all will be forwarded. Please write to:

Kate Freuler
℅ Llewellyn Worldwide
2143 Wooddale Drive
Woodbury, MN 55125-2989

Please enclose a self-addressed stamped envelope for reply,
or $1.00 to cover costs. If outside the U.S.A., enclose
an international postal reply coupon.

Many of Llewellyn's authors have websites with additional information and resources. For more information, please visit our website at http://www.llewellyn.com.

KATE
FREULER

OF

BLOOD
and
BONES

WORKING WITH
SHADOW MAGICK &
the DARK MOON

· FOREWORD BY MAT AURYN ·

Llewellyn Publications
Woodbury, Minnesota

FIRST EDITION
Seventh Printing, 2023

Cover design by Shira Atakpu
Interior art by Eugene Smith on pages 122, 155, and 211. All other art by the Llewellyn Art
    Department

Llewellyn Publications is a registered trademark of Llewellyn Worldwide Ltd.

Library of Congress Cataloging-in-Publication Data
Names: Freuler, Kate, author.
Title: Of blood and bones : working with shadow magick & the dark moon /
    Kate Freuler.
Description: First edition. | Woodbury, Minnesota : Llewellyn Publications,
    2020. | Includes bibliographical references and index. | Summary: "With
    a strong focus on ethics, this book explores misunderstood topics in
    magickal practice, such as ethically collecting and using animal parts
    and bones, blood magick, dark moon energy, hexing, scrying, dark
    deities, graveyard dirt, and spells to assist the crossing of a dying
    loved one"— Provided by publisher.
Identifiers: LCCN 2020010129 (print) | LCCN 2020010130 (ebook) | ISBN
    9780738763637 (paperback) | ISBN 9780738763729 (ebook)
Subjects: LCSH: Witchcraft. | Magic. | New moon—Mythology.
Classification: LCC BF1566 .F747 2020 (print) | LCC BF1566 (ebook) | DDC
    133.4/3—dc23
LC record available at https://lccn.loc.gov/2020010129
LC ebook record available at https://lccn.loc.gov/2020010130

Llewellyn Worldwide Ltd. does not participate in, endorse, or have any authority or responsibility concerning private business transactions between our authors and the public.

All mail addressed to the author is forwarded but the publisher cannot, unless specifically instructed by the author, give out an address or phone number.

Any internet references contained in this work are current at publication time, but the publisher cannot guarantee that a specific location will continue to be maintained. Please refer to the publisher's website for links to authors' websites and other sources.

Llewellyn Publications
A Division of Llewellyn Worldwide Ltd.
2143 Wooddale Drive
Woodbury, MN 55125-2989
www.llewellyn.com

Printed in the United States of America

CONTENTS

DISCLAIMER

This book does not support hurting or killing animals or people for any reason. Please use common sense concerning the subjects of blood and earthly remains. Be ethical and humane when it comes to collecting bones and animal parts.

This book references the use of bodily fluids in ritual. Should you decide to incorporate these into your magickal work, be sure to pay attention to the safety precautions provided. There are several spells in this book that address healing illness and tackling addiction problems. Please note that none of the spells or rituals in this book are a replacement for medical attention, professional care, or legal advice. If you are in any form of danger, please be sure to take practical measures alongside working magick and reach out to the appropriate authorities.

The contents of this book are not meant to replace legal protection or law enforcement. Readers are advised to contact the proper authorities if they experience harassment, extortion, mental health issues, abuse, or immediate danger. The publisher and the author assume no liability for any injuries caused to the reader that may result from the reader's use of content contained in this publication and recommend common sense when contemplating the practices described in the work. Consult your health care provider before undertaking a water fast.

FOREWORD

"A witch ought never to be frightened in the darkest forest, Granny Weatherwax had once told her, because she should be sure in her soul that the most terrifying thing in the forest was her."

~TERRY PRATCHETT, *WINTERSMITH*

One of my earliest teachers once taught me that magick is like a knife. You can use it to carve wood, to harvest plants, and to cut and prepare your food. Like a knife, however, magick can be used in cases of self-defense, and in the wrong hands, it can become an instrument of harm to others and oneself. The way this has been addressed in the past has tended to be either avoiding anything that's seen as dark or harmful or the exact opposite, encouraging the use of the knife to harm oneself and others without much consideration of that responsibility.

Early books on witchcraft often divided magick into two categories, "white" and "black" magick. The implication was that light or white magick was good, and dark or black magick was bad. Not only is this a complete over-simplification of magick, but it also reflects an unrealistic view of nature, life, and the human psyche. Nothing can exist within nature without harming something else, but we can be aware of the harm we do cause and choose to be responsible about the degree of harm we inflict upon others.

A more realistic view of the nature of magick appears in a very unlikely place: a scene from the 1996 cult classic film *The Craft*. In the movie, the protagonist,

Sarah, enters an occult shop with her friends. She asks somewhat suspiciously and mockingly if the store owner is hiding black magick behind the curtain leading to a private room. The shop owner, Lirio, responds, "True magick is neither black nor white. It's both because nature is both. Loving and cruel, all at the same time. The only good or bad lies within the heart of the witch. Life keeps a balance all on its own."

In books addressing and exploring the taboo, forbidden, challenging, and darker aspects of witchcraft and magick, there's so much that can be taught incorrectly and irresponsibly and that can cause real danger and harm. Any witch worth her black salt isn't one to shy away from the darker aspects of magick, whether she chooses to incorporate those aspects into her magickal arsenal or not—a choice that only she can make herself.

Kate Freuler provides an honest, realistic, practical, and thoughtful approach to the aspects of witchery that are often viewed as taboo. From the lens of historical research, she showcases these different aspects of darker practices—many of which may challenge you and make you uncomfortable, as some of them did the author herself. In this book, you will find discussion on not only curses and hexes, but also the history, magickal theories, and purposes of working with different body fluids, using animal and human remains, ritual sacrifice, necromancy, and confronting death. She addresses ethical considerations without ever coming across as preachy and provides suggestions for ensuring that you're working from a place of respect, reverence, and personal responsibility in the most humane way possible if you choose to engage in them.

What strikes me the most about *Of Blood and Bones* is that Freuler, unlike many others who have written about these topics before, writes from a place of inner balance and empathy. Many books that have come before on these topics come across as sociopathic, expressing that anything and everything is permitted without any repercussion or thought about others, animals, or nature. This doesn't mean that there's necessarily a threefold law but that for every type of magickal act, there is a coin to be paid, and often that coin is the manifestation and unfolding of one's curse itself. This is shown again in the movie *The Craft* when Rochelle inadvertently curses her racist bully, only to feel horrible sympathy and guilt while watching the girl sobbing from a place of powerlessness in the school shower as her hair falls out.

Sometimes the coin is paid in other ways throughout the spellcaster's life. Some may disagree with this, but through close observation, we can see it clearly in those who are too quick and eager to cast malefica upon others. Often, we can see all the accumulating problems occurring within their life from an outside perspective, and the spellcaster seems oblivious to any correlation between the issues and their own magickal actions. This is where the notion of justified workings versus unjustified workings comes into play, and it can often be hard to discern when malefica is justified in terms of self-defense.

Yet Freuler explains that there are places and times for darker magick and helps guide the reader to act from a place of personal accountability and discernment. She uses the metaphor and energy of the moon itself, eternally waxing and waning, to explore how the darker aspects of magick are absolutely real and as such should be treated with the same amount of education, precaution, self-discipline, and self-control as any other weapon of defense or offense. She understands that one shouldn't be stuck wandering in the darkness endlessly. The dark moon eventually gives way to the new moon, which again begins its wax toward full moon.

This is also evident in the way Freuler addresses the topic of the shadow, a concept and term coined by the alchemist, psychologist, and metaphysical pioneer Carl Jung. Jung proposed that the goal of working with the shadow was to bring those darker aspects back into the light of conscious awareness so that we were not ruled by our darker impulses and desires but rather integrated them into a holistic balance of self-identity. This is impossible without exploring and understanding the darker nature of ourselves. The shadow has become a popular topic in witchcraft communities recently but is sometimes taught incorrectly as an excuse for bad behavior and a refusal of self-growth, serving as somewhat of a permission slip to wallow in one's darkness. Freuler, like Jung before her, explores the concept of the shadow as an integral part of self-discovery, healing, and self-growth.

Magick is a part of who we are as witches, so it's important to explore the darker sides of magick in safe manners under the guidance of another who is more experienced in these fields. That's exactly what this book offers. While the book is full of so many fantastic practical exercises and workings, even if you choose to never perform them, I still think this is a crucial book for any witch to read. A doctor needs a diagnosis of the patient's ailments before she can assist them, and the same is true for the darker sides of magick, even if it's the ability to understand and distinguish between the signs and symptoms of when someone is working against you or another and when it's simply a stroke of bad luck or paranoia. Freuler also invaluably presents a survey of historical practices and concepts that are often ignored entirely by the magickal community or embraced in an extremely unbalanced manner. Most of all, by exploring these topics, we can make some of the most seemingly frightening aspects of magick and ourselves a little bit less terrifying through knowledge.

In *Of Blood and Bones: Working with Shadow Magick & the Dark Moon*, Kate Freuler tackles some of the most taboo topics within witchery itself, and she does so in a manner that promotes self-growth and personal sovereignty for when those claws do need to come out and less savory practices need to be employed. Most of all, Freuler ends the book with a beautiful optimism often lacking in most other books on the subject. All of this makes the book one of a kind and an invaluable resource for any witch's bookshelf.

—Mat Auryn
Author of *Psychic Witch: A Metaphysical Guide
to Meditation, Magick, and Manifestation*

Introduction
IT'S NOT ALL LOVE AND LIGHT

Here's a blunt truth: we all have a dark side. It's part of who we are. Even the most peaceful of light workers casts a shadow. We all possess the ability to hate, to be angry, to be bitter, and to want revenge. Every one of us can fall into despair and isolation as we experience times of depression. In a physical sense, every single one of us dies. The thing is, if we can learn to acknowledge our own darkness honestly, we can control it and channel it into something productive. In witchcraft, it's important to confront and accept our shadows instead of pretending they don't exist.

To be truly connected to nature, the seasons, and the cycles of life, we must be balanced: we must acknowledge, accept, and embrace the darkness of our spirits and experiences as fully as the light parts. This doesn't mean that we should indulge in negativity and harmful behavior but rather accept these traits as guides and teachers in our personal growth. From there, we can transform our lives.

Facing your own shadow qualities is hard to do. When I first began writing this book, I very quickly realized that I was avoiding some difficult topics and, in doing so, was being inauthentic. I was editing things out, very carefully tiptoeing around some important aspects of shadow magick for fear of offending someone. I was trying to keep the subjects herein "safe" and socially acceptable by omitting the truth. The truth is that our shadows—our personal shadows and those of society—contain a lot of scary things that take more than a cleansing spell to vanquish. It was then that I realized I had to include everything in this book, even subjects I know some people will be horrified by.

It's often encouraged in some modern witchy circles to avoid the darkness at all costs and to stick exclusively to love and light, staying hyper-focused on the positive to the point where darkness isn't acknowledged at all. "Witches only heal and help; we harm none!" some argue. That makes witchcraft very palatable to outsiders, but is it really true? Is it even possible? Some people are more spiritually evolved and empathic than others, but no one is so enlightened as to be devoid of earthly, human feelings. Some of these feelings are negative. Humans have an amazing capacity for love, but we have the same capacity for its opposite.

ON CONTROVERSY

If you've been hanging around the witchcraft world for any length of time, you'll have noticed that there are a few topics that trigger large, loud opinions from all sides. Those subjects mostly revolve around ethics, as in what is "right" and what is "wrong." For example, many people believe that manipulative or controlling magick such as curses is off-limits, based on the premise that using witchcraft to interfere with the free will of another person is as bad as drugging someone without their consent. Not everyone agrees with this theory, believing instead that in some cases the free will of a person is causing harm to others and should be intervened with. This is a decision that's up to the witch.

In that vein, this book discusses other subjects that spark debate, such as blood, sacrifice, and animal remains in magick. These topics polarize the community but are undeniably linked to witchcraft in history and modern culture whether we like it or not. Things that are misunderstood and taboo are often subjects that need to be openly discussed in order to demystify them.

Because I have been working witchcraft for almost thirty years, my practice has cycled through many different phases of growth and change. Like many people interested in magick, I started off with the rule of three and harm none ever-present in my mind, believing that everything I sent out through magick would return threefold. However, over time, as I got older and more experienced with life in general as well as witchcraft, I started to see that things were not so simple, that it was not all fairy dust and white light in magick, life, or nature. Circumstances forced me to think about witchcraft from the shadow side of things. From there, I became drawn to these topics that are so inflammatory, only to discover it was difficult to find detailed and useful information beyond being told "don't do it."

◉N ETHICS

Ethics in witchcraft are discussed endlessly. Some people have very powerful feelings when it comes to curses, manipulative love spells, and blood and animal products in magick, sometimes saying these things are unethical. This book isn't meant to sway people in the direction of dark magick but simply to shed light on subjects that are often kept secret. What you do with the information is your choice.

Remember that the spells you cast have consequences. No matter what rituals and workings you do, it's important to think things through thoroughly first. Whether you believe in the rule of three, karma, or simply that like attracts like, your intentions and actions shape your future even when you direct them outward at others. You're responsible for the results of your magickal work.

Ethics and Cursing

Hindering someone else for your own advantage, however selfish it may seem, is actually natural whether you admit it or not. Everything in nature does it in order to survive, gain dominance, and protect itself. Animals often thwart or impede the things around them. They don't feel guilty about lashing back at the very creature that has set out to kill or harm them, either. When a larger creature endangers them, they fight back and they fight hard. When a porcupine is threatened by a coyote, it doesn't stop to think about the coyote's feelings before letting loose its protective sharp quills. That coyote tried to harm it, so the porcupine defended itself. That's the way it goes. But—and this is a big *but*—you must also understand that there are repercussions, and the interaction doesn't end there. Maybe the quills won't stop the coyote but only enrage it into attacking more violently, or it could become so distressed that it bites another nearby creature instead. What I'm saying is that there's a ripple effect following everything you do, and your spells can have unintended consequences, some of which you might not like or which might even come back to bite you in some surprising way.

It's natural to fight back against someone who wishes to harm or hinder you or those you care about. The emphasis on light and love has spawned the notion that when someone is intolerably cruel to us, we're just supposed to send them healing energy. This idea makes it seem like we're responsible for healing those who hurt us, which I strongly oppose. Not only that, there are leaders and rulers out there right now who are harmful to large groups of people. Why are we supposed to turn the other cheek and pretend we're somehow spiritually obligated to allow it to continue? Bad people exist. They do bad things. Sometimes these people and circumstances can drive you down into a place where literally your only recourse is to curse for the sake of self-preservation.

Curses and Love Spells Have a Lot in Common

Another ethical quandary is that of manipulative or targeted love spells. When you get down to it, the desire to curse and the desire to cast a targeted love spell sometimes come from a similar place: a sense of powerlessness and feeling like you have no other options. When I first began to study modern witchcraft, I was extremely curious about love spells. I experimented and discovered that just as in cursing, the results of love spells were often unexpected. The spells never actually resulted in the kind of perfect, fulfilling, movie-worthy relationship I was after. Sure, it brought a person into my life, but it didn't make them care for me. One time the person spent a couple of weeks with me, only to confess afterward that they were cheating on their girlfriend and regretted it. Another time, the energy in my love spell was so potent and desperate in nature that I'm pretty sure it made the person it was directed at feel suffocated and afraid of me, which was not my goal at all! Not everyone experiences love the same way as you, so you can't predict how a love spell will affect them. Just like that coyote I mentioned earlier, you don't get to choose how someone reacts to your spells, and this applies to both curses and love magick. You can't foresee how anyone, especially someone you don't know that well, will react to magick cast at them. You send them energy and that is all; the results of what they do with that feeling are out of your control.

Free will is a lot more powerful than it gets credit for. If the object of your love spell is fully devoted to someone else, chances are your magick will not overpower their will to do right by their partner, or at least not for long.

In all forms of controlling magick, be it for love or for cursing, looking inward at why you so strongly desire control over another person is one of the most important steps.

WHY FOCUS ON THE DARK SIDE?

While I wish that the only witchcraft I'd ever had to perform was healing and blessing rituals, that simply has not been the case for me. We all have a dark side, and the more we ignore it, the worse things get. But why write a book about such negative things? Well, I think these so-called negative or undesirable aspects of our lives and our characters are important parts of personal development. Every hardship you endure, whether it's the death of a loved one, a traumatic accident or relationship with a damaging person, teaches you a difficult lesson and makes you stronger—as long as you are able to make it out the other side. One of the most important things for surviving life's hardships is facing problems head-on.

Witchcraft, for me, is interwoven into every aspect of my life, guiding me in the right direction so I can try to be my best self. In this way, dark witchcraft has become a part of my life when necessary because whether I like it or not, life has dark times in it.

Like everyone, I've had people in my life who wished me harm. I've had to face very difficult periods of darkness within myself and deal with my own worst qualities. I've coped with some toxic people. In some situations, I thought I was the victim, only to find out I was in fact the villain. I have a shadow side that's probably deeper than my light side. These things are all difficult, but they're part of my journey, and witchcraft has helped me find my way through. That was one reason I chose to write about these topics.

The second reason I wrote this book is because I know that so many people are curious about "dark" magick, but it's difficult to get honest information about it. Most practitioners really do try to avoid causing harm and so have no experience with dark workings. Many times, if you ask about cursing, you will simply be told, "Don't do it—it's bad energy that will come back to you." But this doesn't answer the questions. It merely dismisses them, and it certainly doesn't help explain why witches are associated with the dark side in the first place. We're linked to some spooky stuff, such as blood, sacrifice, and evil, from error and misinformation, yes, but there is a small element of truth in there, in that witches can, and sometimes do, perform dark magick. The controversial ingredients in this book, such as menstrual blood and animal organs, also fall into the shadow category, as these topics are kept hushed up and because they cause so much argument. It's time we really looked at these subjects.

A Blessing or a Curse?

What is a curse to one person is a blessing to someone else. It just depends on where you happen to be sitting. That's why the ethical lines are so blurry. Here is an example from my own experience that sums this up.

When I was quite young, I suspected someone I cared about was committing crimes of theft and fraud. They were doing these things to get money to support a drug habit. I cared deeply about them, but they inflicted a lot of emotional pain on me and repeatedly put me in danger. This was a very difficult position to find myself in, and I didn't know what to do. Going to authorities wasn't an option, as that would possibly put me in more danger.

I did a spell to stop them from further harming themselves and others. I didn't specify how this would come about, just that they would be unable to continue on their destructive path. While this sounds like a reasonable thing, it's actually considered a curse, because it actively targeted an individual and interfered with their life.

Shortly after my spell, the person was arrested and went to jail.

Clearly, to them, this was a curse. However, to everyone they were hurting, it was a blessing.

So what seems like a curse to one person is a blessing to someone else. The opposite is also true. You may think you're doing good with your magick, but is it good for everyone? Is it harming more people than it helps? Does it benefit the whole picture? These are questions to ask yourself concerning your own ethics.

If you are in a dangerous situation, magick is not a replacement for legal counsel, nor is it a means of taking the law into your own hands. My own spell was cast out of desperation, powerlessness, and fear, as many curses are, and I share it here only to illustrate just how complicated the topic of ethics in witchcraft is.

HOW TO USE THIS BOOK

Part 1 of this book focuses on inner work, encouraging you to look inside at yourself, your feelings, and your motives. Before you perform dark magick, it's essential to look inward and understand your own place in the situation and how you got there. Divination helps with this process, as do meditation and dream work. In the midst of heated emotions, the desire to skip the inner work may be tempting, but introspection is absolutely necessary in order to move forward into the spells effectively and with clear intentions. If you jump straight into manipulative magick, there's a good chance it will only make your situation much worse. Understanding the true feelings underneath your motives is imperative for preventing disastrous results. The interesting thing is that once you've fully done the inner work, you may discover there is no need for cursing at all because you have solved the problem within yourself.

The other parts of this book are outer work, meaning actions that can affect the world and people around you. In order for the outer work to be effective in any positive way, it's imperative that you first do your inner work. Both are necessary for balance.

WELCOME TO THE SHADOWS

The dark moon phase plays a dual role in this book: workings are often performed during the dark moon, and the dark moon phase, or current, is a recurring experience in our lives as well. The subjects that this book addresses fall into the category of shadow work, which is the equivalent of the dark moon phase. Most situations that call for the workings in this book occur during difficult life experiences, or when the dark moon phase is cycling through our lives on a larger scale.

Are you ready to face your own darkness? We all have beasts to confront, but with practice and honesty, some of those beasts may become friends and allies, and some of those beasts may turn out not to be as terrifying as we have been taught to believe. Some beasts can be tamed and some may only be lulled to sleep for periods of time. It's how you choose to work with your inner darkness that counts.

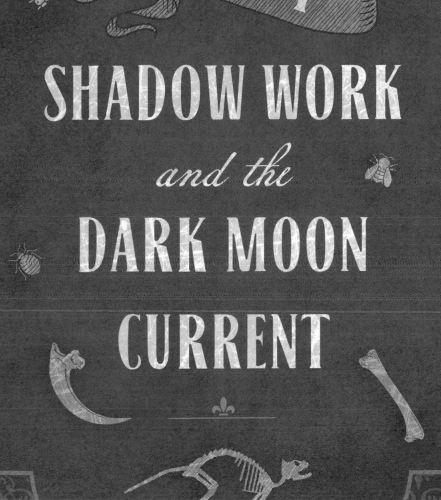

PART I

SHADOW WORK
and the
DARK MOON
CURRENT

The dark moon isn't just a three-day phase that takes place in the sky. The dark moon phase symbolizes something larger that we experience in our lives, sometimes multiples times, as we move through transition and change. The dark moon phase in our lives is the time to do what is known as shadow work in magick.

Our lives are constantly going through cycles just like the moon. Like the waxing moon, we grow and learn. Like the full moon, we see our ideas and plans reach fruition. Like the waning moon, we experience loss. After the waning moon comes another moon phase during which many people choose not to perform magick: the dark moon. Lasting only three days, this is the time of darkness between the end and the beginning. Usually called the new moon on calendars, there is in fact no visible moon in the sky, plunging us into true darkness. As we all know, the dark is full of mysterious things.

When applied to the larger picture of our life's patterns and cycles, the dark moon represents change or, more specifically, the space between when one thing ends and another begins. The gap between death and rebirth is one of life's greatest mysteries. It holds everything we fear and everything we wish for. For example, when trees and wildlife die in a forest, they decompose and become fertilizer for the earth in which new life grows. Without this death, new life couldn't exist. This illustrates that while darkness and death mark an ending, they also contain the next beginning.

Our lives and all our experiences mirror the cycles of the moon. While this doesn't always occur in synch with the actual moon phase in the sky, it's certainly observable. The dark moon energy is no exception and can be felt like a current moving through our existence.

Chapter 1
THE DARK MOON CURRENT AND LIMINAL SPACES

The dark moon current (or shadow current, as I sometimes call it) appears when we endure any kind of ending in our life. This happens in relationships, in projects, in careers, during loss, and when we must fight our way through difficult times.

Sometimes the dark moon current is gentle, and the ending it creates feels natural and complete. Other times it can be a harsh crisis that brings your life crashing down. Either way, it's often difficult and uncomfortable, as growth tends to be. Just as the earth, seasons, and moon rotate through dark and fallow times as they move forward, and just as a seed needs to germinate in the darkness underground in order to sprout, we humans must traverse the shadows on our way to becoming whole. We're as much a part of this great cycle as every seed and star, and our experiences reflect this.

I've heard it said that the dark moon is a time for rest and little magickal work. Likewise, when you're going through emotional upheaval and hardship, it's best to put your wand away and wait it out. This seems strange to me, as these energies have so much to offer. I propose we welcome the dark moon current, welcome the mysteries, and welcome the unknown. Let's stop fearing the uncertainty and instead embrace it. Once we have lived and learned the nature of darkness, we become wiser and more powerful than ever before. That's what shadow work is all about.

WHAT IS SHADOW WORK?

Shadow work is magickal practice that corresponds with the dark moon current in our lives. Shadow work is a term used to describe spiritual practice with our inner, hidden selves. It refers to working through trauma, ingrained behaviors, and facing our demons, so to speak. Shadow work is generally focused inward and involves confronting things that we have shunned from our public personality. Our shadow is where our darkest feelings, such as sadness, rage, wrath, and fear, live, alongside unhealthy behaviors, such as addiction, obsessions, and more. By facing these uncomfortable truths, we're forced to take a more awakened approach. Embracing the shadow means stripping away the ego and really facing ourselves, even the ugly, weak, or undesirable parts.

The workings in this book fall under the category of shadow work for various reasons. Shadow work is represented by the dark phase of the moon; however, as I mentioned, it is not necessarily in synch with the actual lunar cycles in the sky. The need to do shadow work is often brought about by situations outside your control or changes that throw you into chaos. Tumultuous relationships, death of loved ones, breakups, hitting rock bottom in your personal life, and loss are all things that can leave you no choice but to look inward and deal with what you find in there.

Shadow work is absolutely necessary in order to grow spiritually and live a full life. Often when you meet someone, witch or not, who has done their shadow work, you will feel it. They are wise and resilient. They're empathic and strong. There's something about them that says they have wisdom beyond the ordinary. They've walked through the shadows and come out the other side.

THINGS THAT GO BUMP IN THE NIGHT

Venturing into a dark moon phase in life and facing the shadow self is much like entering a mysterious enchanted forest, full of the unknown. There are some dangers that you must conquer in order to move forward. You may unearth qualities of yourself that you've been taught to deny: aggression, fear, anger, and weakness. Sometimes discovering these things is a shock, like reaching your hand under your bed and touching something cold and scaly.

Society teaches us to shove these feelings out of sight and to hide the darkness we have inside us. This makes it seem like these feelings have no place in magick and we should reject them. However, this is unbalanced and only leads to bigger problems, like ignoring a leaky ceiling until the whole roof collapses on your head.

Feelings of anger, revulsion, and dislike are natural. They exist within us for survival. They force us to fight for our territory and our safety and to protect what is ours. War gods and goddesses are not evil or bad; they represent a very real part of our human experience.

This book has a lot of curses in it and employs taboo materials like bones, blood, and body parts. I feel these items and magickal techniques fall under the dark moon umbrella simply because they're hidden out of sight with all the other socially unacceptable witchcraft stuff. Manipulative magick, hexes, curses, and banishing all fall within the realm of the dark moon for various reasons.

The dark moon, being a time of inner work and reflection, can bring your shadows out. If you've been identifying strictly with love, light, and positive thoughts for a long time, discovering these things can be as scary as meeting monsters. I call them monsters because if you ignore them long enough, they grow in strength and ugliness, slowly digging their poisonous talons into your mind, affecting what you do and how you live your life. The dark moon is the perfect time to face and release them, as this is when they are closest to the surface. To be an awakened person and truly understand nature, life, and spirit, you can't ignore or gloss over the dark side. You must accept the invitation when it calls and take the challenge because spirit has chosen this time for you to grow, learn, and become a true master of your own life.

When you enter the dark moon phase of your life, you will be up against some form of combat either with yourself or someone else. This won't always be pretty and you may not win, but you will definitely be wiser because of it.

SIGNS OF THE DARK MOON CURRENT

Nature, God, the universe, spirit, Goddess, the All, Source—these are all names given to a higher power, the force that creates existence. This force, whatever we choose to call it, is constantly giving us signs, symbols, guidance, and warnings in earthly form, almost like road signs along our path. Learning to see these symbols takes quiet effort and patience, but once you become aware of them, your life will drastically change.

The dark moon current (or dark deity, if you prefer) may try to get in touch with you through symbols.

The waxing, full, and waning moon energies—sometimes called Maiden, Mother, and Crone energies—enter and leave your life all the time. Once you're in tune with nature's great cycle, you will begin seeing their messages. Recognizing the cyclical phenomena of progress comes with peaceful acceptance of the hardship life brings because you'll understand it as natural and temporary.

Spirit showing you a symbol is not some bizarre sensational thing like movies would have you believe. There aren't lightning bolts or a big voice booming, "Look out!" The messages are much more subtle than that and often quite mundane, which is why many people fail to pick up on them. Symbols come to you exactly when you need to see them, in the little coincidences and small things that get your attention. Symbols you receive from spirit will always make sense to *you* specifically. Spirit will not send you puzzles to figure out. Usually when you see a symbol, the first association you make in your mind is the first step to deciphering what it means.

There are some "dark" symbols that have been quite consistent within the human psyche across cultures and back through time. Crows, owls, ravens, snakes, serpents, black cats, moons, cauldrons, deep wells, scissors, knives, keys, skulls, and bones are just some of the imagery that may come to you when you are entering a dark moon phase. If you're seeing these things again and again, it is time to pay attention to what is changing in your life.

How are these symbols shown? In the most direct way possible: in your real day-to-day life. On social media, the news, snippets of conversation overheard on the bus, pictures or posters you see in passing, dreams, even cloud formations—any way to get it right in front of your eyes!

If you're consistently encountering one or more of these objects seemingly for no particular reason, there's a good chance the dark deities want your attention. Remember, they don't necessarily herald a physical death. Rather, the shadow current is letting you know that a chapter in your life is going to end soon. This may sound foreboding or even scary, but it really doesn't have to be. Being a witch means accepting, understanding, and even embracing this period of darkness because it is essential to growth. Consider it a quest.

LIMINAL SPACES

The word *liminal* means threshold—any point between entrance and exit. It is a place of transition, waiting, and not knowing. Just like the dark phase of the moon, a liminal space encompasses the gap between an ending and a beginning. Our lives also cycle through liminal times, when we are transitioning from one phase of life into the next or when catalytic things occur that permanently change us.

Performing spells and rituals for shadow work in a liminal space and time can increase their power.

Liminal Spaces:

- Wells
- Where a large body of water meets land
- Cemetery gates
- Where a cliff drops off and meets air
- The crossroads

Liminal Times:

- The dark moon phase
- Samhain (October 31)
- The solstices, when day and night are equal length
- Midnight
- Dawn or dusk

Liminal Experiences:

- Moving
- Breakups
- Changing careers
- Grieving a death
- An unpredictable change
- Loss of all kinds

What all these things have in common is that they are the in-between time, when one thing ends and another begins.

In witchcraft, the crossroads are one of the most popular liminal spaces in which to work magick. Crossroads are literally an intersection of two streets or pathways that make a cross or X shape. This can be country lanes, busy city intersections, train tracks, or any variation of these. They're a place of transformation and change, which is part of the reason they're in so many spells. This is because like death and rebirth, the crossroads represents two intersecting events. They are a symbol of choice and transition.

Folklore about the crossroads abounds. It is where the goddess Hecate can be found, seeing into the past, present, and future. Faeries are rumored to gather there, and even good old Satan is believed to like it there. Some traditions also believe that in these places the veil between worlds is thinner and spirits of the dead can be contacted there.

A liminal space can be used to disperse energy, so place a charm there to carry its vibes in all directions. If you have an important message to send energetically, incorporating a liminal space will ensure it gets carried far and wide. It can also be used in spells regarding difficult choices.

While the absence of the moon in the sky is easy to understand as representing death, it's also a bridge from one place or form to the next, a liminal space that connects two things. That space of "nothing" is where great change happens, and sometimes great change is a result of battle and destruction. The dark moon can represent fighting from one side of a problem to another or overcoming any form of darkness to find light on the other side. Sometimes this darkness takes the form of enemies and rivals who we must face in battle—not necessarily with swords and weapons, of course, but with our will and our heart.

THE DARK MOON PHASE IN MAGICK

The dark moon is just as powerful as its popular, attractive sister, the full moon. When the dark moon rules the sky, you might feel a need to look inward at yourself. This can be difficult but is absolutely necessary. The dark moon energy forces you to see things from a new perspective—the shadows make everything look different. Your own actions and feelings come into a stark exposure, and you're forced to question your behavior, beliefs, and relationships. Your psychic abilities may be enhanced at this time, increasing your sensitivity to the feelings and intentions of others, which can reveal some harsh truths. In the dark, you can see things in ways you never did before, and all the shadows are visible: shadows in others, in society, and in yourself.

Most popularly, the dark moon is a time of meditation, divination, cleansing, and banishing. It's a time for truth seeking and growth. It's a time for clearing out the old in order to welcome the new. These undertakings are all socially acceptable ideas that don't sound so bad after all. They're safe and very politely omit the heavier stuff. However, there's a lot more to the dark moon than house blessings and protection spells. It's also the time when a witch does her dirty work. Dirty work can be unpleasant acts, such as exacting revenge, throwing curses, banishing unhealthy attachments, and drudging up an inner trait to look it right in the face and kill it. These experiences are the definition of *shadow work*, and they make us confront the most painful things and learn from them.

BUILDING AN ALTAR TO THE DARK MOON

If you are feeling drawn to the dark moon phase or are repeatedly seeing shadow symbols in your life (even stumbling across this book could be a nudge), why not create an altar to the dark moon? This way, you have a sacred space within which to commune with it and with your own dark side. Building a dark moon altar signifies your openness to initiation, change, and growth. It's an act that announces to the physical and astral realms that you are ready to welcome the energies of knowledge, wisdom, death, and rebirth.

As with any altar or sacred space, the dark moon altar doesn't have to be expensive or elaborate. It simply must be meaningful to you. You don't have to build an entire dark moon altar unless you want to. Instead, you can add objects to your existing altar during the three days of the moon phase. The rest of the time, keep these special objects hidden in a black box, bringing them out only during the dark moon. Keeping them secret makes them more powerful, and storing them in darkness further sanctifies them for their purpose.

When building a dark moon altar, use certain objects that resonate with this energy. I recommend black, dark red, or purple for an altar cloth and black candles. See if you can find some natural items that are of the dark deities' realm, such as black feathers, black stones, or bones and teeth. Some additional items to consider are figurines or pictures of the dark deities' animals, such as crows, cats, owls, bats, or snakes. Scissors or a small ritual knife is also useful, as is a cauldron-like vessel.

The cauldron is an important part of dark moon symbolism. You don't have to own a big, monstrous cast-iron vat from fairy tales. You can find small cauldrons for sale online and at metaphysical stores that are a perfect size to place on an indoor altar table. You can also use any dark-colored circular bowl made of stone, metal, or other fireproof material. What's really important is what the bowl or cauldron represents: a dark place of creativity, mystery, transformation, and change.

Another important item on the dark moon altar is a knife or blade. This can be a pair of special scissors (there are some very nice decorative sewing scissors out there), a small knife kept aside only for this purpose, a scythe, or even a pocketknife. It need not be sharp, as it is for severing energy only and creating endings in the astral realm. This ritual knife is used for symbolic killing of situations and things—never for objects, people, or animals, and is not meant for physically cutting anything.

From this altar space, you can perform the following rituals and devotionals. Leave your altar set up like this for the three days that the dark moon presides over the sky. In between, store your items in their box in a dark place until the next moon cycle.

CASTING A DARK MOON CIRCLE

If you're reading this book, chances are you're familiar with casting a circle prior to rituals or spells. Casting a magick circle is the act of creating a separate magickal energetic space removed from everyday life within which to do your work. This is meant not only to protect yourself and your working from unwanted outside forces, but also to keep just the right kind of energies and vibrations inside. When you release the circle at the end of your work, you are setting that energy free to spirit to manifest.

You can customize how you cast a circle according to your working. If you are working with the dark moon current or death energy, you will want to customize your circle to suit this. Below is a simple circle casting that compliments most dark moon rituals.

As with a usual circle casting, you will be calling upon the cardinal directions and their associated elements: earth, air, fire, water, and spirit. However, because you're working with death energy and darkness, you're going to be calling upon the elements in their most destructive forms. Just like people, each element has a shadow side.

Here is a table explaining it, along with some objects associated with the shadow side of each:

Element	Direction	Light Side	Shadow Side	Objects for Dark Moon Circle
Fire	South	Creativity, inspiration, sexual energy, victory, success	Destruction, anger, rage, war	Ashes, charred remains of a fire, an object that survived a house or forest fire. A piece of stone or dirt from the site of a fire, especially one that caused significant damage. An object that has been warped and ruined by heat either by your own doing or naturally.
Water	West	Intuition, deep feeling, emotion, empathy, love	Navigating sadness and depression, addiction, being submerged in others' feelings, obsession	Silt from the bottom of a pond or lake. This will contain decomposed plant and animal life. Fish bones (these are often tossed onto the beach by birds of prey). A lost object that has been worn down or destroyed by the water over time and washed up on shore in a state of decomposition and transition. This could be sea glass or some other man-made item that has significantly changed from exposure to water.
Earth	North	Prosperity, growth, fertility, abundance	Physical death; deep, dark change such as compost, decomposition, rot, survival instincts	Animal bones and skulls, dark earth from a deep hole, dead roots of trees from underground, dirt from a grave.

Element	Direction	Light Side	Shadow Side	Objects for Dark Moon Circle
Air	East	Communication, self-expression, connecting to others, writing and art, intellect	Knowledge of the dark arts, communicating with the dead and unseen spirits, crossing information between living and dead worlds, expressing the shadow self through words or art, teaching and learning hard lessons	Crow or owl feathers, burning dark moon incense (explained below), your breath taken during the dark moon phase contained in a bottle.

To perform the dark moon ritual, first choose your space and orient yourself to the directions.

Place your chosen objects facing their associated elements, either around you on the floor or on your altar. Many shadow magick books suggest casting the circle widdershins, or counterclockwise; however, I choose to cast even my dark circles deosil, or clockwise. It feels right to me to do so, as even though I'm making a dark energy circle, I'm still creating it, not banishing it. You can cast your circle deosil or widdershins, depending on what feels right for you.

Stand in front of your altar for a moment and take some deep breaths. Face the west, the place where the sun goes down, the direction of endings. Hold a jar of water and walk clockwise around the circle, sprinkling water from your fingertips as you go. I use dark moon water, which is explained in chapter 3. As you walk, state out loud:

> I cast this circle for protection.
> No unwanted energies may enter here.
> Within this circle we are darkness, we are germination, we are ending and beginnings.

With this I create a sacred space and time.
So mote it be.

Feel the barrier you have created. See in your mind the divide between your circle and the outer world. It may seem like a film of gray or black energy, a veil or a shield. The energy of a dark moon circle may feel heavy, almost oppressive. Contrarily, it may feel empty or cavernous. Dark moon energy is unique and feels different from life energy.

Now face the east. Gaze at the objects you've put there and consider what they mean. Remember the dark side of air: spirit communication and messages from the other side. Say:

> *Hail to the east,*
> *Spirits of air,*
> *Whisperer of secrets,*
> *Voice of the dead.*
> *I honor and invoke thee.*
> *Enter this circle.*

Imagine air swooshing into your circle and lingering there, perhaps in the form of the dead or your ancestors. You may also envision a grimoire that symbolizes dark knowledge.

Move to the south. Gaze at these objects, considering the dark side of fire: destruction, rage, revenge. Acknowledge that you have these inside you. Say:

> *Hail to the south,*
> *Spirits of fire,*
> *Harbingers of rage and revenge,*
> *Powers of destruction.*
> *I honor and invoke thee.*
> *Enter this circle.*

Imagine a violent flame entering the circle.

Move to the west. Contemplate the objects there, the powers of water to shift inner worlds, to feel the truth, to understand the dark side of emotion. Say:

Hail to the west,
Spirits of water,
Keepers of the deadly current,
The undertow beneath our lives.
I honor and invoke thee.
Enter this circle.

Envision a rush of black water running into the circle.

Face the north. Look at the objects, at their lack of physical life. They represent what is left when a life ends. Understand the temporary state of physical death, the fertility hidden within it, and the importance of transition. Say:

Hail to the north,
Spirits of earth,
Place of bones,
Keeper of corpses.
I honor and invoke thee.
Enter this circle.

Imagine a deep hole in the ground appearing in your circle.

Stand in the center of your circle and raise your arms above you to the sky. Feel the energy of the dark moon current streaming down into you. Say:

Hail to the dark moon,
Spirit of death and renewal,
Keeper of the great cycles.
I honor and invoke thee.
Enter my circle.

Now your circle is cast and you can perform your dark moon rituals.

To banish the circle, start in the west. Walk counterclockwise around the circle and say:

I cast this circle into the universe.
The circle is open but never broken.

As you return to the west, visualize your circle spinning off into the night like a wind tunnel or cone of energy.

A DARK MOON DEVOTIONAL

This is a simple way to acknowledge and make use of the dark moon energies each lunar cycle. Perform these monthly exercises each dark moon to acknowledge your shadow self, get in touch with intuition, perform a reading, and take full advantage of this special energy.

⊷ MATERIALS

Small strips of paper

Pen

Envelope

Scissors or knife

Cauldron or fireproof vessel

Matches or a lighter

Strand of your own hair or fingernail clipping

Throughout the entire waning moon phase prior to this devotional, pay attention to those things in your life that you wish to change. Any time you think of something you'd like to get rid of, banish, or outgrow, write it on a slip of paper and place it in the envelope. Keep the envelope hidden somewhere safe. You don't have to add something to it every single day, but having at least three things written down is best. Some examples are discord in the home or workplace, low self-esteem, a creative block, and even a person's unwanted influence over your feelings. In essence, any circumstance you'd like to transform can be written down and added to the envelope.

On the night of the dark moon, while you are sitting quietly at your dark moon altar and have cast a circle as outlined, visualize the dark moon current in your mind's eye. You may see a wise person, a cloaked figure, or simply a black hole. This is death energy. Take all the slips of paper out of the envelope and put them in a pile in front of you. Pick up the first one and read it out loud. Remember how you felt when writing it. Allow yourself to experience the feelings again, and then place the paper in the cauldron. Take the scissors or knife and "cut" the ties between yourself and the issue by slicing the air above the cauldron. Imagine you're cutting threads of energy between yourself and the papers. Feel yourself become lighter as you do this, the threads being released and floating away. Repeat this with each slip of paper. When you've done this process with all the papers, add a strand of your hair or fingernail clipping to the cauldron. This physical piece of your body symbolizes the parts of you being given over to the dark moon to be transformed. Do one final snip with the scissors between yourself and the vessel, separating your current and past self. Then, burn them all to ashes. If you wish, do some scrying or divination to seek guidance about how to move forward. Release the circle.

Scatter the ashes outdoors. Take a moment to present an offering to the dark moon and thank it for helping you grow. An offering can be a coin, a crystal, a pretty rock, or a cup of wine or tea placed or poured on the ground in thanks. As you leave your offering, imagine the vast emptiness of the black hole of change, acknowledging it with your heart.

Chapter 2
DEITIES AND THE DARK MOON

Dark moon energy comes into our lives in many forms: the faceless grim reaper, the fearsome hag, the grinning skeleton riding a black horse. This dark moon energy has many names.

Working with deity is something that many new witches fear. I've often fielded concerns about angering deity, invoking the wrong one accidentally, or offending a god or goddess. While some would have you believe that all deities are loving parental figures who have only your peace and happiness at heart, this really is not always the case.

In most of the workings in this book, you can focus just on the power of the dark moon. This is the most simple and raw way to begin and is something I prefer myself. For those who struggle with this abstract idea and would rather give the energy a face and name, I've made a brief list of deities who are associated with matters of death, renewal, revenge, and other dark moon pursuits. These are meant only as a reference point, for giving sufficient information on all of them would fill volumes.

The simplest way to begin to think about deity in terms of the dark moon is with the Crone archetype.

THE DARK MOON AS THE CRONE

For the sake of simplicity and because it is what works best for me, I often use the word *Crone* when referring to the dark moon influence. It's important to note here that not everyone gives it the same face as I do, and certainly not always a female one. Dark moon energy can appear as a wise man or sage, a faceless cloaked figure with a scythe, or simply a mass of energy. When I use the word *Crone*, feel free to replace it with what resonates with you. The name we give this phenomenon is not as important as understanding and connecting with what the dark cycle really is. The title is just a guidepost for the conscious mind.

Understanding the dark moon current in terms of the Crone archetype is a good start. From there, you can determine your own terminology and find what feels right. When calling upon the Crone (or sage, shadow current, or dark energy), you are invoking so much more than just the image of an old woman or a Halloween witch. You are stirring up and embracing the dark of the moon, the very essence of night, the nature of darkness, the sleep of winter. You are welcoming the primal ancient energy of death, destruction, regeneration, and the "unknown" element of growth.

The Crone is part of the Triple Goddess, who encompasses the three stages of life: Maiden, Mother, and Crone. These phases, and the goddesses and gods that fall under each, fit the moon cycles of waxing, full, and waning. The Crone archetype holds the cauldron of death and rebirth. The cauldron represents the space between endings and beginnings. It occupies a place wedged deeply in the human consciousness, a place of fear, for things disappear forever into that cauldron… or do they? The cauldron ends life but also generates birth. In its most basic, mundane form, a cauldron takes plants and animals and transforms them into life-sustaining food for humans. At its most metaphysical, the cauldron takes away our souls at the end of our lives and renders them into their next incarnation.

Such is the mythology of the Crone, the keeper of the cauldron. She takes life away and she gives life back. When winter comes, the light and warmth disappear into her cauldron so she can turn them into spring. A relationship ends and goes into the vastness, and in its place she presents opportunity and life change. When one thing ends, she always produces something new to take its place.

Eventually everything must go into the shadows. Even you. And that is why the Crone and her moon phase are so feared. The Crone rules over the ultimate unknown: death. She rules over the cold season when fields are dormant and trees shiver barren against the dark sky. She is the moment when the wolf kills the deer. She is disease, accidents, and killing. She is our own death and the death of everyone we know. She, and all the deities she represents, is the one who snips the cord that ties us to the earthly plane. Naturally, everyone fears her and her cauldron. But what people forget is that she is also a creator. Death is double-sided, for on the other side is birth. This is a law of the universe. The Crone and her deities also rule over new beginnings and fresh starts. The abyss of "death" and the unknown is a wellspring of knowledge, wisdom, and power beyond our wildest imaginings. The cauldron, or dark moon phase, is a place of miraculous transformation.

The Crone and the dark moon current are felt at times of initiation in our lives. She beckons us to follow a path full of shadows. Often she does not offer a choice to turn back, but instead forces us to go forward through the darkness and out the other side. She calls us in many ways. There is, of course, our physical mortality, when we are old, sick, or dying, but beyond this, she cycles throughout our lives multiple times, such as at winter. The Crone comes to give us the hardest lessons of all, those of death, loss, endings, and revenge. She challenges us to grow by facing our inner darkness (the scariest thing of all), and once we do, we emerge with a better understanding of ourselves, our nature, and our life's purpose.

The Crone presents us with what are perceived as the challenges and hardships in life, but she is also the opening of a new book. Always. She holds the keys of opportunity and light, but as with any quest, before you open the lock, you must first vanquish the darkness and find the door.

Do not fear endings or death, because there truly is no such thing. There is only change and transformation.

APPROACHING DEITIES

Deities are made of raw, primordial energy. Not all of them are nice and pleasant, just as all the forces of nature are not pleasant. A tornado, for example, is a powerful force of devastation that I would say is the natural equivalent of a god or goddess of destruction. There's nothing gentle and understanding about a tornado though, is there? Many deities are the same way: they don't necessarily have a moral compass that matches your own idea of what is nice or not, loving or hateful, negative or positive. They just *are*. It's up to you to channel them appropriately and carefully. While they may not actively seek to harm you, they do demand a certain amount of respect and acknowledgment, particularly the ones we are discussing here. When you do decide to ask these

deities to enter your life, they *will*. And they don't typically do their work quietly. Don't ask them to come and help you unless you're ready to receive their
lessons and deal with the consequences.

Sometimes people claim deities of death and destruction are bad or evil, but
that's only because they're uncomfortable with the destructive side of change.
This is understandable and natural: change is hard. It's painful. It can feel like
your world has been smashed. However, this destruction is exactly what's necessary to create something new, which the dark gods and goddesses know. The
old adage about having to hit rock bottom in order to activate change is an apt
one. If what you need is a harsh lesson or figurative smack on the head to get
you moving, that's what these deities will give you whether you like it or not.
This requires you to be honest with yourself about your situation and your
own role in it.

When it comes to invoking deity, also bear in mind that it's unwise to go
into it without doing sufficient research first. While it's true I'm only providing a brief list here, the list is only to get you started with a basic idea of what
these gods and goddesses do. From here, I strongly suggest researching each
one in depth before invoking them. In conjunction with research, a safe way to
get to know deity is to meditate with them. Each god and goddess has a different story and personality. To approach them blindly without truly understanding or respecting them can lead to surprising and uncomfortable results. Gods
and goddesses are often multifaceted, and it's important to establish a rapport
with them before asking for their aid.

Many gods and goddesses are alive and well around the world, being celebrated today in specific ways relevant to the culture from which they come.
It's important to learn about these current practices, making sure to fully understand the modern-day traditions associated with that deity. It's no good to
feel an affinity to a deity only to accidentally disrespect it and its practitioners
by not following the current customs for honoring it correctly. It's disrespectful
not just to that deity, but to the people who practice with them and the entire
culture surrounding it.

For example, Santa Muerte is an important death saint/goddess in some
Mexican belief systems that go back for centuries and has recently gained pop-
ularity with witches around the world. It's important to recognize that Santa
Muerte has living, present-day followers with a long line of traditions that

must be valued. While I agree she is definitely appealing and intriguing, that doesn't mean I can just grab her image and start playing around. If I felt really compelled to include her in my life, I would do several things. First, read all about her—history, mythology, modern practice, everything. Second, seek out actual traditional followers of Santa Muerte and learn firsthand how she is included in their personal practice. You can find lots of individuals online and on social media and learn from books written by them. Third, consider what she means to the culture she is part of and why. You will be able to get a feel for what is considered disrespectful to this goddess and how to approach her. Appropriating Santa Muerte, or any deity, by approaching her thoughtlessly is also offensive to her living followers. By insulting her culture, you're insulting her too. That's not a good way to get started with any deity!

This same thorough method can be applied to any deity you wish to learn more about. Pay close attention to the culture they are part of and their place within it.

Personally, I have a very basic and simple approach to deity, and I often see them in their simplest forms. For shadow work, I sometimes literally turn to the dark moon and work with that energy, for I feel it is a direct conduit to the shadow current. However, many people prefer more specific versions of this, with a myth or legend behind them. For some, it's easier to relate to a humanized form of primal shadow energy, something they can see in their mind's eye with relatable traits, features, and personalities.

These deities have been chosen for their associations with shadow magick. Read through and see if one stands out to you, and if it does, research it further before performing the rite that follows. If the deity you're looking for is not on the list, it isn't intentional. I'm only speaking of deities I myself am familiar with—specifically Greek, Roman, Celtic, and Egyptian. There are far more pantheons to examine from all over the world, so don't be afraid to explore all the information you can find.

DIFFERENT DEITIES FOR DARK MOON WORK

Each deity represents an aspect of the human condition, such as war, love, the arts, or fertility. Every pantheon around the world, while its myths and names are different, has a god or goddess representing these archetypes.

Psychopomps

Psychopomp refers to a being who carries the souls of the dead into the after-life. These are the creatures who rule over seeing people safely from this world into the next. Psychopomps come in many different forms, including animals. Their role is usually not to judge the deceased but to merely guide them. Psy-chopomps can be invoked when you are doing spells involving actual physical death. When you have a loved one who is terminally ill, it can be therapeutic to meditate with a psychopomp to gain insight into where your loved one is going and the natural cycle of death. Psychopomps can also be called upon when you feel the spirit of a departed person isn't resting easy and needs help getting to the next world. Sometimes when someone very close to you dies, especially if it is untimely, there can be a real sense of their spirit being restless. This is because they feel like they had unfinished business in this world, or they know you are grieving and having trouble accepting that they're gone. Asking a psy-chopomp for help can put them, and you, at ease. They can help you under-stand the bigger cycle of life and see that death is not an ending but a transition into something else. On a smaller scale, a psychopomp can be called upon to assist you with undergoing any type of ending, such as losing a job, leaving a relationship, or moving. Psychopomps rule over death and endings of all kinds of things, both literally and figuratively.

The Valkyries: The Norse Valkyries are strong warrior women on horses who collect dead soldiers and carry them to Valhalla (the Norse afterlife for fight-ers). They hover over the battlefield, deciding who lives and dies. Once in the afterlife, the Valkyries provide feasts for the chosen soldiers. The Valky-ries are associated with mercy and gentleness because they caringly carry the fallen. However, they are also ferocious and can destroy entire armies.

Anubis: The Egyptian psychopomp Anubis has the body of a man and the head of a jackal. Anubis resides over the purification of the soul and its journey to the afterlife. He also guards tombs and rules over the mummification pro-cess. Anubis weighs a person's heart, which Egyptians believed contained the soul, against a feather, which represents truth. If their heart is lighter than the feather, they are able to proceed to the afterlife. However, if their heart is heavy, Anubis will feed it to a monster known as the "Eater of the Dead."

Hermes: Hermes (known as Mercury to the Romans) is a Greek god usually depicted as a young, athletic man. He is a guide between worlds and the protector of merchants, thieves, and travelers. He is known as the messenger of the gods and can come and go to the underworld with ease, represented by his winged cap and sandals. It is also his job to lead the souls of the dead to the entrance of Hades, where they wait for Charon to pick them up.

Charon: Greek Charon steers the boat that carries the dead souls across the rivers Styx (the river of hate) and Acheron (the river of sorrow). Charon requires a fee for his service, so people would put coins in the mouth of their deceased to pay Charon for their passage across the rivers. Those who couldn't pay the fee were doomed to wander the shores of the river and haunt the living.

Janus: Janus is the Roman god of endings and beginnings in one. He is the God of gateways, doorways, and thresholds. Janus has two faces, one to see the past and one to see the future. He is a mediator between gods and humans and creates bridges between past and present, young and old, primitive and modern. His liminal characteristics to my mind make him a dark deity who can bring both endings and beginnings. It is said he begins and ends conflict.

Grim Reaper: Depicted as a skeleton wielding a scythe and wearing a black cloak, the grim reaper is perhaps one of the most modern psychopomps. This specter of death harvests souls of the living with a massive sweeping blade, severing the life cycle. Mostly viewed as sinister, scary, and even evil, the grim reaper has much in common with other death deities known for "cutting the cord" of the living.

Destruction and Change

Deities of destruction automatically also rule over creation, as they are one and the same. These deities are called upon to bring about transition and dramatic change. You will want to be careful in approaching these forces, as they do not tread lightly once asked into your life. That's not to say they are evil or bad but quite the opposite. They will initiate the change that is best for you, even if you don't realize what that may be. Sometimes change that is best for you is different from what you asked for and these gods and goddesses might surprise you with their results. If you're calling upon these deities, get ready for your life to fall apart and then be put back together. They can smash everything you know and rebuild it in a better way. Just be careful what you wish for.

Set: Set is an Egyptian trickster god whose head is a strange mix of animals atop a human body. Set is best known for his battles with his brother Horus, in which he committed violence and rape. In many texts he uses deception to get his way and is known as the god of chaos. Set represents all things that interfere with peace and harmony, such as destruction and confusion.

Hermes: As well as being a psychopomp, Hermes (Mercury) is extremely devious. A thief and a trickster, Hermes is thought to be a shameless liar. Hermes can be called upon when you wish to outwit or fool someone. Just be warned he might make a fool out of you too.

Eris: Eris is the Greek goddess of strife, hardship, and discord and is called Discordia by Romans. She is summoned to wreak destruction and havoc upon a situation. Her children, according to legend, represent a wide range of human misery, such as pain, murder, famine, and lies. She loves chaos and destruction and starts wars. She is associated with arguments and stirring up trouble whenever possible.

Loki: Loki is a Norse trickster and shape-shifter, sometimes called the god of mischief. Loki causes a lot of conflict for the gods and can change his gender at will. He is playful but can be malicious, and while willing to help in many cases, he is full of surprises. He offended the gods in mythology often and was punished, but he always managed to scam his way out of trouble.

The Erinyes: The Greek Furies embody the spirit of vengeance. They are said to inflict insanity upon evildoers in the form of pangs of guilt. The three Erinyes were named Alecto the unresting, Megara the jealous, and Tisiphone the avenger. They are hideous to gaze upon, described as having snakes for hair, dog faces, bat wings, and red eyes. They are tasked with doling out punishment upon those who interfere with the natural order of things and are particularly protective of mothers. In the underworld, they torture the dead.

War

Gods and goddesses of war are to be called upon in rituals and spells for revenge, victory, destruction, and competition. The energy of war deities is that of brute force and merciless attack. In artwork they're often portrayed as strong and vicious, usually bearing weapons and wearing armor, some carrying grisly trophies of their conquests. Some examples of when the gods and goddesses of war can be called upon are in court cases, beating a rival for a job promotion or recognition, winning the heart of your beloved, and even against physical illness that you are warring with. They can also be called upon for protection.

Horus: Horus is the Egyptian sky god and protector of the pharaoh. Horus takes the form of a falcon or a man with the head of a falcon. His right eye is the sun and his left eye is the moon. In an epic battle, he defeated his enemy but lost his left eye, the moon. This eye was replaced by the gods and became a well-known symbol seen to this day, the "eye of Horus," which is worn for protection and illumination.

Ares: The Greek god Ares (known as Mars to the Romans) encapsulates courage, masculinity, and law. While Ares represents strength and physical ability in combat, he also personifies the ugly aspects of war, such as blood and gore. Ares isn't well liked by the gods or humans but is accepted for his unquenchable thirst for battle and bloodshed. He is seen as dangerous, aggressive, and easily provoked into outrage.

Montu: The Egyptian god Montu is sometimes shown with a bull's head and other times with a falcon's head. He is depicted wielding a variety of weapons, such as swords, knives, and arrows, and represents the destructive side of the sun. He also stands for protecting family values and is strongly opposed to infidelity.

Odin: Odin, the Norse god of war, has a throne in Valhalla, the Norse afterlife for warriors. A raven sits on each of Odin's shoulders. One represents thought, the other memory. Odin is a father-figure god who sees and knows all. While he rules over war and victory, he, like many gods, wears more than one face and also rules over death and creation.

Thor: The Norse god of thunder and lightning has a violent temper and love of battle, which shows itself in his association with storms. He rides a chariot pulled by two huge goats. Thor wears a belt that doubles his strength and wields the well-known hammer Mjölnir, which he uses to defeat giants. His hammer is a protective weapon, but it is also used to consecrate and bless.

The symbol of the hammer of Thor is still seen often today in jewelry and fashion.

Artemis: Artemis (known as Diana to the Romans) is the Greek maiden goddess of the hunt, independent and equipped with arrows. She is called upon in midwifery, and when a woman dies in childbirth, it is believed to be her arrows that cause it. She is a protector of chastity, or, in modern terms, against sexual predators. She killed Orion for committing rape.

Athena: While a goddess of wisdom and art, the Greek goddess Athena (known as Minerva to Romans) is also a warrior goddess. She is depicted bearing military weapons. She conquered Poseidon in a contest over who would rule the city of Athens. However, Athena's energy is not exactly nurturing: she was the one who turned a young girl into the monster Medusa for being raped by Poseidon in her temple. This indicates you shouldn't disrespect or insult her even unintentionally.

The Amazons: These Greek warrior women live in an all-female tribe and only have contact with men once a year for procreation purposes. It is said they only keep their female children, either letting their sons die or sending them back to their fathers. They cut off their right breast to allow them to better perform archery and javelin throwing. Children of Ares, they are devoted to war and are known for their courage, brutality, and aggression. They have no use for males in their group and are fierce fighters who vanquish many. Amazons rejected the typical role of women at that time, which was to be subservient to men. The mythology of the Amazons is often referenced today regarding strong women who reject the rules of the patriarchy.

Rulers of the Underworld

Kings and queens of the underworld are different from psychopomps, who are more like messengers or modes of transport. The ones who rule the underworld reign over all the dead. They are not known for gentleness and are generally feared with good reason. However, they can be worked with in terms of understanding death and facing the darkest shadows inside ourselves. They rule over the empty times in life and can help in understanding the lessons behind loss. Be careful when dealing with these deities, as some are fearsome and merciless.

Re: By day, Egyptian Re traverses the sky as the sun, and at night he descends into the underworld to travel the dark waters by boat. Monsters, serpents, and chaos try to defeat him on this journey, but he slays them all and returns triumphant to shine another day. Re can help you traverse the dark times and come out the other side victorious.

Hades: Hades (known as Pluto to Romans) is the Greek ruler of the underworld. Hades is known for his mercilessness and for forcing Persephone to stay in the underworld against her will as his bride. Hades is the name of the god but also the underworld he rules over. Even though Hades is a lord of the dead, he is also associated with fertility of the earth along with cyclic order. The soul of the deceased is not able to cross into Hades unless the body has been properly buried in the earth. Hades rarely leaves the underworld, as he is not well received by other gods or by humans. It is said he is irreconcilable and does not respond to any sacrifices or pleas. In Hades, the god is accompanied by other ferocious, dreaded beings, and once someone enters Hades, they never leave. Hades's energy is uncompromising and pitiless.

Persephone: Persephone (Proserpina to the Romans) was forced to be Hades's wife in the Greek underworld for half the year. In winter, she is in the underworld, and during spring and summer, she emerges from Hades to rule fertile fields. Persephone symbolizes the shadow self and can be called upon to help you understand and accept the fallow parts of your experience, which we all cycle through inevitably. She can help you go from the darkness into the light and vice versa.

Osiris: The Egyptian god Osiris rules death and new beginnings. Usually depicted as mummified from the waist down, he has green or black skin to symbolize fertility of the land. While he is a god of death, he is also the god of vegetation. He is responsible for floods, drought, and success or failure of crops.

Hel: Hel is a terrifying Norse being of the underworld, her form said to be half woman, half rotting flesh, or half blue and cold like death. *Hel* means "hidden." She is the queen of slaughter and decay, said to trample upon corpses in battle. The realm she rules over is also called Hel, an underground land of desolation in the afterlife. Hel is seemingly viewed more as a metaphor for death than as an actual goddess. She was born of the god Loki and a giantess, so she is not considered fully divine.

THE MORRIGAN

The Celtic Morrigan is a goddess with whom I have a strong affinity, and therefore I'm writing more about her than any of the other deities here. The Morrigan is a triple goddess who encompasses all the aforementioned traits. She is a psychopomp, a war goddess, a harbinger of destruction, and a queen of death all in one, which makes it impossible to categorize her.

During the writing of this book, which was also a time of great change in my life, the Morrigan made herself known to me in no uncertain terms. When this triple goddess decides to come to you, there is no ignoring her. She is the bearer of great change, shifts of mentality, battle, death, and new beginnings. She is a warrior goddess and a symbol of strength. She is the blood spilled in combat. She is the spirit of the crows and ravens who clean up the dead after war, carrying their souls to the afterlife. She is also the queen of sovereignty of the land and the self. She is the terrible mother who kills in order to create, yet she loves her children ferociously.

I was seeing her symbols everywhere, it seemed: crows in the sky, black feathers scattered on the ground, symbols like skulls and bones around me. She made it clear that she was present and that while she brought painful and inescapable change, she was there to help me understand it.

The lessons of the Morrigan are tough ones. She arrives in the form of what seems like chaos and destruction, the end of all that keeps you comfortable and secure … but she only does this when it is in your best interest to move forward and grow. So while she is a harbinger of destruction, she is also a mother figure who will guide you through it.

Understandably, many people are afraid to call upon a goddess of death and war. The Morrigan demands respect, and should you decide to meet her halfway when she's calling you, be ready to accept some big changes. Her allegiance is earned, her wisdom is often achieved by overcoming a battle of some kind, and she has no time for dabblers. She should only be called upon in a curse that is for the greater good of many people and absolutely necessary. Don't involve her in petty squabbles.

About Her Three Faces

The Morrigan is complex and appears in many different forms, an old hag in some myths and a beautiful young girl in others. Sometimes she is a banshee, sometimes a great protector. Her blood-curdling shriek is said to have killed men in their tracks. The most well-known face of the Morrigan is that of a battle goddess. The Celts believed she soared over the battlefield during war, filling her chosen warriors with a supernatural fighting frenzy while striking terror into the hearts of the enemies. After this, she was believed to carry the souls of the dead warriors to the otherworld. Pretty scary, right? But there's more to her than just that.

The Morrigan bears the Maiden, Mother, and Crone aspects all rolled into one. Earlier we discussed the Crone archetype and how it fits with the dark moon phase of our lives. While the Morrigan has all three aspects, they fall on the dark side of the spectrum. To better understand her various powers, it's important to know as much about her as possible. I've gathered some information here, but like I said, it is only a start.

The Morrigan is made up of three sisters known as Macha, Anu, and Badb. They're all separate but part of the same whole.

Macha, the Maiden, is connected with the sun and earth, governing fertility and abundance. She is best known as the one who fights for sovereignty over her rich, fertile land. Macha is the one who swoops over the battlefields, inciting the fighting frenzy in her warriors and bringing death upon her enemies. Macha can be called upon to protect women, especially to fight for what is theirs. She can help you have sovereignty over yourself, your life, and your heart while bringing justice to oppressors.

Badb is most commonly connected with the Crone aspect of the Morrigan. She is the banshee whose screams signify death, she is the infamous washer at the ford who cleans the bloody armor of fallen fighters, and she is also the one who sends the crows to clean the battlefield by eating carnage left behind, thus transforming death into life. In Celtic legend, Badb was the keeper of the cauldron into which souls went to be transformed into their next incarnation. This same cauldron, when overflowing, would destroy everything around it. As the washer at the ford, she was a prophetess, for to see her meant you or a loved one would be next to die. Badb is a goddess of death and rebirth. She can be called upon for protection but also for guidance between endings and beginnings. She can aid with communicating with the dead and helping understand past lives.

Anu is the side of the Morrigan most connected to the Mother aspect, fertility, the land, and wealth. Anu is said to be the mother of all gods and keeper of livestock. Not a lot is known about Anu except that she is associated with the creation of crops and that she is part of the Morrigan. As the ruler of creation, Anu can be called upon for aid in creative projects and growth.

The Morrigan in Our Lives

The Morrigan shows up in our lives when we need her. I've seen her in my life in too many ways to count.

I've acted as psychopomp like Badb, at the bedside of my loved ones as they passed from this life into the next. I helped make them comfortable and tried to guide them through the transition when they were afraid. I've seen her creative Anu aspect in my writing and art as well as in motherhood. I've been a maiden like Macha in the most polar opposite of ways, as a fierce protector and as the provider of love. I've chosen my favorite people in the battle of life and protected and encouraged them.

Some say that you don't choose the Morrigan, but she chooses you. In my case, I would definitely say that is true. Watch for her signs and you will find her. Know that when she is meant to be in your life, she will come.

HOW TO INVOKE DEITY

To invoke a deity is to invite them into your magick circle to witness and lend power to your working. This can be done by having them join you in the circle or by inviting them into your body. In both cases, you will want to prepare an offering of thanks to give them afterward. How to do this is explained on page 40.

Each goddess and god has objects and colors associated with them, which you can use as inspiration to decorate your altar. Get a picture or statue of the deity to help you focus, and surround it with items that are sacred to them. For example, my Morrigan altar has crow feathers, a chunk of black obsidian, black candles, an incense burner, and a dark green altar cloth (I like to keep it simple). When you research your chosen deity, you will learn what items resonate best with them. You will also have meditated with them in order to fully understand their powers and whether or not they are right for your work.

Facing the Deity

One way to bring deity into a working is to invite them into your space as if they are sitting there with you. After you cast your circle, imagine the deity materializing before you. See their physical characteristics, such as attire, hair color, jewelry, and adornment. Now that they're before you in your mind, tell them why you have called them and respectfully ask for their assistance. Some people like to write out an invocation ahead of time to read to the deity out of reverence. This should include:

- Respectfully requesting their presence
- Inviting them into your circle
- Asking them for their blessing
- Thanking them for their presence

After you have read or recited your invocation, spend time with the deity and just *feel* them. Take note of images or thoughts that come to you. If they're part animal, perhaps they smell like it. Consider the texture of their skin, fur, or scales. You may want to touch them to make them more real to you. Are their hands dry and withered or strong and large? Is there light emanating from them, and if so, what color is it? Do they touch you back? Do they speak or tell you something with images or sounds?

You may feel frightened because some of them have great power that is overwhelming. You may also feel love, happiness, or even rage, depending on what they are like and what kind of working you're doing. While this exercise did begin with imagining the deity in your mind, as you do this, you will find they become quite real in the astral realm, with a life and personality of their own.

Now is the time to enact your spell, while the deity is with you in spirit form. When you're done, thank the deity, close your circle, and leave them an offering.

Becoming the Deity

The second way to invoke deity is to actually invite them into your body while you perform your rite. This should be done with caution, and perhaps not alone, as some people claim to be unable to remember things afterward. Sometimes the deity pushes the individual out completely and takes over the mind and body of the witch.

You can read your invocation to them as before, only this time instead of seeing them in front of you, feel them inside you. Sense your body becoming theirs. You may wish to sit or stand in a way that mimics how they are shown in pictures. Feel their attire on your body, whether it's heavy armor, jewelry, or light robes. Sense your face take on their features, their eye color, their hair or headdress. If they are winged or have a tail, feel the weight of the wings on your back and the tail growing from your spine. When done correctly, you should feel like you're partly the deity, partly yourself, kind of like wearing a costume. Perform your spell while they are inside you in this way.

Some would say that assuming the god form like this is reserved only for very experienced practitioners. You may find that in this trancelike state you don't feel like yourself at all but are a different creature.

For this type of invocation, it's very important to separate yourself from the deity when you're done, or you might feel unbalanced and strange for some time afterward. Thank the deity, close your circle, and give your offering as explained next. Visualize them leaving your body and walking or flying away from you. Spend some time focusing on your physical body to realign your energy. Lie on the floor or ground and become conscious of each body part, one at a time, starting at your feet. Wiggle them and feel the muscles working. Do the same for your legs, trunk, arms, and face, anchoring your senses in your physical self. Afterward, have something to eat and, if possible, take a walk to reconnect yourself fully with the present again.

Leaving an Offering

No matter what method of invocation you choose, remember to give an offering to deity after you are done. Leave your offering on the altar for them for several days after your ritual or place it outdoors. Your offering can reflect their characteristics and mythology or can be something general, as long as it is sincere. A common offering is to pour a glass of wine, beer, milk, or mead onto the earth in their name, while thanking them. Incense and flowers are also popular.

Make sure that for the time you are studying or working with a deity, you remember to regularly acknowledge them with daily offerings. This can be a stick of lit incense each day devoted to them in front of their picture or a special candle that you burn for ten minutes each day while meditating with them. The offering is very important; never call upon a deity for help and then forget all about them afterward. You will also find that as you dedicate these small acts to them, they will show up in other areas of your life, developing a relationship with you. Some deities stay with you for a little while as you work through a specific situation in your life and then fade, while others stick around for the long haul.

CHAPTER 3
DARK MOON CRAFTS AND BASICS

Communing with the dark moon in ritual doesn't require a lot of materials or supplies unless you want it to. The following are some simple instructions for items you can make for use in your dark moon practice, to deepen your connection to this special time. You will see some of these items mentioned throughout the book in recipes and rituals, so making them ahead of time can be useful. While they're not absolutely necessary in a spell, they strengthen its intent. For example, a plain black candle will do in a spell, but the death candle described in this chapter is even stronger. The same can be said about table salt versus witch's salt or olive oil versus death oil.

DARK MOON WATER

Moon water is a popular item found in many a witch's cabinet. It is made by simply leaving spring water, rainwater, or even tap water outside beneath the moon to absorb its power. Full moon water is the most well known, but this special liquid can be made at any time of the lunar cycle and imbued with the different qualities of the waxing, waning, full, and of course dark moon.

Dark moon water has a distinctly different energy than full moon water and is best utilized in shadow work such as banishing, cursing, destruction spells, and divination. It can be used for anointing ritual objects, for cleansing and empowering objects, or added to potions and brews suited to shadow work. Dark moon water is not fitting for all the same uses as full moon water. For example, using dark moon water for cleansing prosperity crystals simply wouldn't make sense, nor would using dark moon water to attract love. Dark moon water is reserved for very specific workings regarding dark magick.

⤙⟞ MATERIALS

Small jar with a watertight lid

Water of your choice. I prefer rainwater; water from a natural pond, lake, or river; or melted snow, but any water you have on hand is fine. If you plan on drinking this water in ritual, only use a safe source.

Stick for drawing in dirt or snow, depending on weather

1 black stone. This can be an ordinary little stone you find outside, a black tourmaline crystal, or black obsidian.

Sterile lancet (optional)

On the night of the dark moon, fill the glass jar with water of your choice. After the sun has fully set and darkness has descended completely, take your materials outdoors if possible, to a quiet place. Since the dark moon is a time of endings and beginnings, a crossroads or other liminal space is ideal. Draw an X onto the earth with a stick or branch. Envision the Crone, sage, or dark moon current guarding the cross you have created.

Place your jar of water in the center of the X. Draw a circle in the dirt around this. Spend a moment visualizing this circle acting as a protective barrier against unwanted energy, as well as a target that draws the dark moon. See a big tunnel of vibration between your water and the sky, like a gentle cyclone.

Hold the black stone up to the dark sky. See its blackness against the black of the sky. Say:

> *This stone, black as night, is a magnet.*
> *I draw the powers of the dark moon into this stone.*
> *This stone anchors the powers of the night.*

Drop your stone into the water. It acts as an anchor for the dark moon energy.

If you've read ahead to chapter 5 and learned about blood and understand the safety precautions on page 75, you may use the lancet to add a drop of your blood to the moon water. This step isn't necessary if you're not comfortable using blood or choose not to incorporate it into your work.

Tightly cap the jar. Leave the water outside overnight under the dark moon. In the morning before the sun comes up, retrieve it before any daylight touches it. Keep it handy and use as needed.

Ways to Use Dark Moon Water

- Drink it prior to doing readings with your oracle / divinatory tool of choice (only if you used safe drinking water to create it). By doing this, you will have the intuitive powers of the dark moon in your actual body.

- Add it to scrying water or ritual bathwater.

- Use it to cleanse items on your dark moon altar or ritual items used in dark magick.

- Sprinkle a small amount on your divination tools to boost their efficacy, as long as water will not ruin them.

- Anoint yourself prior to meditation or ritual, by placing a drop on the third eye or heart.

- Wear some on your body while sleeping to invoke intuitive or prophetic dreams.

- Sprinkle it around an area where a situation that needs to change is taking place: for example, an office or home where arguments have reached a stalemate and need to be transformed for the better. The same can be done for a situation that needs to simmer down so that a new one can begin.

- Use in spells for banishing, endings, hexing, protection, and divination.

DARK MOON INCENSE RECIPE

This is a simple incense blend that can be burned on your dark moon altar or during rituals and spells performed during this phase. You can also use it any time you need to be introspective and face changes that may be difficult. This incense doesn't include any specially purchased fancy herbs or resins but rather requires you to gather materials outside during the dark moon phase.

Go outside after dark when there is no daylight left. Go to a wooded area or cemetery. Look at the ground and collect dead leaves, small dry twigs, or shed pine needles. Take only dead debris to ensure they harbor the essence of death and endings. Gather them together in a jar. On the night of the dark moon, repeat the same ritual explained for moon water by leaving the jar of dried leaves and sticks outdoors under the dark moon.

Retrieve it in the early hours before any sun gets on it.

Make sure the plant material you select is completely dried before trying to burn it on a charcoal disk. If you wish, you can chop the larger leaves and needles into smaller bits for easier burning. Like the moon water, store this incense somewhere that it will not be exposed to daylight.

The purpose of this incense is for magickal power more than for scent. This is completely natural incense and will smell as such. Depending on what plant matter you put in, the scent may vary slightly, but generally it has a comforting autumnal smell. I appreciate this for what it is: natural. If you are drawn to more perfumed incenses, try adding frankincense or dragon's blood resin to dress it up.

Ways to Use Dark Moon Incense

- Burn some in a room that has energy in it that you'd like to essentially "kill" or get rid of. For example, use it after an argument or upsetting interaction with someone.
- Sprinkle the dry, unlit incense mixture over a picture or symbol of a thing or feeling you would like to halt.
- Take a small object representing a problem and hold it in the stream of incense smoke to symbolically eliminate it.
- Burn some outdoors while visualizing an unwanted situation coming to an end, allowing the smoke to carry your intent into nature.
- Burn during dark moon divination and rituals or prior to doing dream work during the dark moon.

DARK MOON BATH RITUAL

Occasionally, people who are sensitive to lunar phases may find that the dark moon is a tiring, difficult time. You may discover that you feel irritable, moody, drained, or even depressed. It may seem like performing a whole ritual is a bit much. In that case, a simple spiritual bath is a nice alternative, an easy act that requires little effort. The purpose of this bath is to cleanse away those feelings that come with the dark moon and make room for its benefits, such as regeneration and shedding unwanted influences.

For many witches, the dark moon is a time of letting go, purifying their minds and space. That is the purpose of this bath. Take this bath on the night of the dark moon, right before you go to bed.

⟶ MATERIALS
Dark moon incense

Black candle

½ cup dark moon water

3 tablespoons sea salt or Epsom salt

Purification essential oil such as frankincense, rosemary, or peppermint, diluted in a carrier oil such as jojoba oil or olive oil

Burn some dark moon incense prior to the bath to fill the room with the scent.

Light a black candle but otherwise keep the room dark.

Draw a warm bath as normal. Add ½ cup of dark moon water, the salt, and a few drops of your chosen oil.

Recline in the tub and feel yourself slipping into the cauldron of night. Imagine the dark water and reflections dappled on its surface are the midnight sky full of stars caressing your skin.

Take deep, slow breaths. Inhale the dark of night, and as you exhale, imagine you are blowing out any unwanted energy that may have clung to you throughout the day or week. Imagine a black circle in the center of your chest where you heart is. This is the darkness of the new moon. While it is empty and can feel lonely and dark, it also contains the potential to be filled up again. Spend some time focusing on this dark circle. Imagine it holds the energy that has got you feeling low, whether that's a nagging stressful thought you can't seem to let go of or just a bad mood. Acknowledge this energy, as it has a purpose. Let it speak to you, allowing images or feelings to float across your mind and remember them for later. They may be symbols meant to guide you, letting you know what underlying issues inside you are rising to the surface to be released.

Inhale the smell of the purifying oil and feel the cleansing salt water permeating your skin. Imagine the healing power of these things entering the hole in your chest, clearing it out and opening it up for possibility.

When you're done, dry off and go right to bed. If you have any dreams, be sure to write them down, as they may be meaningful and contain answers to your current problems.

DEATH OIL

This is exactly what it sounds like: ritual oil used in spells to symbolically invoke "death." Different oils are used often in spells: for example, anointing candles with rose oil for love or dripping clove oil on coins to attract prosperity. The same idea applies to death oil, only it is used in spells for banishing, cursing, and endings. You can put a drop of death oil on objects to symbolically "kill" something, such as a feeling, behavior, or action. Put death oil on a symbol of an illness to help quell the sickness, or put some on a photo of something you wish to banish.

Death oil is mentioned in quite a few spells in this book, so having a jar of it premade is useful.

This oil is made to encompass death energy. I warn you—this oil can be downright foul depending on how you make it, and there's nothing pleasant or fragrant about it like the magickal oils we know and love. None of the ingredients that go into this oil should have a shred of life left in them; they must be completely void of life energy. For base oil I recommend jojoba, as it never goes rancid and a little goes a long way. You will put your ingredients in a jar and cover them with jojoba oil.

Below are some suggested ingredients. You can use as many or as few items as you want, depending on what is accessible.

⊷ MATERIALS
Dead insect carcasses

Animal bones

Graveyard dirt or dirt from fallow ground on which nothing grows

Ashes

Dead leaves, plants, and sticks. Choose ones that are completely devoid of moisture or life.

An object that was used to kill something. These objects hold the killing energy they were once employed for. This can be small, such as the tissue used to kill a spider, or large, such as a bullet used in hunting.

Avoid poisons or toxic substances, as you will be handling this oil with your bare hands.

Collect your ingredients under the dark moon and put them together in a small jar. Cover them with jojoba oil. Sit in your sacred space, preferably at your dark moon altar or outdoors under the dark moon, and think about the decay and endings that are in that oil. Bury the jar in the ground, as you would a dead creature, overnight. Mark the spot by drawing a small circle on the ground. Visualize that circle attracting a beam of blackness from the sky into the ground, filling your potion with the energy of the dark moon. Dig the jar up the next day before sunlight touches it. If you prefer, you can strain the oil through a cheesecloth, or leave the items sitting in it. Your death oil is ready for use.

Ways to Use Death Oil

- Put a drop in the shoes of someone whose influence you wish to remove from your life (it will not kill them or make them sick, but rather kill the energy they're putting into bothering you).
- Write down a habit or feeling you'd like to banish, soak it overnight in death oil, and then bury it.
- Anoint candles being used in curses and banishing.
- Use it to bless the items on your dark moon altar.
- Put a tiny bit on your pulse points during rituals in which you are bringing death energy into play or invoking a dark deity.

WITCH'S SALT

Many kinds of salts are used in witchcraft for a range of reasons, sometimes to represent the earth element and other times for cleansing. Salt is an inexpensive and readily available item that is multipurpose in witchcraft.

Witch's salt has basically two purposes: protection and cursing. Here is a basic recipe that can be tweaked to suit your needs.

←·3 MATERIALS

5 tablespoons sea salt or table salt

Handful of ashes from a ritual fire if possible

Ashes from your own burned hair or fingernails

1 tablespoon of your favorite powdered herbs. These can be chosen according to intent, such as rosemary for protection, lavender for love, etc.

Experiment to find your own perfect mixture, replacing or changing the above ingredients as you please. Some people like to add a small amount of essential oils to match their intent or food dye in accordance with color magick. Just remember that dyed salt can stain many surfaces. The intent you add to the salt is the most important ingredient of all.

Some spells call for witch's salt to be eaten, and if so, alter the recipe by only including edible, nontoxic items. Be sure to omit inedible objects like fingernails and ashes if you're going to ingest witch's salt. Also make sure the salt is free of emmenagogic herbs if you are pregnant.

The purpose of witch's salt is keeping things that are harmful away from you or your home. It is used for deflection and for creating a barrier between you and unwanted people or things. Witch's salt is mentioned multiple times throughout this book. However, if you cannot obtain or make any, ordinary table salt will do in a real pinch.

Once it is charged with intent, salt has endless uses. Here are just a few examples, but let your creativity guide you and I'm sure you can think of more.

Ways to Use Witch's Salt

- Sprinkle witch's salt in your doorways and in windowsills to keep negativity out.

- Drop some into the footprints of a person you dislike to make them stay away.

- Include it in curses, hexes, and crossing spells to enhance their efficacy. For example, it can be added to the stuffing of poppets or mixed into candle wax. You can throw witch's salt onto the property of an enemy to make them stay away from you and also give them a taste of their own medicine. It is believed that when an enemy is near the salt, they will intuitively become uncomfortable and want to leave. Have some handy to ward off rude coworkers, nosy neighbors, or toxic people.

- Throw a small handful of salt away from yourself into the wind while envisioning someone you would like distance from.

- Sprinkle it around the edge of your house to form a barrier. If you are having issues with a next-door neighbor, make a line with the salt all along the edge of the property to keep them on their side.
- Pour it onto a picture of a person who is bothering you to make them stay away. You can also pour it onto a symbol or image of a problem for the same end.
- Put a tiny pinch in an enemy's food to quiet their negativity. Put some on your own food to protect yourself.
- Add a pinch to oils, incenses, and room sprays.
- Roll ritual candles in it prior to burning.
- Pour some around your floor and allow it to sit and absorb negativity for a few minutes. Then vacuum it up.
- Add a pinch to your bathwater.
- Make a sachet by tying some salt into a piece of black cloth. Place the sachet under the bed to prevent nightmares or in your home or workplace to absorb bad moods.
- Rub a pinch of salt between your fingers when stressed to absorb the energy. Then rinse it off down the drain or throw it away.

DEATH CANDLES

An easy means of performing a simple banishing ritual is to burn a death candle. It's called a death candle because it is used to end something or bring death upon a situation. This doesn't mean it will kill another person but rather bring about change.

Making a few of these candles ahead of time on the night of the dark moon is useful. When you need to use them, simply carve a word or symbol representing your issue into the side of it and burn it.

⟶ MATERIALS

Dark moon water

Black taper candle(s)

Death oil

Witch's salt

Hard surface to work on

On the night of the dark moon gather your supplies. Invoke the dark moon, inviting it to touch on your candles and bless your activities.

Get some drops of dark moon water on your fingertips and dribble them onto the candles to cleanse them.

Put some death oil on your fingers and massage it into the candle. Start in the middle, massaging the oil outward to the ends. This is a "pushing away" action used in anointing spell candles in banishing.

Generously sprinkle the witch's salt on your hard surface, and roll your oiled candle in it. Salt will cling to the outside of the candle.

Now, hold the candle toward the dark sky and chant repeatedly:

> Absence of light,
> Filled completely with night.

As you chant, allow the power of the dark sky to fill the candle. Feel the dead weight of the candle in your hands, the blackness permeating through it completely. Repeat this with each candle.

You can light this candle for a specified amount of time each day during the waning moon until the candle is gone and so is the problem you wish to end. When you light it, spend about 10 minutes imagining the situation ending or the thing you wish to banish being snuffed out. You can also simply have a death candle burning during any appropriate dark moon spell or ritual to increase the death energy in your working.

To store death candles you've made ahead of time, place them in a box with a lid, and completely cover them in witch's salt. Store the box where it will not be disturbed. When you wish to use one, simply take it from the box and leave the remaining ones covered in witch's salt in the closed box until you need them.

Ways to Use Death Candles

- Banishing foul moods
- Clearing out energy after an argument or other distressing emotional situation
- Breaking unhealthy ties to another person
- Easing heartbreak
- Destroying someone's power over you

- Ending the destructive or hurtful behavior of another person
- Breaking up relationships
- Hindering a person's actions

MISCELLANEOUS DARK MOON CRAFTS

Banishing Ink

You can use this ink in any dark spells that require writing, or simply paint it over a picture of your problem, effectively "blacking out" the issue.

MATERIALS

Tea tree oil

Jar of black ink, such as India ink

Juniper berry

Add 5 to 10 drops of tea tree oil to the ink. Tea tree oil is a powerful cleansing agent and can be used in magick the same way. Next add the juniper berry, which is associated with protection. Let the juniper berry sit in the ink.

Leave the jar under the dark moon for a night, infusing it with dark moon power of endings. Like your other dark moon items, don't allow sunlight to touch it.

Body Paint

Use this paint to draw a black circle over your heart during a dark moon ritual or during meditation to help you understand the dark moon current in your life. The black circle over your heart will connect you to the dark moon and draw upon its wisdom.

MATERIALS

Piece of black obsidian

Small seed like apple or sunflower

Black liquid body paint

Black obsidian was once molten lava that cooled on contact with air or water, forming a black glass. This means that like the dark of the moon, this particular mineraloid is in a state of flux between one form and another. It's a direct product of destruction and transformation.

The seed represents potential for fresh new beginnings.

Place both inside the bottle of body paint and empower it with dark moon energy. You can also use this body paint to decorate your skin with sigils and symbols in future rituals. If you wish to banish something, draw a symbol of it on your body and then let it wash off in a dark moon bath.

Crossroads Charm

This charm is for when you're facing a decision or big change but can't make up your mind which course of action to take.

←─§ MATERIALS

2 small sticks or bones

1 foot string or twine

Hold a stick or bone in each hand. As you examine the one in your right hand, visualize one outcome of the problem you are considering. Now concentrate on the stick or bone in your left hand and consider an alternative option. The sticks represent the two contradicting ways you are leaning. Now tie them together in the shape of an X, binding them with the string.

On the night of the dark moon, go to a crossroads or intersection, preferably one that is not terribly busy. Whisper your question to the charm you made. Hide it somewhere near the crossroads where you will not lose it, and leave it overnight. Some ideas for hiding spots in an urban area are a flowerpot nearby you could tuck it into, a deep crack in the sidewalk, or in a building facade. In the country, where there are fewer people walking, you could wrap it in identifiable cloth before leaving it on the ground so that you can find it the next day.

Collect the charm the next morning and carry it with you. You will be guided in the best direction.

Keep the materials to use again the next time you're facing a big decision.

Crone's Egg

While an egg is typically a symbol of springtime and fertility, it can also represent death and rebirth when used intentionally. The shell in this case is empty and holds both the nothingness of death and the potential of life. Emptiness is nothing and everything at the same time.

To remove the egg from its shell, carefully use a nail to tap a hole in the top and bottom of the egg—surprisingly easy to do without breaking it—and blow the yolk and albumen out, leaving an empty but intact shell. This may sound odd, but it's a common method of preparing eggs for decorating. It also allows you to keep the egg for an indefinite length of time because it won't go bad.

⊷ MATERIALS

An intact eggshell, preferably from a chicken (substitution: empty
    nutshell)

Paints or markers

Decorate your egg with markers or paint, drawing an image of what the Crone looks like to you. This can be a face peeking out of black robes, an image of a scythe, or even just painting the whole egg black.

When it's ready, ask the Crone to come to your altar and bless it with her knowledge and wisdom. Ask her to fill the egg with what you need to know at this moment in your life. Sleep with the egg under or near your bed, and look for answers in your dreams.

Gravestone Crystal

All you need for this charm is a quartz crystal of your choosing and access to the gravesite of your relatives, ancestors, or a friend who has passed.

When visiting their grave, take the crystal with you. Standing or sitting at their tombstone, explain to them what you need guidance or help with in your life right now and that you are leaving the crystal there for them to program with their advice, good wishes, and aid. This can be done out loud or in your head. Leave the crystal on the gravestone or earth for one full moon cycle. When you return to the grave, find your crystal, thank the spirit, and leave an offering of money, flowers, or a libation. Carry the crystal with you to keep their good blessings near. They will be protecting and guiding you in subtle ways anytime you carry the crystal with you.

CHAPTER 4
DARK MOON DIVINATION

The dark moon is usually said to be a time for divination and self-reflection. It's certainly a period when energy leans toward intuition, deep feeling, and introspection. This is true when it's literally the dark moon phase in the sky and also when the dark moon current is cycling through your life in a bigger way. Sometimes you may not feel up to performing spell work during the dark moon, but these vibrations are perfect for divination.

The dark moon phase is a good time to perform a reading for yourself to touch base with what is going on inside you. Since the dark moon pulls our shadow selves to the surface, readings done during this time, whether with tarot, scrying, or other oracles, tend to be especially informative and precise. Occasionally, they can cut to the truth of the matter and even feel a little harsh. While this is not always comfortable, it's necessary, especially if you are considering casting spells that fall into the category of dark magick.

MEDITATIVE STATE

Before you begin practicing the divining techniques explained in this book, it's important to understand that a key element of divination is achieving a heightened or meditative mental state. Here is a simple way to get into the correct mindset.

Sit comfortably in a place you will not be disturbed. Close your eyes.

Become aware of your physical body. Feel the clothing and air touching your skin. Notice your lungs filling with air as you breathe, and note the warm air exiting every time you exhale. What, if anything, is below your feet, and how does it feel? What sounds do you hear around you? This focus on the immediate present creates a mind space that excludes intrusive thoughts and worries.

Now focus on your breathing. Take five deep, slow breaths, and get used to how this feels. You will immediately notice your heart slowing down and muscles loosening.

Imagine a large tree in your mind. The tree has a complex root system under the ground that perfectly mirrors its branches, which reach up into the sky. The branches above reach up to spirit, and the roots below keep it grounded in the earthly plane. You are like this tree, grounded in the earthly plane yet open to the world of spirit in equal measure.

As you inhale, imagine roots shooting from your feet or the base of your spine into the earth. On your next breath, imagine branches reaching up out of the crown of your head.

With every breath, feel your branches and roots extending equally, reaching, growing, and expanding. Leaves sprout and uncurl on the branches, opening to the light to be filled with energy and messages from spirit. The roots thrive in darkness, burrowing their way to water and sustenance, anchoring you.

Hold this image for as long as feels comfortable or until your mind starts to wander.

Now you can perform your divination.

SCRYING

One of the most popular types of divination is called scrying. Gazing into a crystal ball is the most well-known technique, but scrying can be performed in many ways, no crystal ball necessary.

Simply put, scrying is the act of gazing into a reflective surface, seeing pictures, and interpreting them to tell the future. However, since everyone is unique, we all experience scrying in slightly different ways, and unfortunately it isn't as simple as passively staring at an object.

Being familiar with meditation is a must in order to receive messages through scrying. Trying to scry in a distracted mind state will only lead to frustration. In order for your mind to be open enough to receive information, images, or omens, you must be relaxed and receptive.

Scrying can be performed on any surface that is shiny and dark. A black bowl filled with water will work, as will a black mirror or large chunk of obsidian. You can purchase beautiful scrying mirrors or make your own.

Scrying is simple, in theory. You gaze at the reflective surface and relax. Let your vision go soft, do some deep breathing, and allow the messages to roll in. It sounds easy, but it's not. It takes practice.

Scrying is typically believed to be visual, an assumption based on the crystal ball. But real scrying can be, and often is, much more like a full-on sensory experience. Communication can come through auditory means, clairsentience, and even taste. The act of gazing at an object is in fact just a way to focus your mind on one simple thing to the exclusion of all else, clearing and therefore opening your subconscious mind to spirit activity. In other words, gazing at a reflective surface aids your meditative state.

There are different ways to experience incoming information while scrying. Before performing the scrying exercise on the next page, be prepared for any of these types of experience:

Visual: Some people see actual pictures of things in front of their physical eyes. This is uncommon, but it does happen. It's more typical to see clouds or mists of color in your field of vision, in which case pay attention to what the color represents to you in relation to your query. If you relax your eyes while gazing at your scrying object, you may see shapes, swirls, and other forms coming and going. Take note of them without judgment; you can interpret them later. Reflections on the shiny surface may move and look like objects as well.

Mental Images: You may receive a mental visual, which is a picture in your mind and not in front of your eyes. These images flash into your mind as if you're imagining something. This can be moving or still pictures of people you know, places, or objects. These are often symbolic images that you will need to interpret later. If you're having intrusive thoughts about your immediate person—your nose is itchy, you forgot to check the stove burner—you're not relaxed enough. Those thoughts aren't related to scrying.

Auditory: It may sound odd, but there have been times when I was so deep in meditation that I heard actual words said. I understood that this was coming from inside me, but it was very much like physically hearing words, like overhearing snatches of a conversation. If this happens, it's important to remember the phrases you hear and write them down afterward. You may be somewhere you can hear the wind, birds, crickets, traffic, or other noises. Relax into the patterns and swells of the sounds and see if they morph into something else in your altered state.

Tactile: You may have actual physical feelings in and around your body, such as heat, prickles, or chills. Even a sense of pain or pressure in a certain part of your body may appear. This can be spirit attempting to tell you something pertaining to your question or just letting you know it is present.

Some tidbits that have come to me while scrying include a song I know suddenly coming into my mind, and later on when I look up the lyrics, they apply directly to my situation. Other times I'll be shown a hallway or room with objects to look at in it. Another time I was inundated with snowy owls every time I scried and started seeing them literally everywhere I looked in waking life. You just never know what you're going to see.

Scrying Step by Step

My preferred scrying method during the dark moon phase is to use a large black bowl or cauldron of water outdoors where it reflects the black night sky. You can invite the dark moon's energy directly into the water to aid your visions.

On the night of the dark moon, find a secluded spot in which to scry. You can go outdoors or in a quiet, darkened room.

1. Place your black bowl or cauldron of water (or mirror, crystal ball, or obsidian) in front of you where you can comfortably gaze at it.

2. Perform the relaxation technique described on page 57.

3. Envision the blackness of the dark moon filling the water. It holds the liminal space between endings and beginnings, like the Crone's cauldron. In darkness lie answers waiting to be born.

4. Relax your gaze and remain receptive and open. Pay attention to reflections on the surface of your scrying vessel along with sounds and sensations all around you. If you have a specific question, ask it now in your mind and see what comes to you in the forms mentioned earlier.

5. Write down what you saw, heard, and felt afterward. Not all the messages will be immediately understandable to you but may make sense later.

The more you practice, the more accurate your readings will become. At first it may seem like you're receiving random thoughts, but with practice they will start to make sense and form patterns that you understand.

JUNK ORACLE

The dark moon is an ideal time for divination, but not everyone is keen on studying and memorizing systems such as tarot cards, and some may find them difficult to relate to on a personal level. In this case you can create your own oracle to consult. With a junk oracle there are no books to read, symbols to memorize, or layouts to learn. You don't even have to buy anything. The junk oracle is, quite simply, a collection of random objects (often seen as "junk" by others) selected by you that you have associated with a feeling or meaning. The objects are kept in a pouch or bag. When you have a question, you take a handful of junk from the bag, cast it on a hard surface, and interpret the objects that you see. It's very simple, yet the junk oracle is one of the most effective divination tools in my experience, due to its highly personalized nature. You get to choose each and every object in the oracle, and so you will know exactly how to interpret it.

The junk oracle is a good replacement for the bone oracle described later in this book if you do not wish to use animal parts in your divination.

You can put anything at all into your oracle—sticks, toys, coins, nails. The only real limit is size, since you will probably want to stick with small items that are easily handled.

First, you must choose the items for your oracle. This process can take as much or as little time as you choose. While you are out and about in your daily life, be mindful of how you feel, and take notice of small things around you. That is how you will find your oracle objects. For example, if you are taking a walk on a beautiful day and enjoying a peaceful moment, pick up a stone off the sidewalk. Add that to your oracle to represent contentedness. If you go out to lunch with a friend and have a really fun time, keep a token from that meal (like a piece of the paper napkin) to represent friendship. On a day you are feeling gloomy, keep a thread from the sweater you're wearing. This item can later represent negativity when it pops up in a reading.

Almost any object connected to an emotion can be a symbol in an upcoming reading. You may also find objects that have no immediate mental associations but that call out to you at random. Once you've collected as many items as you want in your pouch, you are ready to consult your junk oracle.

Hold the bag in your hands and ask your question or state your issue while gently shaking the bag to stir up the contents. Then reach in with your eyes closed, grab a handful of "junk," and drop it onto the table in front of you.

I like to read from the inside out meaning what has fallen mostly at the center of your work area is the most pertinent or "strong" energy, and what is farther from the center are outside factors that are affecting your question or issue.

What is at the center of the area? What items have fallen near each other? If there is the napkin that represented friendship and it is next to the string that meant depression, it could mean your friend needs you or even that the friendship is in trouble. If you pull out an old coin that represents prosperity, and near it is a paper clip from the office, it could mean a raise or promotion at work. As for the outer items, they represent contributing influences. If one is a child's toy, it could mean family is factored into the issue. Like I said, interpreting the objects is entirely dependent on what they mean to you personally, and only you can honestly decipher what the oracle is telling you.

For a quick read on a situation, simply ask your question and pull one object out of the pouch at random for your answer.

DREAM INTERPRETATION

One of the most personal forms of divination is interpreting your own dreams. Dreams can be especially meaningful when you are experiencing the dark moon current in your life as you go through a transition of some kind, or you can intentionally encourage lucid dreams during the dark moon. The dark moon is a time when your dreams may be meaningful in terms of the active undercurrents in your life, things deep inside you that are stirring and affecting your waking life. If you dream journal for long enough—that is, write your dreams down every time you wake up—you may notice patterns that match the moon phases. For me, straightforward and literal dreams that apply to my mundane waking life usually occur around the full moon, when earthly matters are illuminated. During the dark moon, dreams can become stranger, darker, and even distressing as they turn my attention to inner issues. During the waxing and waning phases, I tend to transition between the two accordingly. While everyone is different, you may notice your own patterns when you start recording your dreams depending on how influenced by the lunar phases you are.

There are literally thousands of books available about dream interpretation, ranging from in-depth self-analysis to lists of meanings and definitions. I lean more toward ones that urge us to figure out the symbolism of our own dreams rather than offer concise lists. While these books are helpful for learning purposes, they can be somewhat limiting, as they're very general. Dream interpretation is intensely personal. For example, say you dream about a snake. Maybe the books say a snake means rebirth, regeneration, and renewal, but all you can feel when you think about snakes is revulsion and terror. That's because dreams are specific to the individual, and so are the symbols. A snake for you personally represents deep-seated fear, not renewal. While a book with definitions can be interesting and helpful, it's a guide only and may not always work for you.

Dreams often reveal what is in your subconscious mind when you haven't even admitted it to yourself yet, providing you with an opportunity for growth and self-actualization.

When we dream, I believe we're directly linked to spirit, or the collective unconscious, in a way we aren't when awake. Spirit can speak directly to us in our sleep to give us guidance. It does so in the most direct, personal way possible. Therefore, it will show you symbols that you know the meaning of, usually. There are exceptions. For example, let's say you can't understand why you keep dreaming about wolves, so you're prompted to research their meaning, only to discover they make perfect sense to your situation. This was spirit directing you through your dreams. All that being said, the more you learn about animals and objects as symbols in the collective unconscious, the more spirit has to work with in terms of getting messages to you.

How to Interpret Symbols in Dreams

Dreams that you have during the dark moon may be especially telling in terms of your inner self and shadow work. Understanding what the symbols in dreams are meant to tell you is important. If you have a dream about an object or animal but you don't make an association, take a pen and paper and make a mind map. Write the word in the middle of the page, and all around it, write down literally every single thought associated with it that comes to your mind. Don't struggle with this; let the thoughts come without forcing them, even if they seem silly, random, or weird.

I'll do one to illustrate. For several dark moon cycles in a row, I had dreams about zebras and had no idea why. At the time I was really struggling with my own social insecurities and anxiety issues while having to fit in with a specific group of my peers, and felt I was failing miserably because I was so different from them (maybe you can relate!). Specifically, I'm a very sensitive, intuitive person and I have a fear of being judged as "weird" because of it. I couldn't figure out what a zebra could possibly have to do with this until I made a mind map. The mind map I made was extremely random, but I didn't leave anything out, even though some things seemed silly. Here is what my mind map looked like:

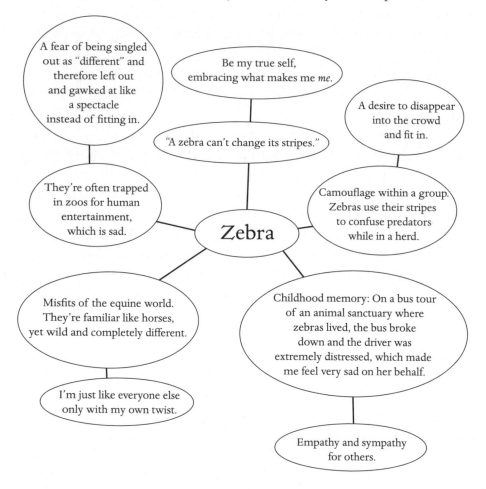

In conclusion, I figured out that the zebra was telling me to be myself, that my uniqueness was what made me interesting and valuable, and that not blending in was okay. I was just like everyone else, but with a twist (my empathy and sensitivity).

As you can see, I even included a little shred of memory from childhood that comes up every time I think of "zebra," just for a flash of a second, but that could be the very reason it showed up in a dream, to remind me of that experience and use it as a guide. Try this mind map trick next time you have a dream you can't decipher and see where it leads you. Don't leave out any details, memories, or thoughts even if they seem unrelated. Be completely present and acknowledge them all. Follow the thought to where it leads you next until it comes to a conclusion. You might be surprised!

Prophetic Dreams

Another type of dream you may have during the dark moon is a prophetic dream. Prophetic dreams warn you of something in the future. Some are very clear and concise, showing exactly what will happen. This has been noted by many people when someone they love is in an accident or passes away; the person appears in their dreams at the moment it happens. In my experience, prophetic dreams are nowhere near so direct; however, when they happen, I know it.

Once I was dating someone and I wasn't sure whether or not I should move in with him. I had a dream where he was surrounded by dancing, smiling blonde women. Sounds like just an embarrassing dream about jealousy, right? When I told him about it, he was surprised for a minute and then confessed that he had actually been dating two other women at the same time as me, both blonde, and that he was still seeing both of them. Sometimes dreams show us things that are worth digging into before making a big life change!

Dark Moon Dream Ritual

Here is a simple bedtime ritual to encourage prophetic or insightful dreams. Perform this during the dark moon phase to gain guidance on deep inner issues.

❧ MATERIALS

Tea made with herbs associated with psychic powers, such as rose, jasmine, or star anise. You can make your own loose tea or purchase tea bags of these flavors.

Square of black cloth large enough to hold the herbs and stones

Bowl of 1 tablespoon each dried mugwort, eyebright, and lavender

Amethyst

Moonstone

Selenite

String

Assemble these things ahead of time near your bed. Let the tea steep while you are in the bath.

Have a dark moon bath ritual, as outlined in chapter 3, and go straight to your bed afterward.

Lay the black cloth out on your nightstand or carefully on your bed. Place the herbs in the center of it, and add the crystals. You will have invoked the feeling and power of the dark moon already in your bath. Hold your hands over the mixture and say:

> *Mysteries of the dark,*
> *Spirits of dreams,*
> *I invite you to come to me.*
> *Show me your messages.*
> *Guide me on my journey*
> *Regarding (your question or issue).*

Tie up the cloth securely with string and place it beneath your pillow.

Drink the tea and go to sleep. Don't forget to write down what you dream and use the mind map technique if necessary.

Visits from the Dead

During the dark moon phase, I have noticed I frequently dream about people I know who have died. This could be because during this time, it's said that the spirit world is closer and more accessible to us.

When you have lost someone you care about, it's normal to dream about them, especially if they were close to you or the relationship you had with them was catalytic in your waking life. Sometimes this is felt to be a visit from their spirit, that they are coming to say hello from the afterlife, and it can leave you with a nice feeling, like you've seen them again. This doesn't apply to night terrors or nightmares about their death. If you have recurring night terrors, it's possible you should seek grief counseling or talk to someone you trust.

When someone who has passed away appears in a dream—not a nightmare —it is often just a gentle reminder that they still care about you. Think about the role they played in your dream: what they said, what they were doing, or the feeling they gave you. Are they trying to tell you something?

Some believe that this is a spirit reaching out from the afterlife to let you know that they are okay and to comfort you. If you keep dreaming of someone who passed from this life who was a negative influence while living, analyze the role they played in your dream. Were they there to symbolize something to you, perhaps past trauma that hasn't been completely healed? They may also represent fears. If you do feel their spirit is intruding on your dreams, a banishing ritual may be in order.

DARK MOON TAROT CONSULTATION

Whether tarot is an old friend of yours or a system you're just learning, the dark moon is always a beneficial time to consult your cards. At this time, you may find yourself questioning deeper things or more self-focused subjects than usual. This is a good time to reflect on your inner self and personal growth, even addressing feelings that are uncomfortable.

This reading is what I call a reflection reading. It will draw your attention to what your current struggle is and what it is meant to teach you. Everything happens in your life for a reason, to encourage you to grow in spirit and mind. A situation that is difficult or unpleasant may exist to initiate important change. Other times, you may discover that your inner issues, such as negative self-talk or personal fears, are the cause of outer problems in the first place.

This is a simple four-card spread.

Shuffle your cards.

Phrase your query. For example, say, "What is my role in this situation?" or "What am I supposed to learn from this situation?"

Lay the cards out as shown here:

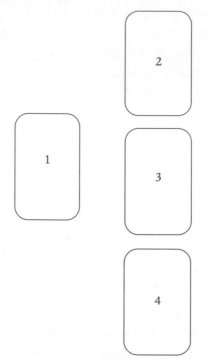

Card number 1 represents the current issue you are experiencing or the general tone of your life right now. This card shows your situation from the outside or as it appears on the surface.

Card number 2 represents you, the querent. It indicates your role in the situation and what part you're playing.

Card number 3 is the most important card in the reading. It denotes your fears, triggers, or ingrained behaviors that are stirred up by this particular problem or even causing it. This card will sometimes show you a part of your personality you haven't considered before or have chosen not to acknowledge. This card is all about you and what is causing your involvement in the situation, not anyone else. That's not to say that you are at fault for a problem, but rather it suggests how your own deeper feelings may be contributing to the outcome. When you sort out your own role in an issue, you will be forced to grow and initiate change.

Card number 4 indicates how you are to grow from the experience. Challenges in life point to very specific lessons we are supposed to learn about ourselves. This card shows what growth is possible if you deal with the issues brought up by card number 3.

As you can see, this reading is very inwardly focused and isn't meant to provide information or guidance about anyone outside of yourself. You can't control other people, but you can and do make your own choices. This is a good reading to perform prior to cursing or hexing.

AUGURY

Augury is the act of interpreting signs from nature, usually in the form of birds or lightning. The Etruscans and Romans were known for practicing augury to determine what course of action the gods wanted them to take.

While many details have been lost in time, bits of information about this practice still remain. The Etruscans divided the sky into sixteen sections and received omens according to where lightning stuck within them. Romans observed the behavior of birds to gain information: for example, if the birds flew in from the left, it was considered a positive sign. Auguries were consulted to figure out whether or not someone should get married, to decide where to erect important buildings, and while planning strategies in war.[1]

You can practice a simple form of augury during your dark moon meditation or during the three days of the dark moon phase. Below is an explanation how to do this, which can be applied to all wildlife in your area, not just birds or lightning. Mine is a much less ritualized version than the Romans had, I'm sure, but the premise is the same.

Find a secluded, natural area, such as a park or backyard, in which you know that birds, chipmunks, squirrels, ducks, or other wildlife can be seen regularly. Sit comfortably facing the east and spend a moment aligning your mind with the four directions. Enter a meditative state as explained on page 57. Then ask your question aloud or in your mind and wait patiently.

Now it's time to interpret the position of the animals. I'll use birds as an example, but pay attention to any creatures you see, even insects. Two things are to be considered when consulting the auguries: the cardinal direction the

---

1. M. Horatius Piscinus, "On Auguries," Societas Via Romana, accessed July 8, 2019, http://www.societasviaromana.net/Collegium_Religionis/augury.php.

animal is in and the behavior of the animal itself. Take note of where the birds are located. Are they perched all in one area, or are they calling across spaces to each other? A large number of birds all in one cardinal direction will be a very clear indication of the answer to your query, but if they're scattered in several directions, there are multiple things influencing your situation. Here is a brief explanation of the cardinal directions to think about while consulting the auguries:

North: Stability, money, finance, business, the home, bills, practical matters

East: Communication, learning, wisdom, arguments, sending messages, interactions with other people

South: Passions, drama, big changes, creation and destruction, life-changing events

West: Emotions, feelings, intuition, mental well-being

The second thing to note is the behavior of the birds. Is one of them calling out the loudest or acting agitated? Their behavior combined with the direction they're in holds answers. A bird making lots of noise carries an important message. The birds in other directions may be calmer, which means their position and meaning is less urgent. Significant actions you may see include a bird eating prey or seeds, an adult bird teaching or feeding a smaller bird, fights, and mating rituals. These are actions that can be applied to your question. For example, if you've asked about your romantic relationship and you see birds fighting in the west, it means emotional turmoil. If you see a calm bird sitting in the north, it means stability. A loudly screeching bird in the east could mean a confrontation.

To take this divination one step further, you can perform it at night under the dark moon while being sensitive to the activity of nocturnal creatures. There are fewer visible animals at night than during the day, but their presence is especially telling in shadow work.

PART II

BLOOD

and

BONES

Now that you understand the dark phase of the moon and how it applies to your life, it's time to discuss some of the oldest tools of witchcraft: blood and bones. Like the dark phase of the moon, these topics are sometimes avoided in popular practice. They have so much power, and yet, somewhat understandably, most people view them as repellent. Of course, blood and bones are linked to one of humanity's greatest fears: death.

These subjects that people find so terrifying make up our very life energy. Blood, semen, urine, menses, bones, and even saliva are literally at the core of survival. Their presence creates life, and their absence takes life away. So while these topics can be gory, gritty, and gross, they speak to people on a primitive level as old as the earth.

This part of the book explores how and why to incorporate blood and bodily fluids (including menstrual blood, urine, and more) into spells and rituals. It also delves into the use of various animal parts in magick, how to source them, and how to safely prepare their remains for use in your spellcraft.

CHAPTER 5
BLOOD AND OTHER FLUIDS

Bodily fluids of all kinds illicit a strong response in people: terror, repulsion, fear, sexual arousal, and more. These associations, along with the fact that they all contain the true one-of-a-kind physical essence of a person, make them very powerful magickal tools. While not to everyone's taste, using bodily fluids in spells is quite common.

In some older spells, there is mention of feeding other people bodily fluids such as blood and urine. Remember that this is in fact an act of assault upon another person when done without their consent. Even with consent, this can be dangerous or cause illness, and I strongly advise against it.

BLOOD

Typically, when we see blood, we're instinctively alarmed and go into panic mode, looking to fight or flee. The sight and smell of it ignites something primal in us, as it does with all animals. Blood represents both life and death. It is vital in terms of mortality and is therefore significant in magick.

Blood has been revered in religion and spirituality since the existence of ancient civilizations and continues to fascinate us to this day. Just look at our most popular media. It's filled with bloodshed, violence, and sexy bloodsuckers, illustrating our continuing obsession with the substance.

Blood often heralds the end of life and, depending on the situation, triggers different emotions. In battle, the blood of our enemies would illicit triumph and a sense of safety. In times of hunger, the blood of prey would spark feelings of success and assured sustenance. Contrariwise, the sight of a loved one's blood heralds dread and fear. Blood is so powerful that some people even faint at the sight of it regardless of context. The primal feelings it invokes in people are undeniable. If you lose too much blood, you will die. If you give blood, it can save someone's life.

In ancient history, blood was used to appease nature. While old rites of sacrificing animals and people are not necessary nowadays, we can learn from them just how important blood was, and still is, in our collective unconscious. Ancient agricultural societies performed blood sacrifice to pacify the gods and the earth, in order to keep crops growing and food supplies abundant, for example, by placing the remains of human sacrifice in the fields in spring. The Mayans pierced their lips, tongues, and cheeks to draw blood, which was then spread upon idols, sprinkled on the earth, or given to divinity.[2] The point of mentioning these old rites is not to say we should continue them but to illustrate just how powerful blood has always been to the human mind and its link to the life force.

When the topic of blood magick comes up, many peoples' thoughts automatically go to a scary place. In reality, blood magick can be implemented in many different ways, not always frightening or painful, and is vastly misunderstood.

Those who practice blood magick in modern witchcraft are sometimes reluctant to talk about it for fear of judgment, and in some circles the subject is completely taboo and considered antiquated and unnecessary. The blood magick I speak of in this book is performed safely and responsibly by consenting adults.

Blood can be offered as a sacrifice or devotional, employed in spells to strengthen the energetic link to yourself or someone else, or used to create a bond between members of a coven. The DNA in your blood contains your whole inherited lineage. This means that every single ancestor you have is present in your blood, making it a substance that reaches further back into time than we can conceive of.

Not everyone is comfortable with using blood in magick, and that's perfectly okay. If the idea makes you uneasy, you can use visualization, energy work, or even hair, fingernails, or saliva in its place.

---

2. Brenda Ralph Lewis, *Ritual Sacrifice: Blood and Redemption* (Stroud, Gloucestershire, UK: Sutton Publishing, 2001), 88.

Those who do choose to partake in blood ritual do so for a wide range of reasons. Adding a drop of blood to a tincture, oil, spell, or charm acts as a binding agent between your physical earthly self and the energy of the spell. Including blood in a spell adds a deep vitality to it. For some, it brings the element of sacrifice (which is discussed in chapter 11) to the working. It also beckons the power of ancestors into your magick. While hair and fingernails are dead cells of a person and contain their essence and DNA, blood is a living substance. This makes it different and, some believe, more powerful.

Safety First

Should you choose to include blood in your rituals and spells, there are some important safety factors to consider to prevent injury and the spread of illness. Many deadly diseases are spread through the blood, and you can make yourself and others ill if you neglect to take proper safety precautions.

- Do not mix blood with someone else unless you know you can trust them. In other words, you know that cinematic "cut our palms and press our hands together" bonding ritual people do in movies? Or when all members of a group put a drop of their blood in a glass of wine and then drink it? Don't do this with strangers or people you're not certain have been tested for blood-borne diseases. In a close relationship or circle of friends, this is something that you should be able to discuss openly. If not, it isn't worth taking the chance.

- When drawing your own blood, use a sterile lancet. These are tiny pin-prick devices used by diabetics for blood testing and can be purchased at any pharmacy. They are single use, sterile, and guaranteed to be disease free when used properly. They don't leave scars and only release a small, controlled amount of blood, minimizing the chance of accidents. Always make sure to dispose of lancets in a proper biohazard container, also available at a drug store. Never share a lancet, and only use them once to avoid infection. Wash the site of the pinprick thoroughly before and after. Be sure to only prick the tips of your fingers with a lancet. Some areas, such as the wrist, are not safe to prick as they can bleed too much.

- Cutting or pricking yourself with nonsterile objects or larger tools such as razors, knives, or pins is not advised. There could be germs or worse on them and you may give yourself a painful infection. Plus, it's difficult to control the depth of a cut using a knife or blade, and you could end up hurting yourself very badly by accident.

- If you menstruate, you can use a small amount of menstrual blood instead of using a lancet. Treat menstrual fluid with the same care as ordinary blood because, again, it can spread disease between people.

- Using a drop of blood in ritual is not the same as self-harming. Blood magick is a special, once-in-a-while exercise for ceremonial reasons only and isn't done for the sake of hurting yourself on a regular basis. If you have a history of self-harm, using blood in magick may not be right for you.

Menstrual Blood

Menstrual blood has been a key component of magick and religion throughout history. This is not to say that all, or even most, witches incorporate their monthly menses into their craft. In fact, there are some very strong opinions about it.

Even within the witch world, there are two strongly opposing viewpoints regarding the use of menstrual blood in magick. One side views it as an incredible source of lunar power and connection to the divine feminine, while the other side dismisses it as nasty, gross, and just plain wrong. To me, the opinion that menstrual blood is shameful and dirty is a twisted belief invented by the patriarchy out of fear. When you look back in time at the role of menstruation in mythology and throughout the evolution of civilization, the ability to create and give life is revered as one of the most sacred phenomena. Over time, feelings toward menstruation have oscillated between two extremes, being worshipped and celebrated while simultaneously shunned and downgraded to the lowest of bodily functions.

In figuring out why it is such a controversial subject, and in order to comprehend any ingrained feelings we may have, we must first understand how ancient cultures felt about menstruation. Early civilizations didn't know the science of the body as we do today. All they knew was that menstrual bleeding was directly linked to childbirth and the propagation of the species. They knew that when monthly bleeding stopped for nine months, a baby would grow inside a woman instead. Once the baby was born, menstruation would soon resume. In a nutshell, they thought that when a woman was pregnant, she was turning her monthly blood into a baby.[3] Therefore, this blood from a woman's womb was revered as a source of life itself. This granted menstrual blood great power.

Menstrual blood is mentioned again and again in mythology from all over the world. The Greeks and Romans believed menstruating women had the power to calm storms and rescue lost ships at sea. There is evidence that Egyptian pharaohs and Celtic kings believed consuming or drinking menstrual blood would grant them immortality.[4] Oftentimes a girl's first bleeding was cause for celebration. On this end of the spectrum, menses has been considered a symbol of life.

There is, of course, the other side of the story, which we are currently more familiar with, and that is one of fear and loathing. This fear of menstrual blood isn't unique to our modern times. In many ancient religious texts, menstruating people are referred to as unclean and cursed.

Pliny the Elder, an influential Roman writer and philosopher, published encyclopedias called *Natural History*, in which he included his bizarre notions about menstruation, and these notions, however outdated they are now, formed a basis for some modern views on reproductive cycles. He claimed period blood could render seeds infertile, kill insects and plants on contact, make crops fail, and drive dogs mad. He wrote that the gaze of a menstruating woman could kill livestock and cause miscarriages in pregnant women. He also said sex with a menstruating woman could kill a man.[5] That's some pretty powerful stuff, which sounds silly to us now. However, this dark interpretation lives on today in some cases.

Menstrual blood has always been viewed as incredibly powerful in opposing polarities: that of giving life and that of giving death, just like the dark moon and just like the Crone goddesses. It was the elixir of life yet at the same time considered deadly. It was a source of fear and terror yet simultaneously viewed in awe as a miraculous source of life. That is some very powerful energy for humans to pour into a substance since the beginning of humankind!

---

3. Elissa Stein and Susan Kim, *Flow: The Cultural Story of Menstruation* (New York: St. Martin's Press, 2009), 35.

4. Stein and Kim, *Flow,* 39.

5. Stein and Kim, *Flow,* 37.

Menstruation and the Moon

How does all this history apply to magick?

First of all, should you choose to include menstrual fluid, also called moon blood, in your rituals and spells, please see the section about blood safety on page 75.

When considering moon blood in magick, it's important to note that a menstrual cycle is in direct correspondence with the lunar phases. This is truly incredible when you think about it. Different times in a menstrual cycle can be utilized in exactly the same way as the phases of the moon to influence spell work.

The monthly menstrual cycle physically and hormonally exactly mirrors the moon's patterns of growth, fruition, death, and rebirth. Here are the parallels:

Waxing Moon: Eggs ripen in the ovaries. The uterus becomes receptive and fertile, preparing for sperm to enter the body. Like the waxing moon, this time in the cycle is associated with accomplishment, high energy, and fulfillment.

Full Moon: The egg is fully formed, ovulation occurs, and the egg is released. Bloody, nutrient-rich lining is created by the uterus to nourish the egg. This is a time of fruition and potential life, of full formation ready to be fertilized.

Waning Moon: If the egg is unfertilized, the uterus lining shrinks and decomposes, taking the egg and the month's blood with it. This is a time of letting go and moving on. This is a time of diminishing and approaching endings.

Dark Moon: Menstruation. The body releases the blood and the egg. This represents great transformation and release, much like death. This is a time of clearing the way for new beginnings.

After this the cycle begins all over again, just like the moon, the seasons, the cosmos, and time. A giant cycle of life, death, and rebirth reflected right inside our bodies.

Menstrual blood has been defined both as giving life and as a toxic killer. It logically follows that magickally speaking, it can be used for either of those ends. It can be used to protect, to bless, to create sympathy between a witch and an object, to curse, to hex, and to maim. A person's moon blood is deeply and intrinsically theirs alone and can be used to send an extremely strong message to spirit or to boost the power of spells. It sounds multipurpose, and that's because it is. The conflict surrounding menstrual blood has created this amazing catchall of energy. Such extremes invoke gut-level emotion. Strong emotion creates powerful energy. And powerful energy makes for successful magick.

There are a few spells at the end of this chapter based on the vast range of powers associated with moon blood. Not everyone is willing to use it, but I felt it was important to discuss this topic due to its misunderstood nature.

SEMEN

Semen is somewhat the male equivalent of menstrual blood in magick, although it has never gotten quite the same bad reputation. No one has ever accused semen of destroying crops or killing livestock, for example, but that's a discussion for another time.

Semen, like moon blood, creates life. Using semen in spells is a practice as old as time, and yet another one that is not discussed openly in most modern witchcraft circles. Like menstrual blood, it's been viewed as a potent ingredient in spellcraft all over the world.

Semen is symbolic of divine masculinity, fertility, action, and virility. These are all forces that can boost the general strength of a spell. Semen can create a link between objects and the practitioner just like blood. Both semen and vaginal arousal discharge can be used in the place of blood in magick.

Semen can be utilized to anoint a candle in sex magick, as can female arousal fluid. To attract a man, carve a heart or an appropriate symbol into a candle and anoint it with ejaculate (you can even buy penis-shaped candles for this). To attract a female, putting semen into a bowl or other round vessel representing the womb can aid in finding a mate. These actions can be mixed and matched for any sexual preference. Before performing love spells on a specific person, please review the points on pages 4 and 5 regarding ethics and targeted love spells before going forward.

Semen can also be used in dominance spells or when you wish to energetically mark something as belonging to you, like a job or position of rank within a group. While it is best that this be done with one's own semen because it contains your personal energy, given its symbolism, anyone can use semen in this way as long as they have permission from the person. A woman can use her own arousal fluid in this same way or obtain semen from a willing donor.

In love magic, semen can be dried on a piece of cloth then added to poppets and charms. It is said that when collected from the target of a love spell, it will keep them faithful. Semen is especially used in spells meant to bring growth and new beginnings. Fertility abounds in all aspects of existence, not just in procreation. Job prospects, relationships, and any other area of life that needs to be fertilized and encouraged to grow can be considered for a fertility spell.

A simple ritual is to collect some of your semen and imbue it with an intention that you would like to grow and develop in your life. Bury it in the earth, like planting a seed, and your goal will come to fruition.

URINE

Gross, right? But since we're talking about all the other uncomfortable things, we may as well discuss this too. Urine (or any bodily fluid, for that matter) is by no means obligatory in magick, and certainly not everyone is comfortable including it. Since this book is written in the spirit of learning, I'm going to discuss using urine in spells to help understand what it is for, even if you never use it.

In nature, animals use urine to mark their territory. When other animals come along and smell it, they know to stay away. This is especially true for large or dominant creature such as male cats. When approached from this perspective, urine can be used in magick to mark a person, idea, or thing as belonging to you, protecting it from others.

Urine isn't always territorial, though. For many species, it is also part of the process of locating suitable mates through scent, and from this we learn that it can be used in love and attraction spells. It's said that putting urine in coffee and serving it to a lover will bind them to you, but as I've mentioned, please do not feed other people your bodily fluids.

Urine is waste and toxins—garbage from the body, no less—and this lends it to being used in curses. There's nothing more insulting than to be "pissed on," as in the saying "I'd piss on his/her grave." It would seem peeing on someone's good name is the ultimate insult and act of disrespect.

Witch bottles are a well-known example of urine being used in spells dating back thousands of years. Some contained rusty nails and hair and were meant to protect a person from witchery. It's also said that you can put the name of your enemy into a bottle and fill it with urine to curse them.

On the other side of the coin, urine carrying unwanted waste from the body is linked with removing curses or energetic refuse. Done with intent, urinating can be integrated into a banishing spell.

As you can see, the use of urine in spells is, like everything, entirely dependent on the intent behind it. It's used to attract love, to bind, to hex, and to lift curses.

Using urine in magic is a very personal choice, and should you decide to experiment with this, always remember that urine, like blood, carries pathogens and should be handled with care and cleanliness. Do not consume it. While using urine in spells is not something I personally prefer, I'm not one to tell other people what they should or shouldn't do. Like menstrual blood, opinions and feelings about urine are strong, and this lends it powerful energy by association.

SALIVA

For those who are uncomfortable with using blood, semen, or urine in magick—and many people are—but still feel compelled to add a bodily component to a working, saliva is always an option. Blood or other bodily fluids can be replaced with spit in any spell.

Saliva can be used in sympathetic magic just like blood, to create a bond between yourself and a magickal object. It can be used in love magick for its association with kissing and sexual pheromones, but on the contrary, spitting is also considered rude and offensive, making it useful in curses.

Multipurpose like all bodily fluids, saliva is no exception in that intent is everything. Spitting in a person's face, for example, is one of the most disrespectful things you can do. In this train of thought, you can integrate it into a curse by spitting on a poppet of someone you dislike or on the ground where you've buried a spell item meant to curse someone. Meanwhile, you can integrate it into love magick to attract a compatible mate.

SPELLS USING BODILY FLUIDS

This section focuses on spells using blood and urine. For spells using menstrual blood, you can substitute regular blood, and vice versa. If you're not comfortable using blood at all, you can substitute saliva.

Family Protection Spell

Moon blood is our connection with the Great Mother, the divine feminine and the source of life itself. For this reason, it is perfect for use in family protection spells, especially the protection of children. This blood is connected to matters of nurturance, caregiving, midwifery, giving life, raising children, and love. However, on the flip side, mother energy is certainly not always hugs and flowers. Woe unto anyone who interferes with a lioness's cubs! This primal, protective energy can be applied to spells designed to guard your families, children, and relationships.

This spell takes several days to perform, so be sure you have some time available each day for the next week or so.

⊷‑⁊ MATERIALS

Athame, ritual knife, or sharp object for cutting into wax

White taper candle

Several drops of moon blood (menstrual blood)

Pin for each member of the family

3 thistle plants pulled from the ground. These invasive weeds can be found almost anywhere, but wear gloves when you pick them. They're painful!

Lighter or matches

Heatproof dish

10-inch square of black cloth

Cast your circle and invoke your deities.

Using your knife, carve the names of your family members into the taper candle, or if you all share the same last name, carve it from the top to the bottom of the candle.

Next, anoint the candle with moon blood. You will do this by starting at the top of the candle and rubbing it into the wax, down to the middle. Then, anoint it from the bottom up. This attracts protective energy. As you massage the blood into the candle, imagine a powerful field of fiercely protective energy surrounding the name(s) carved there. Now, pick up one of the pins. Say the name of one of the people you wish to protect, and then insert the pin into the candle, all the way through. Repeat this with each name, inserting a pin to represent each person. You will need to remember which pin represents whom, so perhaps positioning them from oldest to youngest from top to bottom is a good idea. If you find it difficult to push the pin through the candle, try carefully heating it up with a flame first to help it ease it through.

Arrange the prickly thistle in a circle around the candle, further defending it from outside interference.

Light the candle at the same time each day. As it burns through each pin, chant or mentally say:

> *(Name) is protected by the power of my blood,*
> *The power of creation and destruction that resides in me.*
> *As I will it, so mote it be.*

I suggest burning through one pin per day. Remember which pin represents whom, and while the flame burns through each one, focus very strongly on protecting that individual. Visualize a steely bubble around them physically, while they live content and free of all threat. When the candle has burned down, wrap the remaining wax, pins, and thistle in the black cloth and bury it near your front door.

This kind of protective spell is not limited to family or children. You can perform a similar ritual to protect property, a job or position, or a romantic relationship that is being threatened by outside forces. Simply alter the words on the candle as well as your visualization to fit what is needed.

Heart's Blood Fidelity Spell

It is said that feeding your menstrual blood to a lover will ensure that they never stray, that they will always be faithful to you alone. It's believed that if the victim unknowingly consumes the blood, they will be loyal to the spell-caster forever. For this reason, it is often used in "bring back my love" spells.

Don't feed menstrual blood to anyone without their consent. Instead, I've come up with a spell for fidelity that uses blood but doesn't involve ingesting it.

Some say that fidelity spells interfere with the free will of another person. I share this spell trusting that the reader is able to make their own decisions.

⟶ MATERIALS

2 red candles

3 drops lavender, rose, or ginger oil

1 crumbled dried rose petal

Small chunk of clay that can fit easily in the palm of your hand (See the recipe outlined in chapter 9 about poppets, or you can buy some air-drying clay.)

3 apple seeds

Several drops of your menstrual blood

Cast a circle and invoke deity if you wish. Light the red candles.

Using your hands, knead the rose petal and chosen oil into the clay. Imagine that you are in fact holding the heart and emotions of your partner in your hands. See them in your mind; imagine their smell, the sound of their voice. Picture the two of you loyal to each other, with no desire to stray.

Mold the clay to make a heart shape. While you do this, chant:

(Name), I hold your heart in my hands. From me you will not stray.

As you press and work the clay with your fingers, feel the aspects of your partner—their looks, their energy, their personality—flowing from your hands into it.

Place the heart on your altar before you. Hold one apple seed in your fingers and declare:

(Name), your heart beats only for me.

Push the apple seed into the center of the heart. Hold the second seed and say:

(Name), your heart sees only me.

Push this seed into the heart. Hold the third seed and say:

(Name), your heart belongs to me.

Press the third seed into the heart. This will have made a dent in the center of the clay heart. Into this dent, put a drop of blood. Mold the clay over the top of the hole you've made, completely covering the blood and seeds.

Close the circle. Allow the candles to burn out.

Let the charm dry and keep it under your bed or hidden in a secret place where no one will find it.

This spell should not be taken lightly. If you are fickle-hearted and just playing games on a crush, this will be a big mistake.

Blood and Vinegar Revenge Spell

This spell is to get revenge on someone who has wronged you. In many ways, revenge spells are like reversal spells. You will gather up all the malevolence behind their actions toward you and send it right back at them with extra force. This will hopefully cause something worse to befall them than what they've done to you.

━━ MATERIALS

 3 thorns cut from a plant
 Small dish
 Sterile lancet
 Jar with a tight lid
 1 cup vinegar
 1 tablespoon ashes from a fire, incense, or another source.

Gather your items at your altar. Cast a circle and invoke deity if you wish.

Place the thorns in the dish. Think about how the person has wronged you, and allow your anger or other negative feelings to build. Envision the person experiencing the same pain they have inflicted on you, whatever that may be. When these feelings are at their peak, use the lancet to prick your finger and put several drops of your blood onto the thorns. This release of blood is carrying all the pain and torment they've caused out of your own heart, through your blood and into the thorns.

Put the thorns in the jar. Fill the jar with vinegar and then add the ashes. Tightly cap the lid, and then shake it and watch the chaos you've created inside the jar: sharp thorns swirling around in burning vinegar, with ashes making a cloudy veil throughout to obscure their vision and protect you from their radar.

If possible, you should dump the mixture onto their property, outside their home, or outside their place of work. If this isn't possible, you can dump it into a sewer grate or river that flows in the direction of where they reside.

As you walk away, take note of the lightness your heart feels now that you've removed the anger and vengeance and sent it back to where it belongs. Wash and recycle the jar.

Reversal Spell to Teach a Lesson

If someone is behaving in a way that is harmful to others, sometimes the best way to stop them is a reversal spell. This will cause them to experience that which they have inflicted upon someone else, giving them a taste of their own medicine.

This spell makes use of sunlight but can still be performed during the dark phase of the moon.

⊷ MATERIALS

> Pencil
> Paper
> Small hand mirror
> Direct sunlight
> Sterile lancet
> Nail
> Hammer

Cast your circle and call your deities.

Draw a picture of an eyeball and write the person's name inside it. This represents their vision or perception.

Hold the mirror in such a way that it reflects the sun, making a visible reflection onto the eye. Focus the reflected light onto the center of the eyeball, "blinding" the eye with it. Imagine that the light you're reflecting holds all the pain and fear this person has inflicted on you. Imagine the scenario in which they played the villain exactly as it happened. Feel it again, and then transfer your emotions into the reflected light. Burn those feelings into the eye through the beam of light.

Chant repeatedly:

With this curse, I reverse.

When you feel your attention waver, set aside the mirror and eye.

Use the lancet to draw some blood from your finger, and put several drops on the nail. Then, using the hammer, nail the paper into the ground right through the pupil. This act symbolizes that they will understand or "see" for themselves the pain they have caused and hopefully change their ways. For example, if they have stolen money from you, then money will be taken from them. If they have used or manipulated you, someone will do the same to them.

Once they've changed, dispose of the spell items. You can cleanse the mirror by running it under water or passing it through incense smoke, and you can reuse it in future spells. Recycle the other materials.

Eating the Life Force Spell

It's said that people once believed they could take on the qualities of the animals they ate. This spell is based on that idea.

Often we find ourselves wishing we could harness the traits, energy, and power of another person. This can be someone you admire or someone who is your rival. Rivalry isn't always negative, and it can even be healthy if channeled correctly.

This spell is to ingest the energy of another person, living or dead, so that you may have similar abilities or circumstances as them. It isn't meant to weaken the other person in any way but rather to tap into the same forces that have touched them and made them successful. The universe has plenty of abundance for everyone, and doing this spell isn't meant to steal anything from the person you are focused on.

This spell uses a photo of someone who represents that which you desire. For example, to increase your drive for success, use a picture of a famous person who is known for their determination and hard work to achieve their goals. If you'd like to give your arts career a boost, consider a renowned artist. For love and attracting mates, find an image of a famous sex symbol. For prosperity, choose a photo of someone who is already successful in your field.

If you choose to use a picture or image of an individual you actually know in your day-to-day life, make sure that the energies you are imbibing in are positive ones. Using an image of someone you have feelings of jealousy and resentment toward will taint the spell entirely, and only gorge you on more unhappy feelings of inadequacy.

This spell calls for a piece of red meat, as you will be symbolically ingesting the blood and life force of the person. A vegan alternative is cooked beet root, which has bright red juice that can represent blood.

If the person is an artist, author, or inventor, have one of their works nearby, such as a copy of their book, a print of their artwork, or the object that has made them successful.

⤙⊰ MATERIALS

Pen

Paper

Sterile lancet

Photo or drawing of the person you admire, 5 by 7 inches at the largest

Edible portion of frozen red meat, wrapped in butcher paper. A bite-size
piece is fine. (substitution: beet root)

Lighter or matches

Firesafe dish, cauldron, or firepit

Place the items on your altar and cast your circle.

Invite the energy of the person into your circle. If they're famous, tap into their public persona, which is imbedded in the collective unconscious. Famous peoples' images live in the minds of large groups of people, similar to an archetype, and this collective image can be drawn into your circle almost like a deity.

Write down exactly what it is about the person you admire so much. Make a list of traits and accomplishments that inspire you and that you wish to take into yourself. While you do this, you can pretend you are talking to the person (if they're dead, they might just hear you!). Tell them how much you respect their work and that you wish to channel their qualities. When you're done, prick your finger and place a drop of blood on their picture.

Next, take the piece of food and set it on top of the picture. Envision them pouring their creative force and success into it and this energy transforming into blood (or juice), taking on physical form. See the food engulfed in the light of their power. Wrap it in butcher paper, and then wrap your own paper list around this. Thank the energy of the person, close your circle, and place the package in the freezer for 3 nights where no one will touch it. After the third night, take the food from the freezer. If it is meat, cook it rare so the "blood" is visible. If you used a beet, thaw it out and take note of the red juice.

At your altar, eat the food while contemplating the traits you're taking into yourself. Feel them enter your body, go into your bloodstream, and pump through your heart. They're a part of you now. Use this power wisely to accomplish the task you set out to complete. Burn the photo, list, and butcher paper afterward and scatter the ashes outdoors.

Urine Spell to Remove a Curse

Make a tea from dandelion leaves (dandelion is a diuretic and therefore cleansing). You can purchase dandelion tea made from the root or leaves, or you can make your own. Make sure you gather your dandelion leaves and roots from an area you are absolutely certain has not been sprayed with herbicides or pesticides, and wash them thoroughly before use.

As the tea is steeping, hold your hands over the steaming pot. Imagine it is glowing with cleansing, purifying energy. As you imagine yourself free and clear of the hex that has been placed upon you, chant:

Reverse, reverse, remove this curse.

After it has steeped for about 10 minutes, drink the tea. With each sip, imagine the warm liquid filling your body and coursing through all your capillaries, carrying its toxin-removing properties with it, gathering up all the negativity that has been put upon you.

Eventually, as the tea makes its way through your system, you will need to urinate. Imagine that inside your bladder is all the remnants of the curse put upon you, gathered there by the dandelion tea. As you urinate, see the curse leaving your system, and then being flushed away down the toilet.

This spell can be used to remove any unwanted energy from your person, whether it is a curse, an energetic tie to another person, or just the creepy-crawlies from being near someone who bothers you.

CHAPTER 6
ANIMALS AND THEIR PARTS

The subject of using animal parts in shadow magick often offends people and even creates a divide between members of the Pagan community. However, using animal parts such as hearts, bones, and horns in magick is rooted in the history of many traditions around the world, starting long ago when hunting food and keeping livestock were a normal part of everyday life. We're all familiar with the stereotype of a witch sacrificing chickens, sticking pins in toads, and slicing open hearts. This stereotype creates a lot of fear and misunderstanding, which can hopefully be assuaged by discussing it openly.

Animal remains can be used in ritual and magick in countless ways. Bones are so important in magick that chapter 7 is specifically dedicated to them.

An animal's traits come through their body parts into your magick, so choosing which creature to include in your practice is important. Snakeskin encompasses self-activated change and growth. One can carry cat claws for stealth and hunter energy or fox fur for cleverness. Every animal has different associations.

Preserved animal parts can be placed on the altar to attract the spirit of a certain creature into your practice. They're added to sachets, worn as jewelry, ground up to add to powders and incense, or engraved with runes or symbols for use in divination.

FINDING ANIMAL PARTS

Animal components can be salvaged in many ways that don't involve hurting an animal. That being said, there are various means of obtaining them, and peoples' values differ as far as what is "ethical" and what is not. As with everything regarding ethics, it's a fluid gray area that can be debated endlessly. Where you stand on this is your own personal choice. Personally, I would never kill an animal for use in magick. The following are some different sources of animal parts with various pros and cons for your consideration.

Natural Death/Predators

I put this one first because in my opinion it is the best and most fortuitous. If you pay attention, you'll be surprised just how often you find remains left by a predator or dead from natural causes. Larger animals attack and eat smaller ones, leaving a pile of bones and fur. Older animals fall behind the pack and pass away, to be consumed by vultures and scavengers. Babies are rejected from the nest. House pets like cats and dogs sometimes attack and kill smaller creatures because it's their natural instinct. Other times, an animal is found dead and intact, appearing mysteriously unharmed.

Finding dead animals seemingly at random happens to me so frequently it's honestly impossible to ignore. Here are just a few examples. On the morning of my fortieth birthday, I opened up my front door and right there at my feet were, literally, the wings of a dove. The dove's body was completely eaten, and all that was left were two perfect wings, connected by a bit of bloody bone. It was so jarring and seemed like a symbol sent straight from spirit, telling me, "Okay, lady, this is an important year for you. Get ready to grow wings and fly." Another time, on the night of a full moon in spring, when I was thinking about all the new projects I was undertaking, I went out to the garden and stumbled across a dead rabbit lying across the path perfectly intact. Its placement seemed so intentional, put directly where I had no choice but to find it. Rabbits represent beginnings and springing forward into new projects. Another time, when I was feeling discouraged about writing this book, I was given a crow that had been killed by a hawk to clean. Crows are definite symbols from dark deity, so it felt like this was a symbol from spirit to buck up and get writing. I can't help but think of these things as gifts and omens that arrived to give me a nudge in the right direction or help me make up my mind about something. Needless to say, I respectfully honored, cleaned, and salvaged the remains of all these creatures.

Some animals die from disease, and while it's not possible to always know for sure, there are some indications. If numbers of a species are found dead regularly, there's a good chance that disease is involved, and you should contact wildlife control. If you suspect an animal was diseased, it's best not to handle it at all.

Finding animal remains in nature is often a symbol sent to you from deity, the cosmos, spirit, or whatever you choose to name it. Of course, live animals are omens as well, but nothing stops you in your tracks like a dead creature placed in front of your nose. Pay attention, because when an animal dies at the hands of nature and is presented to you, you are being sent a very clear message. No bones about it.

Human Accidents (Roadkill)

An unfortunate reality of living in times of excessive cars and trucks is that many animals fall victim to road accidents. There's nothing sadder than a little skunk or squirrel squashed on the road, driven over without a single thought given to its life. Unfortunately, we see this all the time, especially on country roads and long stretches of highway. You may wish to collect animal remains that you find this way. My personal thoughts are that you are in fact honoring its life by cleaning it off the road and removing it from further thoughtless disrespect. You will need to follow the instructions later on in this chapter for cleaning bones and health and safety tips for collecting dead animals. As you gather the animal remains, say a word of thanks over them, acknowledging the animal's shortened life and sending love to its spirit. Tell the animal's spirit what you intend to do with its body, such as use it in magick that benefits the greater good. You will be able to feel the energy of the animal near you. It may have something to tell you. Send it love and respect.

This technique can be applied to any animal you find that has died directly or indirectly because of humans.

Some people feel that these animals have been tainted by human carelessness and disrespect and choose not to include them in their craft. Others, like I said, feel they are honoring an otherwise abandoned spirit. It's a personal choice. What you feel deep down is the answer. If you feel there is negativity attached to an animal whose life ended this way and don't want to use it in your magick, consider just giving it a respectful burial instead or at least moving its remains off the road away from further harm.

If you're unsure whether or not an animal is dead, do not touch it. An injured animal will bite. If it's a small animal, you can get a long stick and nudge it to see if it moves. A large animal can be deadly due to its size, and I wouldn't go near it at all if there were any question. A good indication that it's dead is that it will have begun to stiffen with rigor mortis. Its limbs will be frozen in position and it will be hard.

There is no way to know if an animal killed on the road was diseased, but you're better safe than sorry. Wear gloves when you handle it and do not get fluids on yourself.

If you find an animal that is in a severe state of decay and there are maggots crawling on it, you might not want to take it into your house or vehicle for hygiene reasons.

Purchasing

Believe it or not, there are entire businesses out there based on scavenged animal parts salvaged from natural sources. Some of these sellers live in remote areas where finding animal remains is commonplace, and they sell the bones, teeth, and claws already cleaned. This is a good alternative for those who would rather not do the dirty work of bone cleaning (and believe me, *it's dirty*, but more on that later). If you're concerned about animals being harmed by humans, most of the time you can contact the store online and ask. Many sellers are forthright on their website explaining where they source their wares. If the tooth, claw, or bone came from an endangered, rare, or extinct species, it was definitely not a cruelty-free salvaged item, and you'd best stay away from it. It's also probably illegal. On that note, there are laws in place about buying and selling animal remains depending on where you live, especially from one country into another. Certain things are banned completely. For example, in Canada and the United States it is illegal to have the remains of most migratory birds.[6] Reputable sellers will not have banned items on offer anyway, but it never hurts to do some research about legalities in your area while shopping.

---

6. You can read more about the Migratory Bird Treaty Act of 1918 here when sourcing your materials: https://www.fws.gov/birds/policies-and-regulations/laws-legislation/migratory-bird-treaty-act.php.

Some animal parts, such as faces, tails, and pelts, are left over from the fashion industry or hunting. Many people are against this. That being said, other practitioners believe that these discarded animal parts are better off being honored by someone using them in magick than just going to waste, similar to their feelings about honoring roadkill. Some people feel that these animals were killed long ago, or in a way that they themselves have no control over, and that refusing to use the parts is pointless and not helping the problem anyway. This is a conundrum for your own moral compass.

Hunters

Hunting is another way to source animal remains, which may or may not be appealing or ethical in some circles. Where I live, it is legal at certain times of the year to hunt turkeys, deer, coyotes, and more. Fishing falls into the hunting category as well. People who hunt typically eat the whole animal, and often the skins and fur are used as well. If you know someone who hunts, you may be able to ask for discarded parts they do not want or need, such as antlers, skulls, teeth, claws, hooves, and other parts not needed for meat. If you are against hunting or eating wild game, this would perhaps not be an option for you.

Factory Farms

Most of the meat you buy at large chain grocers comes from factory farming. The problem with factory farming, and the reason so many people are against it, is that it is thought that the animals there are mistreated and that the process is harmful to the earth. While one person may argue that using remains of factory-farmed creatures is unethical because the animals were mistreated in life, another person would argue that since the animal was already dead, using their parts is okay and even honoring the animal in a way by including them in something spiritual. This side of the argument believes that these animals are being killed and slaughtered in a way that they cannot help or control, as mentioned earlier, and that using them in ritual is better than them going to waste.

It is your choice whether to use factory-farmed animals in your witchcraft, just as it is your choice whether to eat them or not.

ANIMALS AND MAGICK

How do animal and insect parts factor into witchcraft? Animals, including teeny-tiny insects, are interwoven in a witch's craft. Every animal is an archetype for a larger energy current, which can be tapped into for use in magick or shown to us as an omen. Here we're going to discuss two ways that animals and insects play into our magickal experience: first, as messengers carrying omens from divinity; and second, by integrating them into ritual. Following that is a list of animals and their associations in terms of symbolism and magickal properties.

Animals as Messengers

I am a firm believer that there are no coincidences in this life and that everything we experience has a purpose. I believe that spirit is constantly communicating with us through any means possible—what we see, words we hear, people we meet. Spirit is guiding us all the time. We just need to know what to look for.

One of the major conduits spirit uses to communicate with us is nature. When in touch with the dark moon phase in your life, you may find yourself coming into contact with like-minded creatures, by which I mean creatures of the night. These are mostly nocturnal animals or are animals that have what we conventionally consider "dark" or mystical aspects. For example, during my own shadow work, I was very connected to owls and vultures. One is a nocturnal predator and the other a beast of carrion. Both are associated with death energy. These birds showed up for me on a daily basis during my own time of darkness. Knowing what I do now, I could have noted all the owls I was seeing and realized I was headed into the cauldron for a big, mind-expanding transformation. Now I know to pay attention next time.

Animal guides may appear in the flesh as you go about your day or night, or you may find yourself inundated with imagery of a specific animal. This is not a coincidence. The energy of that animal is trying to give you a message, offer guidance, or even issue a warning. Many wild animals are mostly hidden, especially in our industrialized society, which means the sighting of a bat or coyote is truly a gift and very meaningful. When an animal spirit has information for you, you will know it: a ton of imagery about one animal suddenly, coincidentally, being thrown in your path will be difficult to ignore once you see it. If you find that everywhere you look, you seem to see pictures of owls, you need to pay attention to what an owl means!

The trick is figuring out what the animal is trying to tell you. Consider that animal's traits, talents, and special abilities, and those will be clues. Books and websites are great starting points, but it's worth mentioning that what message an animal has for you is highly dependent on how *you* feel about the creature, regardless of what any outside resource says. If you have a terrifying phobia of cats, then seeing a cat is a definite warning for you, no matter what nice things a kitty represents for me.

My Lesson from Vultures

I had an interesting experience with vultures a few years ago that illustrates how clearly spirit communicates with us through animals. Vultures, sometimes called buzzards, are birds of carrion, which means they eat other dead animals. Many people erroneously dismiss them as disgusting, lowly scavengers. The most common vulture in my area is the turkey vulture, which is a massive black bird with a six-foot wingspan. When turkey vultures roost, they gather their magnificent black wings around their bodies like a vampire cape, adding to their foreboding appearance. Usually, they travel in groups and can be seen high up in the sky riding the wind in spiral patterns. Vultures appear when death is literally near. They spy a sick or injured animal down on the ground and gather to circle it from above, waiting patiently for its demise. Then they descend on what is left of its dead body and consume it, integrating its shed earthly shell back into nature's cycle. When we look at death not as a scary ending, like we've been taught, but as a beginning and fresh start, the vulture takes on a whole new meaning. No longer just a scavenging eater of death, the vulture is here to carry creatures to their next incarnation, much like a psychopomp, escorting them to the other side, into the spirit world. They come to warn us that they're about to carry us through a transformative, probably challenging, experience that changes us permanently.

During the several years when my mother had cancer, a group of vultures started nesting in a public park right near my home. It's very unusual for vultures to nest in a busy place with all that noise and activity, yet this is where they chose to live. Every time I left the house, I would see them soaring around and around in the distance, sometimes right over my yard. This went on consistently for the years that my mother was suffering her long, treacherous illness. The vultures were a constant circling presence in the sky, much like my mother's declining health was a constant thought in my mind. Shortly after she died and I was deeply grieving, I decided to take a walk on the natural pathways in the park one day. Suddenly a bizarre, huge black creature appeared on the path ahead of me. I stopped and stared. I'd never seen such an enormous, strange bird up close. It was monstrously scary looking. I froze. After a moment, it spread huge cape-like wings and took flight, its feathers so big I could almost feel the wind they made on my face. It felt like the vulture had stopped me on the path to get my attention. It showed me that it was flying away now, as if to say, "Our work here is done." After that startling confrontation, I gradually stopped seeing vultures in the sky and their numbers decreased locally, parallel with how I began to heal from my loss. In this way, vultures came into my life to signify the death that was coming, as well as the huge personal transition I would experience as a result. They saw me through the harrowing experience of illness and death of a loved one, with their message about the unending cycles of life, and then went on their way.

Another time, I was going for a run in the park at dawn and saw five vultures roosting on a tree over the river, hunched there like grim reapers. I stopped to admire them for a moment, and they all took flight. A minute later I almost got killed by a car running a red light and was only saved because another person pulled me back out of the way. That time, the vultures were warning me to watch out.

If you pay attention, it's amazing how often nature reflects what is happening in our lives. Nature works in mysterious, coincidental ways, always in synch, never by accident.

Incorporating Animal Remains in Ritual

The second way that animal energies factor into witchcraft is when we use their bones and other parts in our spells and rituals. There is a lot to learn about this, from the very practical details of cleaning bones to what different body parts mean and what to do with them. We'll expand further on that and get specific about the powers of different animals and how to integrate them into our witchcraft.

Toward the end of this chapter is a list of animal meanings. The animals on my list are mostly found in North America because they're what I'm familiar with. Since this book focuses on the dark moon energy in our lives, the animals listed are mainly nocturnal, beasts of carrion, or underground animals that spend their lives connected to the shadow current and darkness. Research animals from your own area to find out their history and what they may mean. Some of the symbolism for certain animals bridges cultures and spans civilizations. For example, the symbolism of the fox in Western, Asian, Indigenous Canadian, Native American, and Druid folklore is all similar: diplomacy, cunning, slyness, and sometimes trickery. The fox having the same symbolism in societies so separated by time and space is meaningful, as it indicates a larger archetype in the collective unconscious. It means that fox spirit is real and alive all over the world and not something made up by one group to suit their purposes or immediate needs. Similar worldwide patterns can be seen with the spider, the snake, and countless others. When working with animal energies, it helps to do some background research on top of your own feelings toward the animal, as these collective beliefs are powerful indeed.

Animal lore is rich and bountiful. When choosing an animal or insect to work with in magick, I focus a little bit on mythology but also on the behavior of that particular creature, including its strengths and characteristics, when calling upon it in spells or rituals.

ANIMAL PARTS IN SPELLS

There's evidence to support that mentions of animal parts in spells in old texts, specifically Shakespeare, were actually simply folk names for herbs and not to be taken literally. This is true in many cases. However, to say that old-world witchcraft never made use of actual animal parts is just as dubious as claiming those same people never ate meat. Hunting and farming livestock was a natural part of life. Killing and eating animals, preparing them for food, and making use of the leftover parts were all very ordinary parts of living.

While many witches prefer to stick to bones and skulls for magick, there are of course other animal parts to consider. We've all seen rabbit's feet made into key chains. While some animal parts are much messier to handle than others, they do have their uses in magick and a history therein. The following is a brief list of different parts and what they might be used for in spells. Please keep in mind that organs can spread germs and illness.

Antlers and Horns

Antlers are very common items and are readily available. Each year, male deer and other antlered mammals drop their racks naturally and grow new ones in their place. If you're a serious hiker or spend a lot of time in remote areas, seeing deer or moose antlers on the ground is an ordinary sight. Almost all animals with antlers are male (except reindeer—which means Santa's sled just may have been pulled by does). Males use their antlers against one another during mating season in feats of strength as they battle for female companions. They do this by locking their antlers together and wrestling; the buck with the strongest rack wins female attention and also leadership in the hierarchy of the group. This same technique is used to battle for territory. Sometimes antlers are employed as weapons in a fight, but mostly they are a visual signal to communicate power and dominance. In this way, antlers are associated with strength, victory, and sexual attraction. Antlers and horns are also associated with gods with horns, such as Pan (Greek) and Cernunnos (Celtic). The horned gods generally encompass fertility, warrior energy, action, sexuality, protection, and power. Horns and antlers can be used in magick to channel all these energies.

Horns, such as those of sheep or goats, do not shed annually like antlers do.

You can purchase antlers and horns whole or in pieces to make into your own jewelry or charms. You can even powder them with a file to add to soaps, oils, sachets, and incense. However, be warned: antler and horn are not known for smelling pretty when burned!

Teeth

For predators, sharp fangs are not only used for protection and defense but also for survival and the conquering of prey. Teeth can therefore be used as protection charms or as part of spells for victory and power. If the tooth comes from a carnivore, they are most likely at the top of the food chain, making them useful in dominance and personal power spells or to protect yourself from the emotional "predators" you encounter in day-to-day life. In the animal world, showing the teeth when threatened by another animal is a way to ward off attack and danger. An animal will bare its fangs to threaten an enemy and scare them away. Sharp animal teeth can be used in a spell of this nature and send off the vibe that you are not to be threatened.

Teeth that are not fangs are also considered protective. Even herbivores will bite when provoked, and it hurts! Molars are used for chewing food and can be integrated into spells for abundance and prosperity.

Claws

Much like teeth, claws are a mechanism of defense and protecting oneself. Any animal, even a tiny herbivore, will use its sharp claws for defense, and size doesn't matter—even mouse claws bring pain. They can be used in protection magic, in deflective magick to "fight back," or to bring pain upon an enemy. Many animals such as cats organically shed their claws, leaving behind a husk that naturally falls off and maintains the shape of the claw. This can be added to spells or mixtures for protection or any working in which a claw would be appropriate.

Bird Feet

You can make charms from bird feet according to what kind of bird the claw came from. You can figure out its qualities based on its behavioral patterns or folklore about the bird.

The most popular use of bird feet is in protective magick. Most birds have big and sharp claws, and the idea is that they can scratch and gouge, a quality that can be used in defensive magick. Also, a charm made from a bird's foot looks scary all on its own. However, bird talons can be used in many other ways, from love to prosperity.

Chicken, turkey, and duck feet can be purchased at specialty grocers or from people who hunt wild game. They are affordable and come in bulk; however, they do require some work and preparation for use. There are several spells using bird feet in this book, but the feet must be properly prepared ahead of time, which is explained later in this chapter.

Hooves

Hooves are part of an animal that typically doesn't get used by hunters or butchers. You can find these sometimes with the legs still attached, dried and made into ornaments. Hooves can be powdered and added to magick powders and salts or placed whole on your altar. There are different kinds of hooves:

Cloven Hooves: A cloven hoof is divided in two and seen on goats, sheep, pigs, and cattle. The cloven hoof is a popular symbol of Satan and evil. Cloven hooves have ties with the Horned God, Pan, the Green Man, and more. Cloven hooves are associated with carnal desires, sex, fertility, prosperity, and, if you believe in it, the "evil" of Satan.

Equine Hooves: These hooves are one solid piece and don't share the demonized reputation of the cloven hoof. Because they are associated with horses, they represent power, strength, virility, capability, and beauty. They can be used in spells for all those things.

Feet

Feet are of course all about movement. They mean different things depending on which animal they come from, but some stand out through time as having had specific purposes. They're used in spells for travel, forging new paths, and stability. The rabbit's foot has a long history of bringing good fortune to the one who carries it and has an association with money and gambler's luck. Rabbits are symbols of fertility, growth, fresh beginnings, and procreation, so use rabbits' feet, or bones from rabbits' feet, for spells of these kinds. When it comes to the feet of other animals, consider that animal's magickal associations and then combine it with the idea of movement and travel.

Ears, Eyes, and Tongues

While the thought of actually touching and using any of these items in spell work is off-putting to say the least, it has certainly been done. Eyeballs of animals are used in spells for truth seeking, ears represent wisdom and learning, and the tongue is all about communication. These items, which typically are harder to preserve and dry, unlike bones or claws, can be replaced with alternatives such as cat's eye shells or cat's eye stones.

Hearts

The heart is the very core of every living creature and is very powerful. Hearts are most commonly used in love spells. They can be added to a poppet to act as the heart of the person it represents or dried and added to powders, incense, and spells. They can be pierced with needles to inflict emotional turmoil and heartbreak or lovingly wrapped and used in healing spells.

Fur and Pelts

Fur can be used for camouflage, which for us translates to protection. You can also add a sprig of fur to your spells to share characteristics of the animal with your working. For example, adding some cat fur to a spell for stealth would make sense. The pelt of a carnivorous animal, such as a coyote, can act as symbolic protection. Furs can be placed on your altar to attract the energy of an animal just like bones.

Skin

Reptiles such as snakes and lizards shed their skin naturally. If you find bits of molt, add them to spells for change, renewal, fresh beginnings, and shedding the past. Molts can be utilized in any spell for letting go of something or banishing unwanted qualities.

Wings

While possessing parts of wild birds is illegal in many places, you may be lucky enough to find an intact domestic bird and keep its wing. You can stretch it out and dry it in borax or salt. You can also purchase intact bird wings. These make wonderful fans for smoke ceremonies. Because wings are associated with air, they are used in spells for communication, learning, intellect, ideas, and sending messages. The type of bird dictates further what it might be used for. For example a peacock feather is very different from a rooster feather, so whatever feather you find, do some research and meditation to figure out what it is meant to show you.

Feathers

These are much like wings, associated with air energy. Their purpose depends on which kind of bird they came from and what color they are. You can apply the usual color associations of magick to the feather: for example, red for love, yellow for communication, or white for spirituality. Again, these are useful in communication spells and sending messages.

Tails

Animals use their tails for many things. The type of tail you have and what it was used for in life will give you insight into its magickal properties. Cats use their tails for their incredible balancing feats, whereas canines use their tails for communicating through body language. Birds use their tails to steer as they fly through the air, and fish use their tails the same way in the water. Tails can be included in spells for communication, travel, and stability.

Other Internal Organs

While I personally usually prefer not to make use of entrails or innards of animals due to mess and other reasons, these parts do have their place in religious ritual and divination. Haruspicy was the act of inspecting the entrails of an animal to glean information about the past, present, and future. In Rome, animals that were sacrificed to the gods were then sliced open and their organs examined for signs and portends. The liver was believed to be especially important in divination.[7]

Substitutions

In part 2 of this book, when describing spells using animal parts, I've included at least one suggestion in each for plant-based substitutes. Perhaps you do not wish to use animal parts in magick whatsoever, and that is perfectly okay. If this is the case for you, but you find a spell that appeals to you, here are some suggestions for replacing animal parts with vegetable matter instead.

Animal Hearts: Any small dehydrated fruit or vegetable can be used in place of an animal heart. Some suggestions are prunes, dried apricots, artichoke hearts, cherries, and beetroot.

Antlers: Use branches.

Bird Feet: A twisted root that is very strong can be shaped and dehydrated just like a bird foot. Choose your root according to intent. Dried invasive vines, such as bindweed or ivy, can also be tied and twisted in such a way as to keep a certain shape, such as a foot.

---

7. Lewis, *Ritual Sacrifice*, 59.

Blood: Some replacements for blood in spells are beet juice, walnut ink, milk, and egg yolk.

Bones: Depending on intent, consider twigs and stems of various plants. The sticks can be dried and cut into random shapes for divination or tied onto an amulet just like a bone can be. Sticks can be drawn or etched on once they are dry, just like a bone. Research the magickal properties of trees in your area and use them instead.

Eggs: Try bulbs or large seeds. Walnut or other large nut shells can replace an eggshell.

Fur or Pelts: Instead of fur, you can use fabric in the color aligned with your magickal intent. You can also obtain fur that was clipped or shed without affecting the animal.

Skulls: Pumpkins or gourds painted to look like skulls can replace the real thing, especially when dried or with their insides removed.

Teeth or Claws: Use thorns.

GATHERING AND CLEANING BONES

Though every once in a while you'll be lucky enough to find bones and skulls that nature has naturally cleaned up on its own, usually it requires more elbow grease than that. I have to be honest: cleaning bones is not a pleasant task, and that's why it's a business all on its own. However, if you're up for collecting and cleaning your own, there are a few different ways to do so depending on where you live, what kind of space you have to work in, and how much time you're willing to invest in it.

Some basic tools you may need are rubber or plastic gloves, plastic or metal tubs for soaking, plastic bags or reusable containers for transport, and large pots or bowls. Any dishes you use should be set aside only for bone cleaning and never used for food or anything else. You'll also need sea salt, borax, peroxide, and biological washing powder.

Never touch bones you find with your bare hands until they have been cleaned. They are a host to disease and germs—and sometimes an unfortunate stink. Wear gloves when picking up bones you've found, placing them carefully in a plastic bag or washable tub for transport. If you can avoid plastics by having reusable gloves and a metal box set aside just for this purpose, instead of a plastic bag, that's great. However, remember these objects will be contaminated and can attract germs, so be sure to disinfect them between uses.

Sometimes you'll find bones that are already cleaned by nature, but often they will need a little extra work before they are safe to make into jewelry or touch without gloves. Some people place bones in the freezer until they're ready to clean them, which will kill any bugs or parasites on them, but I wouldn't personally recommend taking a stinky, bug-ridden corpse into your home. I prefer burying it outside to let nature cleanse most of the flesh off before working with the bones, although this isn't an option for everyone. If you cannot bury an animal, I would suggest that for now you seek out an ethical place from which to purchase precleaned bones. This is a messy business and best done outside!

There are four steps to cleaning an animal you find in order to make use of the bones: burying, maceration/soaking, filing and picking, and degreasing.

Burying Bones

Burying bones involves simply digging a substantial hole in the earth on your own property, placing the dead animal in the hole, covering with dirt, and letting nature run its course. Burial is an ideal way to begin if you have found a mostly intact animal.

Keep in mind there are bylaws in some cities that make it illegal to bury animals on your property for various reasons, so check the rules where you live before doing this.

If you have found an animal that's still partially intact, my personal preferred method of cleaning it is burial. I'm fortunate enough to have a yard to work in. Burial is the least smelly and messy method I have tried, and it lessens or eliminates the time you will have bones sitting around soaking in peroxide or water. The biggest problem I've encountered with burying bones is timing. If left in the ground too long, the bones will start to rot and you will lose part of your animal. If not left long enough, when you dig it up, it will still have flesh and moisture on it—this experience is not for someone with a weak stomach.

How deep you bury your animal depends on its size. For a small creature like a bird or mouse, one foot is plenty deep. For something larger, such as a fully grown raccoon, I recommend around three feet deep. Before burial, wrap the animal in burlap, a piece of sheet, muslin, or wire screen to ensure the bones all stay in one place while still allowing insects and bacteria in to break down the flesh. Pack the earth over the top thoroughly, and place heavy rocks or cement blocks on top of the site. Do not skip this step! This is not just a way of marking the spot for when you return. If you neglect to put a weighty object on top of the burial, it will be dug up by scavengers. This can be a disturbing sight to say the least, not to mention you will have lost your animal.

Now comes the tricky part: timing. Figuring out when to dig up bones varies greatly, depending on several factors: the size of the animal, how much flesh was still on it when buried, soil quality, and the time of year. For a small animal, waiting one to two months is long enough to check on it. Larger animals you may leave for three or four months. Be prepared for some trial and error; you may have to rebury the animal and wait another month. It is okay to leave the animal buried over the winter. The earth, and it, will freeze, and then it will continue to decompose in the spring. The freezing also helps kill germs and bacteria that may be living on it. Even after being buried, bones may still have cartilage and connective tissue on them, which will have to be removed by maceration or by hand, which are methods explained next.

Maceration

Maceration refers to covering the bones completely with water, letting them sit, and allowing water to very slowly work away the flesh. After you have dug up your bones after burial and they still have connective tissue and gristle on them, maceration is the next step. Maceration is also appropriate for an animal you find that has mostly deteriorated and only has a small amount of flesh on it still. Maceration is a long process but leaves bones clean and intact and allows more control over the outcome than burial because you can keep a closer eye on the process.

Simply place the bones in a bowl or bucket of water and patiently leave them, changing the water every few days. This is considered the most effective method of flesh removal and the least disruptive to the physical makeup of the bones. The downside is that it can take one to ten months and is extremely stinky. It also requires space to store all this smelly stuff during the process. Some people prefer to add enzyme detergent, also called biological washing powder, to the water, although it's not absolutely necessary. This is a type of powdered laundry soap containing enzymes that break down grease, proteins, and fats to effectively remove stains on laundry and, incidentally, gristle and soft tissue on bones. Non-enzyme detergents will not have the same effect. Many popular brands of laundry soap use enzymes; simply read the label to see which ones. Dissolve one part soap in three parts water, and let the bones soak covered in this. Change the water every few days. When you remove the bones, rinse them very well so that the enzyme detergent doesn't continue to eat away at the bones.

Cleaning with Hydrogen Peroxide

The next step is to clean the bones with hydrogen peroxide, which can be purchased from hair salon suppliers or in small amounts at the pharmacy. It is available in varying concentrations, but the higher percentages are harder to purchase because they are dangerous. I've personally used peroxide from the pharmacy, which is only a 3 percent concentration, many times, and it works fine for small critters. Some taxidermists use peroxide that is up to a 35 percent concentration, but this can be dangerous and difficult to obtain. Even when using low concentrations of peroxide, wear gloves and eye protection when handling it. Do not get it on your skin, eyes, or even your clothes. You may add peroxide to your maceration water in a fifty-fifty measurement to help break down fats or cover the bones completely only with peroxide for faster results. Do not use peroxide and enzyme detergent at the same time.

Peroxide will whiten and sterilize the bones while softening tissue and making it easier to remove by hand.

Contrary to popular belief, bones should never be bleached or boiled. Bleach will turn them to powder, and boiling weakens them considerably.

Filing and Picking

Even after all this work, no matter what method you use, there can still be gristle and cartilage on your bones. Now begins the real manual labor of bone cleaning—peeling and prying by hand, flossing with wire, and sanding off soft tissue with a metal file. There's no magickal trick to make this go easier. You just have to do the work. Believe me, you don't want any gristle and cartilage left on your jewelry or on your altar. It will smell terrible and attract unwanted pests.

Degreasing

After you've removed all the soft tissue you can, cover the bone in sea salt or borax and leave them there until they are completely dried. Letting the bones sit in borax or salt also leeches all the remaining grease out of them. You can change the borax or salt once a week until the bones are dry.

When working with any animal flesh of any kind, please wear gloves and remember to avoid cross contamination—that is, do not touch raw meat and then your wand or chalice with your dirty hand, as this spreads bacteria that can make you sick. Wash your hands thoroughly after every time you touch flesh, meat, fresh bones, or organs. Once the bones are completely cleaned of gristle and totally dry, you can touch them without worry.

Gathering, burying, and cleaning bones can be a very long process, sometimes taking months. There is no quick way to get it done, and you must be in synch with nature for it to be successful.

Dehydration

A food dehydrator can be used on parts of animals such as claws, feet, and even small organs. I don't recommend trying to dehydrate anything fleshier than bird talons, as it would take far too long.

When drying bird feet, remember that they are raw meat and must be treated as such. Avoid cross contamination when handling them. Bird feet must be dried thoroughly to prevent rot and unwanted smells. One way to do this is with a normal food dehydrator. Space the feet in a single layer and not touching one another on the racks, and dehydrate them for about three days. You want to make sure they are absolutely, certainly, 100-percent dried. If your bird feet still have moisture in them when you store them, they can grow mold, attract pests, and smell bad.

The second way to dehydrate them is by putting them in a dish and covering them with borax or salt. This can take several weeks. Be sure to check them every few days and change the salt or borax as needed. Borax and salt draw moisture out of the feet and keep bacteria away as well.

Depending on the spell you are doing, you may want to shape the feet before drying them. This can be done by tying them into the desired position with string so they will harden that way. Some examples are tying the two side toes down and leaving the middle one up (like it's "giving the finger" or "flipping someone off"), shaping them to hold something (like money in a prosperity spell), or positioning the middle claw down and side claws up (like horns). To shape them to hold on to things, try tying them around a marble and drying them that way. You can remove the marble afterward, and your claw will be ready to hold whatever you put into it. Sometimes you can dry the feet while holding the item included in the spell, such as a coin or crystal. This is fine too, as long as your object isn't flammable and will not be ruined by the heat of the dehydrator or salt.

ANIMAL LIST

The following is a list of animals that are often seen in and around my area and what they mean magickally. These are mostly animals that appear during the dark moon current in your life and are generally associated with shadow work.

Bat: Bats live their lives at night and are dependent on sound and echolocation to hunt and navigate the world, rather than their vision. A bat sighting indicates you need to look deeper into a situation than what is right in front of your eyes, that there's more going on than you can see. Bats symbolize messages coming to your intuition or through your dreams. Unseen energy is guiding you, just as invisible sound guides the bat. Bat energy can be used in spells for learning secrets and asking for guidance in murky situations. Add bat parts to dream pillows to aid in prophetic dreams, keep them with divination tools, or carry them with you when intuition is needed.

Cat: Stealthy, aloof and independent, the cat is a fierce, dominant hunter. Cats answer to no one. They do as they please and are their own masters. They often win fights against much larger creatures and saunter coolly afterward. Cats teach you to do the same: to be in charge of your own actions and destiny and embrace your fighting spirit. During a cat nap, a cat looks like it is sound asleep when in fact it is wide awake, listening, smelling, and planning; unbeknownst to any observer, the cat is pulling in information and plotting its next move. They appear placid but are actually very much alert and aware of everything around them. When unsure how to proceed in life, use the same technique. Cat parts can be used in an endless amount of spells; protection, hunting, psychic ability, lunar workings—and are a favorite witch's familiar.

Crow: Entire books and movies have been made about these wonderful birds. Crows are a witch's best friend, and for good reason. The crow represents the death of one thing so that another may begin. They are the blackness between the end and the beginning. Crows are present at war and sacred to the Morrigan. The presence of crows heralds death. Crows can travel between this world and the next, making them symbols of knowledge, wisdom, and the unknown. Like witches, crows have one foot in each world—that of the living and that of spirit—and perhaps that is why we like each other so much. When crow energy is present in your life, you are being guided to look to the occult, the esoteric, and the witchy side. The crow calls on you to explore your dark side, and it will appear to remind you that magick is real. Use crow energy for spells for death, endings, occult knowledge, and spiritual journeys.

Coyote: Coyotes are able to survive and breed in any environment, including secretly in the middle of cities completely unseen by humans. Coyotes are a miracle of evolution, wile, and adaptability. Much as humans try to trap and control these animals, they continue to thrive and outsmart us again and again, outwitting those who try to interfere. Coyotes are cunning, intelligent, and strategic. Coyote energy is crafty, tough, and determined to succeed. Use coyote remains in spells for outwitting your rivals and enemies.

Frog and Toad: Frogs and toads are another witch's favorite. Frogs and toads have figured into folklore since the times of ancient Egypt and Mesopotamia. They're associated with predicting weather and bringing luck and fertility. On the other end of the spectrum, frogs and toads were demonized as witch's familiars and agents of the devil during the witch hunts. Stories abound from this time of their body parts being used in various curses and hexes. In your own practice, they can encompass either of these extremes depending on how you personally feel about these warty, slimy creatures.

Mole: The common mole can be found all over North America and beyond, though we rarely see them. The most we ever glimpse of these underground rodents is a mole hill or what looks like lines of disturbed grass on the lawn where they've been tunneling below the surface. Underground, these blind animals create and navigate entire complex subterranean mazes. Moles rely almost entirely on touch to live and eat. They feel their way through life. Mole energy is useful for feeling your way through new or uncharted territory.

Mouse: Mouse energy tells us to be quiet, lie low, and keep our mouth shut. A mouse can signify that you're potentially prey in a situation, so make yourself scarce. Mouse energy is good for keeping yourself hidden and thriving while unseen and unnoticed. Mice are good animals to work with when your best defense is to just appear to disappear. In some contexts, mice are believed to spread disease and illness and are associated with the destruction of crops and food sources. Mouse bones can be added to spells for destroying things or symbolically setting pestilence upon a situation.

Opossum: The opossum is the only marsupial in the Americas and is most famous for its ability to "play dead" when faced with a predator. When under attack, an opossum will seize up and lie still for hours, letting off a bad stink to keep itself safe. This is where the saying "playing possum" comes from. It means to just lie low, play dead, don't stir up a scene, and literally do nothing. If you see an opossum, this may be the message. Opossum parts can be used in spells for deflecting enemies and shielding yourself from harm.

Owl: An owl spends the majority of its life watching and waiting for prey. It is an observer and an outsider who travels alone. In many cultures, owls are a portent of death. This death association can also be linked to representing big life changes. Owls are one of the few predators who ingest an entire animal for prey, leaving nothing behind; they can literally stomach anything. This can represent an ability to withstand, ingest, and learn from whatever life throws at you, no matter how unpalatable. Owls also draw attention to matters of the mind, wisdom, occult mysteries, and lessons. Owls represent the pursuits of a spiritual seeker. Use owl energy for magick involving boosting your own mystical powers. Owl pellets also contain bones of the creatures they've eaten, which may be identifiable enough to use in magick as well.

Porcupine: Proceed with caution. The porcupine represents a seemingly harmless situation that can turn into disaster quickly. It's also a sign that you need to protect yourself. Act prickly to shield your soft heart. Use porcupine quills or bones in spells for protecting yourself against enemies or stopping someone from inflicting pain on you or others. Simply stabbing a porcupine quill into a picture of a person or thing is a spell in itself to quell their negative energy and protect you.

Raccoon: These scavengers are not afraid of anything. Brazen and brave, raccoons are able to use their handlike claws and discerning minds to solve any problem in order to get what they want (which is usually food). Raccoons are considered a nuisance in cities because they are so good at figuring out humans' traps, locks, and defenses against them. They can figure out how to open complicated containers and garbage bins. Undoing puzzles and overcoming obstacles are the raccoon's strengths, and their energy can help you negotiate your way through a difficult scenario. Raccoons go after what they want fearlessly and with determined focus and will fight what gets in their way. The striped tail is especially indicative of a sleuthing nature, containing both the dark and light. Raccoon parts can be used in spells to boost one's determination, to unlock the puzzles or deceit of another person, or for stealing. Raccoon penis bones are associated with love and luck.

Rat: Rats are a real source of horror for many. This is most likely because of their association with spreading disease and destroying homes and crops. Rats are also amazingly cunning and clever, adaptable to almost any situation or habitat, and true survivors. Rat bones and teeth or dried rat tails can be used in pestilence spells as described in the mouse section. Rat parts can be used for spells involving cunning, discernment, and trickery. The phrase "I smell a rat!" means something seems dishonest or untruthful. Another saying, "the rats are abandoning ship," refers to disloyal associates. Rats can be used in any spell regarding disloyalty, exposing a scam, or an otherwise bad person.

Skunk: When skunks are provoked, their reaction reeks for several miles around them. They really know how to clear a room. If they spray someone, the stench is almost impossible to wash out. Skunks warn that there may be someone or something in your life that is a dramatic stink bomb waiting to happen, and once the situation explodes, it will have lasting, unpleasant affects. Look out for that person who may be a ticking time bomb of drama and disaster. Skunk parts can be used in spells to dramatically hinder the actions of others or to spread a "big stink" symbolically that ruins a situation (think a skunk at a picnic). Use bones, teeth, claws, or the tail with fur on. Warning: never approach a skunk. I guarantee you will regret it!

Snake: The snake is one of those iconic animals that have represented both good and evil over time. Some people have deeply entrenched phobias of snakes, whereas others are beguiled by their strange beauty. The snake outgrows and sheds its skin and is therefore connected to rebirth and self-generated change. One of my personal favorite symbols is the ouroboros, in which the snake is shown eating its own tail. The ouroboros is a reminder that creation and progress are always a result of destruction. Snake energy can be included in meditation or magickal workings for renewal, for letting go of the past, for banishing unwanted habits and traits, and for blessing a new beginning. If you are someone who deeply hates snakes, you can draw on that repulsion for curses and hexes. Shed snakeskin is easily found in nature, and sometimes bones as well.

Vulture: A vulture can spot a sick or dying animal from afar; it will hang around patiently gliding on the air currents until the suffering animal expires, then seemingly ruthlessly descend on the corpse to eat it. Vultures take what has died, eat it, and transform it into energy for themselves, thus assimilating it into the great cycle of life, death, and rebirth. Vultures represent taking the past and learning from it. They also herald big important changes in life that affect your future. Vultures often have a negative connotation. For example, to call a person a "vulture" means they search for ways to benefit from other peoples' misfortune, such as when a family member dies "the vultures" come along hoping to get money or property from them, pouncing in to pick at the corpse, so to speak, before it has even gone cold. If this is the association in your mind for vultures, next time you see one you may want to be on the lookout for human ones! Vulture energy can be used in spells to remove aspects of you that are holding you back, resolving the past, overcoming trauma, and letting go of that which no longer serves you.

Weasel: Weasels are known to hunt relentlessly night and day. They are among the most successful of hunters, often killing more prey than they can eat and saving it for later. Weasels are solitary and capable of killing animals much larger than themselves. They can be called upon for hunting skills, dominating others, and abundance. In the modern world, this translates into making money and beating down competition for position and rank.

Wolf: Wolves were given a bad reputation in fairy tales, known for eating people and ferociously destroying the homes of little pigs. While wolves are carnivores that eat smaller creatures, underneath their strength they're shy, intelligent, and wise. The imagery of the wolf is a strong one that resonates with many people. Wolves represent loyalty, strength, survival, and warrior energy. Due to stories of children being raised by wolves (whether true or not), they are also associated with maternal instinct and nurturance.

CREEPY-CRAWLIES

Not much has been written about bugs from a magickal perspective, mostly because they are considered "lower" than bigger creatures and because the idea of touching them makes many people shiver.

Insects are just as important to our ecosystem as everything else living here on earth. Some of them, like the dragonfly, have relatives dating back to when dinosaurs roamed the earth! These are ancient, powerful beings and their energy can contribute to your magick just as much as birds or mammals. This list of insects is not limited to shadow work. Unlike animal symbolism, which has been written about extensively, I feel like insects have been overlooked somewhat, and for that reason I've included all kinds of common bugs and their magickal uses in this list.

Ant: A colony of ants is like no other community in the animal world. Thousands of ants work together to build entire cities underground, each with their own job, working as a team for the betterment of the whole. In this vein, ant energy can be utilized for making friends, cooperation, and attracting like-minded people into your life. Every single ant in a colony has its own task and is never idle, so ants can be used in employment spells. Ants are amazingly strong for their size and can carry fifty times their own body weight, so ant energy can help when you need the strength to shoulder many burdens. Fire ants, known for biting and stinging, can be employed in spells to cause destruction or pain.

Bees: Bees, in particular honeybees, are masters of industry. Honeybees represent being a productive part of your community, as well as working hard toward a positive goal. A honeybee is useful in magick pertaining to studying and schoolwork, starting a business, or any other industrious pursuit that requires you to buckle down and put your nose to the grindstone. The honey produced by these bees is, among many things, said to have healing properties, so if you consider yourself a healer in some capacity, using a honeybee in your working can increase your powers. Honeybees devote their lives to serving and nurturing their hive, protecting their babies (larvae) and looking after each other. A honeybee can be used in a home protection working or spells for family harmony.

Beetle: Some beetle species have been around for over 300,000 years. Their hard shell is strong and provides a shield, making them useful in protective magick. Because they've been around so long, beetles represent ancient wisdom. Their energy is useful in spells relating to study and learning and spells to provide a wider view on life.

Butterfly: It's easy to guess the associations of the pretty and beloved butterfly: beauty, attention-getting, and standing out in the crowd. Butterflies are the end result of the transformation of a caterpillar, and they signify success and change for the better. They symbolize grace, joy, and lightheartedness. Butterflies cannot hear the way we do, but instead they can feel vibrations. Use a butterfly in your magick to increase your awareness of happy, carefree vibes around you.

Caterpillar: The caterpillar curls up inside a cocoon before a big change. Energy of the caterpillar can be called upon when facing life's shifts with courage and acceptance. The caterpillar carries within it the potential to be anything and everything. Its energy is great for any new beginning or while learning a new skill.

Cicada: Cicadas have one of the most interesting life cycles of insects. They are birthed on a tree branch, then fall to the ground and burrow for roots for anywhere from two to seventeen years, depending on the species! This is a long journey into the underworld, during which many things are learned. A cicada spends most of its life underground and then emerges with a loud, strong song. Its time above ground is extremely short in comparison and limited only to the very end of its life. Perhaps you've been through a long time of darkness and learned many important things, and now you're ready to share your message with the world. Cicada is all about self-discovery followed by communication and sharing an important message. The cicada is a voice of things learned in the shadows. They can be included in spells regarding meditation, vision questing, divination, and communication.

Cockroach: These unpopular guests can survive literally anything. Cockroaches are horrifying to many people and have a very strong energy because of this. Cockroach energy can be used to thrive in an ugly situation that you have to get through. It can also be used to repel and disgust another person. I've never met a person who didn't squirm at the mention of cockroaches, which makes them excellent in the worst kinds of curses.

Cricket: Crickets are all about getting your voice heard. Crickets spend their lives singing loudly in the darkness, and so are associated with communication and getting a message out. If you feel you have an important message for someone who is not hearing your words, or if your words are being ignored and overlooked, cricket energy can put some volume behind your voice.

Dragonfly: Starting life as larva underwater, this insect crawls onto land and then transforms into a dragonfly. For this unique reason, the dragonfly is called upon to combine the essence of both water and air: emotion and communication. This equals pure self-expression. The dragonfly tells us to be brave enough to voice our feelings and tell the world who we really are. Come out of the dark, still water and fly in the sun and air.

Earwig: These guys get their name from an old myth that claims they will crawl into your ear while you sleep, tunnel into your brain, and drive you insane. There is no proof that they actually do this. However, they do like small, dark, damp areas. Because of the superstition attached to them, you could use earwigs in a spell to find out information. Charm the earwig to reveal the information you seek by getting inside someone else's head.

Firefly: Fireflies are symbols of pleasure and delight. Male fireflies light up to attract females. Fireflies are all about attracting mates and friends. They signify love, lust, and fatuousness. Romance, flirtation, young love, and the beginning stages of relationships are all part of the firefly's life. Doesn't sound like shadow magick, does it? However, if you find a dead firefly (please don't kill one on purpose), its remains can be included in spells to end relationships, to kill the glow on a partnership that needs to end, or to otherwise "snap off the light" in a situation where people are so beguiled by love that the stars in their eyes are blinding them to the truth.

Fly: Most common flies have compound eyes that allow them to see many things at once, giving them a wide range of vision. For this reason, a fly can be used in workings for foresight or for seeing a situation from many perspectives. Flies are able to multiply at a rapid rate, and so they can be used to increase or multiply your own abilities or talents. They are incredibly adaptable, thriving in almost any situation, making fly energy useful for toughing out new situations. Flies help break down and transform waste into sustenance, so they are also associated with transformation. In that sense, they can be viewed as a reminder to take the lessons you've learned from the past and move on with the knowledge you've acquired. Alternately, flies have a dirty, nasty reputation as pests and, as such, can be used for cursing.

Grasshopper: Grasshoppers are always jumping forward: ahead of the competition, into new situations without fear, and over obstacles. Grasshopper energy can help you cast off what holds you back and jump into the future with enthusiasm. This can pertain to any number of risks, including employment, following a dream, starting a relationship, or other leap of faith. The grasshopper urges us to follow the joy in our hearts and see where we land.

Ladybug: The fun, bright polka-dot pattern of the cute little ladybug signifies happiness and carefree feelings. In nature, their bright colors actually scare off predators, just as you can use positive vibes to keep negative people away. Ladybugs can be used in spells to dispel negativity, attract joy and peace, and promote friendship. People will often exclaim in delight when they see a ladybug, because they are considered lucky. Ladybugs evoke the childish joy that resides in all of us, and by using them in magick, you can have some of their lovely charisma for yourself.

Maggots: Studies have found that maggots have antimicrobial effects on wounds and can be used for healing. In other words, maggots eat disease and cure infected flesh wounds. When properly applied to a flesh wound in a human or animal, maggots will ingest the "necrotic" or dead tissue, thus cleaning out and disinfecting the injury. They ingest that which is rotten and no longer needed. Maggots are fly larva, and they eat rotten food and meat to gain the energy required to transform into flies. Maggots can be used to remove unwanted or "rotten" energy in your life and transform it into something useful.

Mosquito: It's hard to find nice things to say about mosquitoes. As bloodsuckers, they are useful in hexing when you wish to drain someone else's energy or glean some of their traits for yourself. Although they're an important part of the ecosystem, there's no denying that they are pests who spread disease and can be employed to spread bad energy if you desire.

Moth: Everyone knows moths are drawn to the porch light, the flame of a candle, and other bright sources. An interesting fact is that when unimpeded by human-made light, moths normally navigate by the stars and moonlight. The moth can be used in spells for nocturnal knowledge, understanding moon mysteries and astrology, and seeing truth behind the shadows. If you are in a dark place metaphorically, moth energy can help you find the light at the end of the tunnel. Moths are masters of camouflage, and many species are known for imitating other animals as a disguise to confuse their enemies and predators. Moth energy can be used to conceal yourself when you wish not to be noticed.

Snail: The patient, unhurried snail reminds us to slow down and relax. The spiral in the shell represents the constant ongoing cycles of life, and within this universal spiral, the snail patiently plods on and lives in the moment, trusting its fate. Snail energy can be harnessed for grounding and learning to accept that we are part of something larger, encouraging us to live in the moment. The snail represents devotion to a slow and steady spiritual path. If you are feeling vulnerable, carry a protective snail shell to shield your personal growth from others.

Spider: Spiders are almost as popular as snakes when it comes to the occult. Love them or hate them, the sight of a spider triggers a strong reaction either way. Spiders are believed to be keepers of the primordial alphabet and so are associated with the written word. A writer looking for inspiration or battling writer's block could benefit from spider energy. Spiders also represent wisdom, cunning, mystic knowledge, and psychic ability and can help us understand the grand web of existence. The spider weaves its web all of its own creativity and lives in it, yet the web also kills prey for the spider to eat. This is a creature that is entirely self-sufficient and independent; this energy can help you create your own reality and make your own dreams come true. Seeing spiders in life can symbolize that you are able to deal with a situation all on your own and be the master of your own future.

Wasp: Wasps are tough, very threatening, and do not play around. They can sting repeatedly, and their venom lets off a pheromone that alerts other wasps to become more aggressive alongside them. Wasps are great for protection and defense magick. They can be used to promote courage to stand behind your words even if others may not like it—in other words, when you must deliver a necessary sting. Wasp energy can be employed to rally like-minded people to take your side or help you get your point across in an important debate, discussion, argument, or legal dispute. If you associate wasps with fear, pain and unpleasantness, you can use this association while crafting curses to "sting" an enemy.

Worm: Worms get a pretty bad rap, being associated with death the way they are, and it doesn't help that they are slimy and wiggly either. However, when we understand the role worms play on our planet and the gifts they bestow upon all life on earth, it is possible to appreciate them in a whole new way. Worms are associated with the dark moon and shadow magick because they spend most of their life in darkness. They're commonly called "night crawlers" because they only come to the surface after dark or when it rains. Worms are sightless and deaf but are minutely sensitive to invisible vibrations, which links them to intuition, psychic ability, and spirit connection. Worms consume dead vegetation and transform it into nutrients for the soil, taking what is old and no longer needed and transforming it into something new and useful. Like all our scavenger friends, they represent renewal, change, and growth. An interesting worm fact is that if they get ripped apart, they are able to regenerate new segments of their body, further symbolizing creativity.

If you pay attention, you'll notice that deceased insects can be easily found at almost any given time. Usually, things show up for us as we need them, exactly when they should. This is part of the amazing way that spirit communicates and shows itself to us. Yes, even through bugs! So the next time you notice a dead wasp on the windowsill, don't squash it in a tissue. Keep it for later, for chances are you will need it in a spell soon. Here are some ways to use deceased insects in magick:

- Include them in sachets.
- Put one in a tiny glass bottle and make a hanging amulet.

- A dead insect will get very dry and brittle over time. Grind it up with a mortar and pestle and add it to incense, herb mixes, and casting powders.

- In a small amount of oil such as jojoba or grape-seed, soak the dead insect. Allow it to infuse the oil with its energy for three days. Strain the oil through cheesecloth. Dab a small amount on your skin to absorb the energy of the creature. You can also use this oil to anoint candles and other spell tools. I know this sounds disgusting, but no one ever said dark magick was pleasant.

- If you're really crafty, you can try setting a bug in clear resin jewelry to wear as an amulet. Supplies for this craft are obtainable and reasonably priced; however, making resin jewelry does take practice. Try it out a few times with different objects before using your special insect, just to make sure you don't waste it.

SPELLS USING ANIMAL REMAINS

This section focuses on spells that make use of animal remains, bones, and organs. For those who do not wish to make use of animal remains, a plant-based substitute is suggested.

Antler Dominance Amulet

Since antlers are associated with the qualities of the Horned God—fertility, warrior energy, dominance, victory, power, and protection—this amulet will attract those qualities. An amulet like this may be useful when in a competition of any kind, whether it is recreational (sports), professional (career), or personal (relationships). This amulet is carried or worn when you wish to exert power over an opponent.

To create this amulet, you are going to make a magickal sigil. A sigil is an esoteric symbol or character created personally by the witch, which is imbued with magickal power toward a specific end. You can design your own sigil and make it as simple or complex as you want. What is really important about a sigil is the intent and focus that is put into it, as well as its deeply personal nature. I will be providing an example of a sigil for this spell, but it is preferable that you design one yourself so only you know its meaning.

✎ MATERIALS

Orange candle

Lighter or matches

Wood burning kit, carving tools, or marker. This will be used to put your sigil onto the antler. Wood burning kits are available at craft stores, but if you cannot get one, you can carefully carve or scratch the sigil into the antler with a sharp object or draw it onto the antler with permanent marker.

Small piece of antler (substitution: a small disk cut from a tree branch)

Sterile lancet (optional)

30-inch cord (optional if making a necklace)

There are entire books written about creating sigils, but the simplest way to create one is the layering of different letters of a word on top of each other, creating a symbol. You can also link the letters together in a visually appealing way, adding shapes or designs to put your own twist on it. We are going to use the word *DOMINATE* to create this sigil. I do this by removing the vowels and repeated consonants, leaving me with *DMNT*. I then take those letters and my pencil and paper and play around with different ways to connect them to create a symbol. Here is mine:

If you look hard enough, you can see the letters. I also added a few fitting artistic details, such as sun rays, dots, and a black space that resembles the head of a horned animal. You can use my sigil for this charm or create your own.

You can incorporate your own initials, name, or astrological symbol into the sigil, creating a link between it and yourself.

When you are happy with your design, it's time to create the amulet. Light an orange candle while you work to represent victory and success.

Wood burning or carving are preferable because both will create a rhythm as you work and require extended physical effort and energy, allowing you to transfer your intent into the amulet while working away on it. While you burn your sigil into the antler, you will see the antler burning, small amounts of smoke rising from it, and smell it changing form. These things are energy being transferred into the amulet. Visualize your desired outcome (winning the game, getting the promotion, gaining someone's interest) while the smoke and scent carry it off into the spirit world. Also see the blackened marks you make in the antler as physical proof, a declaration stamped into the world, that you are manifesting your goal right now. If you're carving, the physical acts of scraping, clenching your hand muscles, and digging into the antler are transferring the energy of your intent into the amulet. Make sure during the drawing, burning, or carving of the sigil that you are strongly visualizing.

Cast your circle and light the orange candle again. Hold the amulet in your hand, and see your sigil pulsing with power and energy. Optionally, prick your finger with the sterile lancet and rub your blood into the sigil. Now, the energy of dominance and power are embedded in the symbol and directly linked to you.

Close the circle.

Let the orange candle burn out.

Carry your amulet with you, or string it into a necklace that you wear close to your skin.

For some, a dominance spell may sound aggressive and therefore seem unethical and a gross display of greed and control over others. You can use your own judgment about whether or not you think this type of spell is right for you.

Bird Claw Protection Charm

This charm can be hung on the interior mirror of your car, if legal in your area, or the doorknob of your home for protection against accidents, theft, and break-ins. I suggest using a bird foot with very large, sharp talons.

←--ᵌ MATERIALS

Prepared bird foot (substitution: a strong twisted root with multiple
   appendages)

Glue

3 black feathers

3 small jingle bells

3-foot black ribbon

½ cup witch's salt (see page 49)

Nail file

Blood-red nail polish

You will need to construct and decorate the charm beforehand, with the exception of painting the fingernails. Dry the bird foot as described on pages 109 and 110. Glue black feathers to the top and tie a few of the small jingle bells around it with the black ribbon. The jingle bells make a sound both to warn the potential predator to stay away and also to alert you to unwanted energy entering your space.

Use the black ribbon to make a loop at the top for hanging.

Cast your circle.

Make a ring of witch's salt on your altar and lay the bird foot inside it. Focus on how scary and intimidating it is. Its claws are sharp, curved, and vicious, and its energy may even seem repulsive. This is good because it is meant to scare things away; the more repellent it is the better.

Using the nail file, sharpen each claw to a point. They will already be naturally sharp, but you are making them even more so. As you do this, chant:

> *Sharpened claws and bloodied nails*
> *Act as a warning sign.*
> *No thieves or enemies come near*
> *The lives of me or mine.*

Paint each nail blood red and, as it dries, imagine the red paint is blood dripping from the claws as if they have just shredded an enemy.

Close the circle.

Hang the charm in your car or on the doorknob of your home.

Bird Foot Money Amulet

Livestock birds such chickens and turkeys represent abundance and prosperity, since once upon a time people depended on them for food. The following amulet is created with the intention of attracting wealth and money to the place you hang it in.

⟶ MATERIALS

Dried turkey or chicken foot (substitution: dried braided stalks of wheat or barley)

Green paint

Golden nail polish

7 sparkly silver and gold beads

3 feet green string, cut as needed

Scissors

7 sprigs of dried peppermint or other money-attracting herbs

Coin or rolled-up bill

Paint the bird claw green, the color of prosperity (if you're using wheat, there's no need to paint it green). Use the nail polish to paint the nails of the claws (or tips of the wheat) golden. Place the coin or bill in the claws of the bird. The idea is to get and keep money, so it is important the money be permanently "caught" in the claw. Tie it in with green string to ensure it stays put. Glue the sprigs of dried herbs to the top of the foot and secure them with green string. Put the beads on the green string and tie them to the claw as well. Charge your charm by imagining that you always have money set aside for emergencies, a bank account that is always in the black, and plenty of money to do fun things. Hide this charm near your front door or in the place where you make money to welcome prosperous energy in.

Heartbreak Reversal Spell

This spell is to be cast when you have been betrayed in love, when someone has lied, manipulated, cheated, and used you thoughtlessly and without remorse. It will send the feelings they've created back to them.

←-3 MATERIALS

Small animal heart, such as bird's or rabbit's (substitution: cooked artichoke heart or dried apricot)

Piece of their clothing. If clothing isn't attainable, a picture of them or a description of them with their name on a piece of paper will do.

Death candle (see page 51)

Rose stem with thorns

Charge the heart with the person's essence. Imagine it is beating in conjunction with their real heart. Hear the sound in your head. Then place it on the clothing or paper, wrap it up, and leave it overnight to absorb their energy.

The following night cast your circle and light a death candle. Open the clothing or paper the heart is in. Hold the rose stem in your hands and feel the prick of the thorns. See the thorns pulsing with red bloody light. Chant:

> *Vicious thorns*
> *For your vicious heart.*
> *The pain you cause*
> *Rips you apart.*

Chant this repeatedly while raising anger, power, and hurt, then transfer your betrayal into the rose stem, filling it with red, bruised light. Now take the stem and stab the thorns into the heart. Use the thorns to rip the heart apart, pulling, and tearing. Poke it full of holes and wounds while visualizing the person suffering from their own actions in a fitting way.

Afterward, note the absence of a heartbeat in your mind.

Close the circle.

Wrap the heart in the cloth and dispose of all the items in the garbage. Allow the candle to burn out.

Breakup Spell with Chicken Hearts

If a relationship needs to end because one or both people are being hurt, are toxic to each other, or are engaged in an unhealthy cycle of abuse or manipulation, then it is time for a breakup spell. Keep in mind that their desire to be together may still be more powerful than your magick. Toxic relationships are very hard to end, especially for the people trapped inside them. These types of relationships are much like an addiction, and just as powerful. You may have to perform this spell more than once if that is the case.

⟿ MATERIALS

    2 chicken or bird hearts (substitution: 2 artichoke hearts)

    Black plate

    3 feet red cotton thread

    3 drops death oil (see page 48)

Put the two hearts side by side on a black plate on your altar during the dark moon. Choose which heart represents each person. One at a time, charge each heart with the energy of the person it represents. Hold it in your hand, and imagine their face, affectation, and voice clearly in your mind. Send that image into the heart; imagine it beating in synch with the individual's heart. Repeat this with the other heart, charging it with the essence of the other person.

Next, wind the red thread all around both hearts, binding them together tightly. As you wind the thread, think about their relationship and their bond: how they interact together, their arguments and problems, and what it is that keeps them so unhealthily attached.

Place the bound hearts back on the plate and put 3 drops of death oil onto them. Imagine the death oil snuffing the life out of the bond.

Spend some time thinking about the hearts, imagining the couple as broken up. Do not concern yourself with how this will come about; think instead of the outcome, seeing both people as separate individuals who have moved on with their lives. See them as happy and independent, one at a time.

Declare to the dark moon or your deity:

> *These are the hearts of (name) and (name).*
> *As these hearts rot, so shall their bond decay,*
> *Setting them both free.*
> *As I will it, so mote it be.*

Bury the charm in the ground.

Close the circle.

The decay of the hearts can in fact represent "rot" in the relationship, the bond between two people going sour and foul thus bringing it to an end. Because the thread is made of cotton, it too should eventually decompose, ending their attachment.

Bird Heart Love Spell

This spell seems simple on the surface, but don't be fooled. It's to make someone love you. Make sure this is what you really want before proceeding. Also review your real reasons behind wanting to perform it. This is a very controlling spell and definitely doesn't fit under the "harm none" category.

I feel this spell, unlike other love magick, leans toward the dark side because it borders on violence in its ferocity. It's a last resort, a desperate act when everything else has failed. It employs the dark moon circle casting mentioned earlier in the book, as it requires the destructive aspects of the elements.

⟶ MATERIALS

Red candle anointed with a drop of your own blood or sexual fluids

Lighter or matches

Heart from a bird. This can be dehydrated or fresh. If you're using a
   fresh heart, have a plate to set it on. (substitution: a cherry)

Hair of the person the spell is directed at, if possible

3 pins

Your own hair

6-inch square of red cloth

1 foot red string

Cast your circle and lay out your materials on your altar. Light the red candle. Pass each of the materials one at a time over the heat of the flame of the candle, infusing them with sexual fire energy.

Hold the bird heart in your hand. See it vibrating with raw emotion and deep feeling.

Declare out loud:

This heart belongs to (name).

Visualize the heart becoming swollen with the energy of the person. Imagine the sound of their beating heart inside their chest, wherever they may be at the moment, how this core of their being pushes the blood through their very veins. The heart is the center that keeps them alive and the home of their love.

Hear the sound of their breathing. Feel the warmth of their skin against yours and the blood beneath it.

Wind their hair around the heart and knot it tight. If it's not long enough to do that, just place it firmly on top of the heart.

Set the heart down on the plate when you feel it is infused with energy, and pick up one of the pins. Shove it into the heart, piercing it in the center, and say:

> *One to see me.*

Insert the second pin, saying:

> *One to feel me.*

Insert the third pin, saying:

> *One to love me.*

Wrap the strand of your own hair around the pins creating as much of a tangle as possible. Use several strands if necessary, weaving them in and around the pins while you visualize your beloved seeing you, feeling your energy, and then loving you. If your hair is too short for this, you can place it firmly on the heart instead. Imagine they are fixated on you completely, like they've dropped everything to notice you.

Hold the finished charm in your hand and say:

> *(Name), you will know no peace until you come to me.*

Place the charm inside the red cloth and tie it securely with red string.

Close the circle.

If the heart was dried, hide it in your bedroom. Otherwise, bury it outside where it will not be disturbed. Allow the candle to burn out.

The recipient of the spell should begin to feel piercing emotional discomfort and longing, which they eventually connect to you, causing them to seek you out.

A note on love spells: When thinking of doing a very controlling love spell, consider that your obsession with the person may not be based in reality. They represent an ideal. The same can be said for someone you strongly dislike but who isn't directly harming you in some way—there's a good chance you don't actually know a whole lot about them, but they are instead a symbol. A crush exists almost solely because of what you *don't* know about the person, allowing you to fill in the blanks with all the traits you wish for, which you then project onto them. Once you get to know them, you will quickly realize that they were mostly imaginary in your mind. If you're trying to force a partner to stay with you against their will, you need to look inward at why your own happiness is so dependent on them.

Shut Up Spell with Cow's Tongue

This spell is to stop someone from verbally causing you or someone else harm. We encounter this type of thing all the time in life, whether it's a gossiping coworker or someone who hurls deeply scathing insults just to get their way. Often the people guilty of this underestimate the power of words and have no idea just how much harm they are causing with what may seem like casual remarks; other times, they know exactly what they are doing and are intentionally causing problems with rumors or lies. This spell is appropriate only when all practical measures to stop the situation have been attempted, such as communicating with them directly if possible, reporting the person to management, or otherwise solving the issue logistically.

This spell usually uses a cow's tongue, which can be purchased in a butcher shop and some Asian markets. You can replace it with the tongue of any found animal that is already deceased.

⟶ MATERIALS

Cow's tongue (substitution: slab of soft fruit, such as a very ripe peach or cantaloupe)

Black plate

Large sewing needle

3 feet black thread

Photo or drawing of the person no larger than 4 by 6 inches

Black pen or marker

Scalpel or sharp knife

3 drops death oil (see page 48)

Cast your circle during the dark moon. Have the cow's tongue unpackaged and ready on a plate and the needle already generously threaded.

Place the photo of the person where you can see it. Imagine their words and hear their voice. Contemplate the things they are saying that are causing harm. Using the black marker, draw an X over their mouth. Now, hear how muffled they have become; imagine them unable to speak, as if they've lost their voice. See them become powerless. Say:

> *Your harmful words have no more power.*
> *Speak no more—your voice is gone.*
> *No one hears you, no one listens.*
> *Lose your speech, be gone, move on.*

Using the scalpel, cut a slit down the center of the cow tongue. Do not cut all the way through. Place several drops of death oil into the slit you have made, and then slide the photo into it. Fold the tongue over on itself in such a fashion that the photo is inside. Chant the above phrase and imagine the person unable to talk. Using the needle and thread, stitch the tongue over on itself so it is "sewn shut" around the photo. You have symbolically sewn the person's wagging tongue still. See them as fully silenced. Handling the tongue may be unpleasant and unsettling, but that is fitting, seeing as the things that leave the person's mouth are equally undesirable.

Close the circle.

You can bury the tongue (remember, bury it at least 1 foot deep and place something heavy on top so it is not disturbed by scavengers) or pop it in your freezer and leave it until the spell has worked.

This spell doesn't mean the person will physically actually stop talking, but that the power of their words will in some way be rendered ineffectual or used against them.

Sea Sponge Energy-Draining Spell

This spell is meant to siphon negative energy off a person who is causing harm to those around them. The saying "one bad apple spoils the barrel" is true for people too. One person's bad energy can throw off an entire household or place of work. This charm is meant to suck away some of that negativity over time and restore balance to a place, group, or community.

←—३ MATERIALS

Sea sponge (substitution: a piece of moss)

6 white tea light candles

1 tablespoon witch's salt (see page 49)

Cast a circle. Place the sponge on your altar, with the 6 tea lights in a circle around it.

Place a little pinch of witch's salt into each tea light to give them an extra personal boost. Light all the candles. Feel the heat that comes off the flames. Imagine that heat permeating the materials you have placed at their midst. This heat is empowering the sponge with the ability to soak up the unwanted energy. The heat from the flames will warm the sponge, enlivening it (be careful; don't let it catch fire). Mentally, tell the sponge its purpose. Picture the unwanted emotion as a color (such as red for anger or muddy brown for sadness) drawn to the sponge from all directions. The sponge attracts this color like a magnet and draws it right into itself. Visualize until your attention starts to waver or your own energy drains. Close the circle and allow the candles to burn out.

Hide the sponge near the person it is meant for. It can be under the side of the bed they sleep in or near their work area in a place of employment. If they are a long distance away, hide the sponge in your own home wrapped in black cloth.

If possible, every so often, rinse it under water, ring it out, and put it back in place until the job is done.

Snake Spell to Break Addictions

All too often when we enter a dark phase in life, we don't know how to handle it in a healthy manner. Instead of facing our shadow, we find all kinds of ways to numb ourselves to it instead: drowning it with alcohol, scrambling it with drugs, distracting ourselves with food, sex, or some other diversion. People look to outside sources to ease pain, halting their personal growth in the process. When you spiral into the darkness in an uncontrolled way, fighting it with drugs or other vices, you will only have that much more trouble finding the light again. Sadly, as in the classic haunted woods in a fairy tale, many people who take this path never come out again, and their addictions result in terminal illness and death. They go into a dark place and never come back.

This spell can apply to any kind of habit, addiction, behavior, or dependency that needs to be faced and released. The snake sheds its skin and bursts forth triumphant, bigger and better every time, all of its own volition. It requires no outside assistance to make this change: it is completely self-generated, as is the decision to move forward in life.

For the sake of simplicity, I'll be using the example of addiction when outlining this spell. This can pertain to food, relationships, fears, or other habits too and is not restricted to substance abuse.

⊷ MATERIALS

Small piece of snakeskin, about the size of your palm (substitution: birch tree bark)

Amethyst crystal

Several sterile lancets

Small black cloth bag

Sit at your altar with your materials and cast your circle.

Place the piece of snakeskin before you. It will represent the "old" you. It is a husk containing what you used to be before you made this decision to reinvent yourself and become stronger and better. The snakeskin will hold the energy of the addiction or habit you are shedding. Place the amethyst on top of the snakeskin; amethysts are associated with sobriety and self-control. Spend some time visualizing what you'd like to purge yourself of. See yourself experiencing the negative parts of the behavior. You may feel shame while you do this, and that is okay: the shame or embarrassment are things that must be faced in order to move forward. This can be a painful exercise, but it is entirely necessary to be honest with yourself during this visualization. There may be feelings of regret or sadness as you see and feel your own actions. Accept them. When you're brimming with feelings of your addiction, prick your finger with the lancet. The pain you feel in doing this is a powerful release of energy. Put your blood onto the snakeskin and, with it, all your shame and sadness. Now the snakeskin holds the power of your addiction.

Place the snakeskin into the bag, along with the amethyst, and keep it closed.

You can close your circle for now. However, this spell is not done. When it comes to addiction, there are triggers and cravings. A trigger or craving urges you to engage in the negative habit and can be anything from having a stressful day to hearing a certain song. Keep your amulet with you in the closed bag. Every time you experience a craving or trigger, you need to channel it into the amulet to be neutralized and taken away. A way to do this is to use a fresh lancet and add a drop of your blood to the snakeskin, releasing the craving through pain like you did the first time. Feel the uncomfortable, awful energy, and release it with your blood. If you are not comfortable using a lancet again (or at all), this can just as effectively be done by visualizing the craving as a black cloud streaming from your forehead into the amulet instead. Triggers and cravings can go on for a long time, so you can repeat this every time you have one. Some people need to keep their amulet for years as a means of dealing with relapse. Only you will know when you are truly ready to let the amulet go and either bury it or take it apart.

Every time you acknowledge your feelings and send the energy of the habit into your amulet, you are funneling its power away from your present and into your old, cast-off version of yourself. You are telling spirit again and again that you are emerging as a new, stronger, bigger, and better self as you reject the unwanted behavior. Each and every time you use the amulet, you are affirming to yourself and to the universe that you are moving on. You may find that the amulet feels utterly disgusting and repulsive to you over time, as it takes all that unwanted energy into itself.

If you are struggling with drugs or alcohol, this spell is not intended as a replacement for treatment. It can be used in conjunction with counseling and professional attention, and as always use common sense.

Teeth Intimidation Spell

Animals in the wild have many visual signals they use to converse with each other. Body language is one of many ways animals and humans communicate. Just observe any two or more animals together and you are sure to see subtle correspondence. For example, a dog will lift its tail to signal friendliness, flatten its ears to show annoyance, or fluff up its fur to appear threatening. Something that is quite universal among carnivores is that they will bare their teeth at each other to act as a warning. If you've ever seen a dog peel its lips back from its fangs and rip out a snarl, you know that this sends a very clear message to back off or be torn up. The human equivalent would be flashing a weapon at your enemy to indicate that you mean business.

I'm not saying you should go about your daily life flashing weapons at people. Don't. First of all, it's illegal. Second of all, physical violence is not the solution to anything. This spell is not about physical harm or any harm at all; rather, it is about sending out an aggressive, defensive warning signal to another person or people to back off and to scare them away before any harm happens at all.

When we consider teeth in magick, especially those of a predator, there are many uses for their energy in charms. Wearing an animal tooth charged with defense, even when no one can see it, sends out a warning vibration to those who wish to harm you that they'd better not bother. This sentiment, unfortunately, can be applied to many aspects of our lives as we navigate the workplace, school, and social networks. All too often we find ourselves around people who, for some reason or another, would wish to harm us, intimidate or manipulate us, slander us, or steal from us. Carrying a charged tooth of a predator is like flashing warning energy at these people. Even though they may not see the tooth or know you have done any magick, if you have imbued it with enough power, something inside them will get the message and leave you alone.

←⁃ᴢ MATERIALS

Tooth of an animal. Drill a hole in the top with a power drill and string a cord through it if you wish to wear as a necklace, or you can put it in a little charm jar. (substitution: jagged shard of a walnut shell or large thorn)

Photo of the animal in attack mode. Find an image on the internet of the animal that is intimidating or scary and print it out. If you'd prefer, you can use a photo of an intimidating character that you admire. Whichever you choose, make sure it is vicious and merciless looking

½ cup witch's salt (see page 49)

Red candle in a holder. A small chime candle is best for this spell.

Knife

Lighter or matches

Cast your circle.

On your altar, place the tooth on top of the photo. Around the tooth and photo, make a circle of witch's salt, being sure to leave room for the candle. If someone specific is bothering you, carve their name onto the red candle with the knife. Fill your red candle with the energy of bloodshed by visualizing gnashing teeth tearing flesh as you light it. This is hostile, war-like energy. Do not see yourself being attacked, but rather project the energy outward. Place the candle within the salt circle with the tooth and light it. For the duration of the burning time of the red candle, hold the tooth in your right hand and gaze at the picture. Hold the tooth in the warmth of the flame (don't burn yourself) and let it absorb the heat. Imagine all the things that picture brings to mind: the threat, the power, the dominance, the protection. See the name in the candle with the person's name on it lose its power as it melts away under the fire.

When the candle is burned out, you can close the circle and wear your amulet.

Dispose of all the salt, candle drippings, and picture outdoors or in the garbage to get them off your property.

Store your tooth amulet in a dark piece of cloth or in a box to contain its energy when you're not wearing it. You don't want it sitting out and making everyone who enters your house uneasy.

LIVE ANIMAL SPELLS

This section focuses on performing spells in the proximity of live animals while enlisting their help, without disturbing their natural habitats. No animals are to be disturbed, moved, or touched during the working of these spells.

Ant Spell to Ease Community Discord

As grownups, we don't often pay a lot of attention to the little critters beneath our feet, but I think we all can remember a time when we were children, looking at an operational anthill and being mesmerized. Underneath the sidewalks are utterly miraculous ant-built worlds that rival our own human cities in innovation and efficiency. We can take a lesson from the ants when our own home, workplace, community, or group of friends is in discord. This spell can be done to help create harmony, community, and a sense of camaraderie among a group of people when power struggles are holding back the whole of the group.

You can find ants in the warm months. Their nest is usually indicated by a little mound of dirt that they enter and exit through a small hole. Do not disturb the anthill during your working.

⤙ MATERIALS

Jar or container with a lid the right size to hold the fruit
Slice of apple or other sweet fruit
Functioning anthill

Take the jar containing the fruit with you the next time you're with the group that is experiencing discord. Keep it hidden. Anytime during the meeting or event when you notice disharmony or conflict, mentally guide the energy of that conflict into your jar. It may look like dark, cloudy energy. Put the lid on when you leave.

Later, sit beside the anthill and cast your circle. Explain mentally to the ants the discord that is inside the jar, and ask them lovingly to transform it into teamwork and community. Remove the apple slice from the jar and place near the anthill. Thank the ants and offer them respect. Imagine the conflict in the group being resolved and everyone getting along well and happily. Release the circle.

Over the next few days, the ants will harvest and consume the offering, transforming it into nourishment for the group. This symbolically transforms that negative energy into productive, communicative energy.

Soon after, the problems or power struggles within the group dynamic should be resolved and harmony should take its place.

Earwig Spells

Just mentioning the word *earwig* is enough to give people the chills. The name itself is part of the problem. The word *earwig* comes from the myth that they like to bore into human ears while people sleep and lay eggs inside their brain, making the host go insane. This story is entirely untrue—there are no medical accounts of this ever actually happening. Earwigs can typically be found inside ears of corn, lettuce, celery, cabbage, and leafy greens in the garden. The disturbing lore of the earwig can be applied to magick for spells that require getting inside someone else's head or, as another saying goes, "put a bug in their ear" about something you wish them to know, understand, or warn them against. Don't worry—these spells do not involve putting an earwig in anyone's ear! The point of these spells is to instill an idea in someone's mind, wiggling energy into their head and helping them see things differently. I'm going to share two different methods for using earwigs for this purpose. One uses live earwigs, and the other uses a dead one.

Earwig Spell for Eating Negative Thoughts

This spell is to remove negative thoughts that are holding a person back, such as self-doubt, low self-esteem, unhealthy influence from others, or bad habits.

⊷ MATERIALS

Area outdoors where you know there are many earwigs, such as a garden or damp forested area you have located beforehand. Earwigs often live in large groups under rocks. Locating such a group is ideal for this spell if possible.

Death candle, in a jar for burning outdoors (see page 51)

Lighter or matches

Ear of fresh corn with leaves and corn silk still attached or head of cabbage (both available at a grocery store)

Natural ink that will not harm animals or insects if consumed. Beet juice or blueberry juice is great for this.

Small paintbrush

1 drop of death oil (see page 48)

Go to the place where earwigs live. Sit down on the ground and cast a circle. Light your death candle. Imagine it glowing with purification energy, burning up intrusive, useless, or harmful thoughts.

Hold your vegetable in your hands and quietly contemplate what you want removed from the mind. Then, using your choice of ink, write the person's name on the vegetable. Say out loud or in your mind:

> *I ask that all self-doubt (or other problematic pattern) be gently*
> *and lovingly removed from (name's) mind, setting them free to*
> *grow and be their best. Insect friends, please aid me in my working,*
> *cleaning up the bad thoughts and influences that plague (name).*

Place a drop of death oil on the vegetable. Imagine the earwigs coming and wiggling into the leaves and folds of the food, eating away parts that they wish. This represents nature's power to cleanse and purify the thoughts and feelings in one's brain. As the earwigs consume parts of your offering, so too should the negative aspects be removed from the thoughts of the targeted person. Leave the vegetable near the earwig colony. Release the circle and leave the space.

Keep the candle and light it occasionally over the next few days until it burns out, while thinking about how the bad thoughts are being eaten away.

Do not go back and disturb the earwigs. Just trust that they will do their work.

Earwig Spell to Get into Someone's Mind

This spell is meant to get inside someone else's head and send a message to them or implant a thought in their mind. It could be that they are in denial about something that is harmful to them and they need to see the truth, or their thoughts are holding them back from growing. It's also suitable to use when someone's beliefs are making them hurt those around them.

⚹ MATERIALS

Light blue candle

Lighter or matches

Small paint brush

Natural ink, such as blueberry or beet juice, that will not harm animals if consumed

Head of iceberg lettuce

Dead earwig or molt (substitution: a burr from a prickly plant)

Knife or long object to make a hole in the head of lettuce

Cast your circle at your altar. Light the blue candle.

Use the paint brush and juice to mark the head of lettuce with the name of the person you wish to communicate with. Lettuce tends to be quite watery, so don't worry if your writing gets smeared, absorbed, or marred; it's the energy in the words that is important. As you write, imagine the lettuce as the head of the person. See them as they are, with their current problematic thinking or habit.

Set the lettuce aside and hold the earwig in your hand. Close your eyes. What is the message you want to send into this person's mind? Your message will be tailored to the situation. Keep your message short and sweet, just a sentence or two. Repeat this sentence as a chant while pouring your intention into the bug.

When you feel the insect is saturated with energy, set it aside and pick up your knife or long object. Pierce a hole into the center of the head of lettuce, without cutting all the way through. Blow your breath into the hole you have made. Then shove the dead earwig down inside it.

Now the new thoughts are symbolically inside the person's head. Spend a moment seeing the message in the earwig spreading throughout the veins in the lettuce leaves. Visualize the person having the desired realization, idea, or awakening and how that might play out positively for everyone.

Bury the lettuce or compost it. Let the blue candle burn itself out.

Maggot Spell to Heal a Broken Heart

Maggots are gross. I get it. Believe me. However, amazingly enough, these offensive wigglers have been used to cure infections and diseases of the flesh for thousands of years. Therefore, maggots, despite their bad rap, in fact ingest disease and are said to be healers. That being said, please don't try this method at home—lucky for us, nowadays we have antibiotic ointment. Instead, you'll be calling upon the healing energy of maggots in your magick.

This spell is for healing a broken heart. A relationship that ends badly can leave you with a heartache that makes it difficult to trust new partners or even send you into dark places of mourning, loss, and isolation. This is a very dramatic and visceral spell using the heart of a small animal to ease the part of your heart that is in need of healing. You must have access to an outdoor location away from people in order for the maggots to find the heart and go to work on it.

↞∙⊰ MATERIALS

Animal heart or piece of meat (substitution: rotting onion)
Container to put the heart in
Sewing needle
5 feet red thread

Cast a circle and place the heart in the container before you.

Visualize the person who hurt you, the words they said, and the way they betrayed you. Feel the pain all over again and transfer it into the heart. You can do this by holding your palms over the heart and visualizing the pain as murky energy flowing from your hands into it.

Thread the sewing needle with the red thread. Pierce the heart through its center and then securely tie the thread. The heart should be dangling securely from a length of red thread.

Release the circle.

Take the charm outdoors and tie it somewhere high in the air, such as on a tree branch or secluded balcony, where it will be safe from scavengers. It is best if it is hanging isolated, completely surrounded by air, so that only flies will be able to get to it. As the heart begins to rot, it will naturally attract flies, which lay eggs in it. The eggs become larvae. Nature will do its work, and the maggots will eat away the rotting heart, using its energy to transform themselves into flies. When the heart is all gone, you should be free of your pain and ready to move on.

Worm Spell to End a Relationship

The following is a spell employing worms to end a relationship. Since worms are associated with death in that they're said to eat buried corpses, they can be integrated into spells for endings.

MATERIALS
Shovel

Carving tool such as a small knife

2 fruits or vegetables, to represent each person in the relationship. Traditionally, a phallic-shaped vegetable such as a carrot would be used to represent a man and a round, womb-like food such as an orange for a woman. These can of course be used in any combination for any kind of relationship. If gender binaries are not your thing, you can select a fruit or vegetable based on some other association that resonates with you and your partner, such as color or shape.

Container of 2 cups of fresh soil

About 5 worms. You can easily find them crawling on the sidewalk after it rains. When you pick them up, gently put them in the container of soil to allow them to be comfortable throughout the spell. You need to do this spell within 24 hours of taking the worms to avoid hurting or killing them.

This is an outdoor spell, best performed on a dark moon. Before you begin, use the shovel to dig a hole in the ground about a foot deep and a foot wide.

Cast your circle.

Carve your name into the fruit that represents you. As you do, pour your energy into it. Carve your partner's name into the other, filling it with their image. Imagine their face, smell, voice, and other characteristics while you do so. Next, join the foods together. If you are using a carrot and an orange, for example, insert the carrot into the orange to represent your union. If you are using two carrots or two oranges, push them together tightly.

Hold them above the hole in the ground. Consider the energetic ties that bind the two people together. Since this is the end of a relationship, these may be things like obligation, fear of change, familiarity, stability, boredom, or money. Avoid the temptation to focus on the good times past with rose-colored glasses: most relationships that are at an end are being held in place by stale, unhealthy things like those stated above. It's important to recognize what is keeping you in a dead relationship and face it. See those tangled obligatory things holding you together like black energy threads snarled all around the foods. When you are ready, slowly pull the foods apart and imagine the threads falling away and disappearing into the dark hole you have dug. Now, observe each piece of fruit as peacefully separated and unique, unattached to the other, each in its own bright, thriving circle of light.

Lay the fruits in the hole in the ground, peacefully side by side but not touching each other.

Now, hold the container of worms in your hands. Be aware of their wise, primal, benevolent energy. Remember, they can feel your vibrations and energy as well. In your mind (or out loud if you want), ask them to help you separate from the relationship, and ask them to transform that which has stagnated into something new and beneficial. Tell them the relationship is over and ask them to recycle what is left. Because worms feel vibrations, the better you are at energy transfer the more effective this will be. Imagine your message traveling down your arms, through your hands, and into the dirt, or else streaming from the center of your forehead. Send them your appreciation and gratitude, and then gently pour the contents of the container into the hole in the ground with the fruit. Refill the hole with the dirt, close the circle and walk away. It is done.

Over time the worms and other critters will eat away the fruits you have buried and change will come to you.

This spell can be altered for many other applications. It can be performed to help you let go of someone who doesn't love you back or to get rid of someone who is enmeshed in your life in an unhealthy way. The idea is not to hurt this person but to remove their hold on you and transform it into something positive. You can also use this spell to break your bond to an object, substance, or habit.

Bird Spell to Banish Illness

This spell was originally written to banish an illness or ailment. It can be reworded to banish anything one wishes to get rid of. It involves feeding wild birds, so make sure to find a place where this is legal. You will also need a general knowledge of which birds inhabit your area and what they eat.

For this spell, you will be using suet. Suet is fat taken from around the organs of sheep and cows. You've probably seen this kind of bird feeder before. Suet is available at animal feed stores already cubed and coated in bird seed, or you may be able to acquire some from a butcher shop. Most birds that eat insects also eat suet. It has a consistency similar to clay or wax and can be cut or molded into the shape needed for this spell.

← ⋅⋅⋅ₛ MATERIALS

Mold shaped like a person (such as a gingerbread man mold from the holiday season) or a knife for cutting the suet into a human shape

1 suet cake

Lock of hair, a fingernail, or drop of blood from the person who is ill

Small lump of almond paste or marzipan, about the size of a large marble. This can be purchased at baking stores.

Pin or sewing needle

1 cup bird seed

First consider what it is you wish to banish. This illness can be an actual physical ailment you wish to help someone overcome (along with proper medical attention) or spiritual in nature. Beforehand decide on a simple symbol that represents the ailment. You will be tracing this symbol into the marzipan with a pin. If the illness is depression, it can be represented by a sad face. If it's a broken bone, a simple bone shape will do. If all else fails, you can use the pin to write the actual name of the illness in the marzipan in tiny letters.

Gather your materials on your altar on the first night of the dark moon or during the last quarter of the waning moon. Cast your circle.

Using your knife or mold, make the suet cake into the shape of a human. Don't worry about making it look perfect—the intent is much more important than appearance. As you work with the figure, imagine the person you wish it to represent. Feel it becoming warm with their life and energy. See their face. Hear their voice. Add their hair, fingernails, or blood to the suet.

Now take your marzipan or almond paste. Hold it in your hands and knead it until it is soft like a piece of dough. While you do this, imagine the illness. Feel its heavy, rotten energy. Carve the symbol or word into the marzipan with the pin. Then, push the marzipan into the body part of the suet figure affiliated with the disease (head, heart, liver, etc.). Seal the suet over top of it.

Roll the figure in bird seed until it's covered.

Close the circle.

Take the suet to a deserted outdoor place in nature (not a public park or somewhere people and pets are likely to be). Take a moment to sit with it, and feel the energy of the birds that live there. Listen to their chirping. Call on their attention with your mind. Even if you do not see any at that exact moment, know they are there and that they can feel your intentions. Explain to them that you wish for them to enjoy the treat in exchange for carrying away the sickness. Listen to their songs and feel their presence while you do this.

Through the birds, nature is carrying away the illness and transforming it into something new.

Put your treat in a tree in a suet cage, or some other high place that won't be disturbed by land animals.

Chapter 7
BONES AND SKULLS

Bones are believed to house the true soul of the animal they came from, creating a direct link to the spirit energy of that creature through all time and incarnations. For example, a single coyote bone contains the life force of every coyote that ever lived. The DNA in that single bone is a direct conduit to the archetype of that species. The bone brings all the qualities, mythology, personality traits, and history of the coyote into any working you include it in. This concept applies to the bones of any animal, including people.

ON HUMAN REMAINS

Using human remains in magick is a lot more common than many people realize. Utilizing human bones, or even ashes, is a fairly common practice among magickal practitioners, at least for those who are able to obtain them and who wish to work with spirit in this way. That being said, using human bones in spells and rituals is not so different from using animal parts except that instead of working with the pure energy of a plant or animal, we are dealing with a much more complex human spirit.

Human bones house human characteristics. This means that in terms of magick, they can be employed in spells for things that people value most, such as love, prosperity, and connection. A spirit can be asked to retrieve information, send messages, and pull strings, so to speak, in situations in which otherwise you do not have much control. Human bones will have energetic characteristics of the person they belonged to in life and reflect their personality traits. The same can be said of animal bones. If the creature the bones come from experienced a difficult and traumatic life, this can sometimes be felt in their remains.

I include information here on human bones for research purposes only. I prefer working with animals and plants. For this reason, I don't have any spells in here employing human remains. As an empathic person, the unpredictable personalities of living humans are enough for me to handle in this life, never mind the dead ones! However, some people do choose to get human remains ethically and use them in their practice.

If you decide you'd like to include human remains in your practice, please never, ever, under any circumstances, go into a graveyard and steal body parts. Not only is it far more physically difficult than you can probably imagine, it's illegal and you can go to jail. It's disrespectful to the spirit, and it's insulting to the family of the deceased. There have been some documented cases of grave robbing across North America in which the skull is stolen for use in spells. The illegal trade of human remains has been, unfortunately, a lucrative one. People will pay lots of money for a human skull, especially those who believe it possesses the magic powers to grant their heart's desire. However, there are many legal ways to obtain human bones, such as through established online shops who sell cleaned and legally sourced remains. There are laws surrounding the sale of bones across the border or overseas, so you may have to hunt around a little to find them in your own country. The bones in these stores come from people who willingly donated their bodies to science and whose bones have been used in a classrooms and labs for educational purposes or scientific research. This is much different from tearing into the grave of someone's grandmother and stealing her head!

When you purchase bones online, there is no way to know for certain who they came from. You can attempt to find out from the dealer, but often all they can tell you is its country of origin. For the rest, you will have to rely on your own meditation and divinatory work to figure out what the bones can be used for, what kind of person they came from, and whether or not they wish to assist you with your work. You can do this by keeping the bone near you when you sleep and asking the spirit respectfully to come to you in your dreams and make themselves known. You can hold it in your hand during meditation, ask for information, and see what drifts into your vision. We all have varying levels of skill when it comes to communicating with the dead.

When working with any bones, it's important to be respectful to the spirit who resides there. Some people like to make offerings of food or drink to their bones, particularly on special days the spirit may have celebrated in life.

When you possess a piece of human bone, the spirit attached to it can aid you in your magickal workings. They can gather information about situations that you cannot, and can give your spells a push in certain directions. The spirit in the bones has journeyed to the other side and experienced the afterlife. They have walked between the worlds and know the secrets of life and death. They know what our purpose here is even when we don't. The spirits of the dead have wisdom we do not because they've evolved beyond our world of the living into the next dimension. Working with human bones is different from working with those of animals because animals are such pure creatures; they don't know what evil or hatred is, and their energy is far clearer and easier to understand. Humans are a whole different story, in life and in death, which is why I tend to be very wary of them in either form!

The Human Skull

Human skulls have been sought out by necromancers, spiritualists, shamans, witches, and magick workers of all kinds since the dawn of time. Some believe a human skull is the most powerful tool a practitioner can possess. It is considered a literal link to the spirit world of humans. While a fox skull can connect us to the archetypal spirit of fox, the human skull does the same with the most primordial essence of human spirit and our earliest beginnings. Some believe they can communicate directly with the dead through a human skull, either vocally or with visions, and that they can use the skull as a tool in summoning the deceased. Obtaining a human skull can be expensive, so some people will use a skull replica, a crystal skull, or even a photo in place of the real thing for these purposes.

Along with being linked to the archetypal spirit of a being, human and animal bones will also contain elements of the individual from which they came, depending on their personality traits. I believe that the older the bone or skull is, the less of the individual personality will be clinging to it as the energy fades over time.

The human skull has been a prized possession in magic throughout history. But why?

Cups and bowls from days past fashioned from human skulls have been unearthed. These were elaborately decorated drinking vessels, possibly used in ritual settings. Archaeological digs in parts of the Pacific, South Asia, and the Americas have revealed ancient temples filled with carved skulls. These have been labeled "skull cults."[8] Sometimes skulls were positioned in a place of reverence, while other times they appeared to be trophies of vanquished enemies. There's no way to know exactly what these so-called skull cults actually practiced or how they felt about their strange treasure, but chances are they believed the heads were a conduit to the Divine or the afterlife. Regardless, their existence is proof that the human skull has been a powerful object the world over, forever.

Most current spiritual practices that use human skulls do so for creating a connection with ancestors and bring power and luck to their practice. It's not necessarily anything evil or scary, simply different from what many Westerners are used to. In some parts of the world, purchasing a human skull is as easy as buying an ordinary household item. There are some rare instances when a family member can bequeath their skull to their kin in their will, although doing this nowadays is mostly unheard of. In many cases the use of human remains is done respectfully and viewed as an act of reverence to spirit.

The skull image has now become a commonplace thing in fashion and home décor, particularly the colorful Mexican sugar skull, which is rooted in Day of the Dead ceremonies. This image is seen in the mainstream regularly, with many people not understanding its importance in Mexican culture as part of honoring ancestors. At one time, skull and bone images were thought to be foreboding and only for heavy metal bands or pirate costumes, but now they're everywhere. I like to think the prevalence of the skull in popular culture indicates a shift in thought regarding death and the afterlife, if even subconsciously. I feel it could be the deities of death and rebirth making themselves known, indicating that we're currently in a time of transition as a whole. The deaths of old paradigms are upon us, and we're shifting into new ways of thinking, communicating, and existing together. The skull symbolizes the death of outdated ways of being as we evolve and change for the better.

---

8. Shaena Montanari, "Hints of Skull Cult Found in World's Oldest Temple," *National Geographic*, June 28, 2017, https://www.nationalgeographic.com/news/2017/06/skulls-cult-turkey-archaeology-neolithic-gobekli.

All in all, whether a skull is a trophy from a vanquished enemy, an oracle through which to speak to the dead, a thing to respect as housing ancestors, or a warning symbol, it's a powerful icon. To look at a human skull is to face death.

Animal Skulls

Animal skulls represent a true connection with the creature. The skull is the most important part of an animal you can have on your altar. The head is where the brain lives, the eyes see, and the ears hear and where all the animal's experiences are processed. While all bones are a conduit to animal energy and archetypes, the skull is the most powerful.

WORKING WITH BONES

Let's say you've decided to use bones in your magickal work and have bought some online or found and cleaned your own. Purchasing online means you've skipped the bonding process of finding, cleaning, and intimately handling the bones, which can create a feeling of disconnection. In a nutshell, the bones are strangers to you and you've not developed a rapport. When you receive them in the mail, they might not feel "right," or perhaps you'll feel nothing at all. The good news about feeling nothing when you handle them is that there is no malevolence attached to them. To put it another way, the spirit in the bones is "at peace" with you, and you should be easily able to work with them once woken up. Bones that you've found and cleaned yourself can also sometimes have dubious energy.

If the bones are giving you a bad feeling and you're reluctant to use them, it's possible they were disrespected on their journey to you, or maybe the spirit of the creature is unsettled.

Take the time to develop a relationship with the spirit in the bones. Give them a special spot on your altar and make an offering to them of food or drink. This is as simple as setting the offering before the bones and saying it is meant for them.

Sit before them in a quiet place and take some deep breaths. Hold your hands in front of you as if you are holding a ball. The ball is pink or white. It is pulsing with a gentle glow. Feel your positive intentions, respect, and reverence, and send those emotions into the ball of light. Then, place the ball of light over the bones and imagine it permeating them. This is your way of sending a message to the spirit that you mean no harm and that you want to be friends and allies. Don't expect immediate results. You don't know what traumatic events may have led to the death of the creature, so allow time for a relationship to develop between you. Repeat this process every so often until the feeling of unease leaves the bones. At this point, you may be able to commence dream work and meditation to find out more about them.

Remember that a spirit, whether human or animal, is not your servant. Do not approach them with a demanding attitude. This spirit is your ally and friend; treat them as such. If not, they will either go silent and not work with you at all, or worse, spoil your plans.

Giving Thanks to Animal Spirits

When you are working with parts of an animal, whether you find them or purchase them, it is very important to offer thanks and gratitude to the spirit of the animal. You're thanking the one rabbit you found for providing the bones, but you are also honoring all rabbits and all that they represent in our world, their special archetype of fertility, newness, virility, and new beginnings.

Besides uttering a thankful chant or prayer over the parts you are using, consider giving thanks through your actions. There are many practical ways to honor animals that also provide useful aid to the environment and natural habitats. While pouring a libation to the spirit of the animal is nice, also consider the following:

- Pick up trash in a naturalized area.
- Make a donation to a wildlife fund or nature center.
- Put out high-quality birdseed in winter.
- Always recycle and reuse as much as possible. Garbage and plastics have destroyed so many habitats already. Every time you choose to reuse and recycle is a step toward helping the planet.
- Plant herbs, flowers, other plants, or trees.
- Volunteer at an animal shelter.
- During extremely dry weather, put out dishes of water for wildlife.

Just having an animal's bones in a place of honor on your altar is in many ways an act of respect and thanks. When you're not using the bones and have stored them away, every so often be sure to handle them and feel appreciation for them. This is a form of "feeding" them with your energy, explained in further detail on page 153. Some people prefer to put a drop of their blood on them now and then or blow incense smoke onto them. As you handle the bones, imagine the animal and all the wonderful traits it has and the archetypes it represents and feel grateful.

THE BONE ORACLE

A bone oracle is a collection of bones from one or several animals, stored together in a bag or box, that are used for divination. The bones are gently dropped onto a surface and then interpreted according to how and where they land in relation to each other. You can ask questions or request guidance from a bone oracle the same way you would with tarot cards or tea leaves.

As you work with your bone oracle, the spirits inhabiting them lend their power to your reading. For this reason, you have to show respect to the bone oracle and "feed" it with your energy, blood, or breath.

Collecting the Oracle Bones

You can use any small bones you have found in nature and cleaned yourself. The collection may be a range of different animal bones that you've salvaged over time or all from one skeleton. You can also purchase pieces of cleaned animal skeletons online.

If you're a meat eater, you can salvage the bones of a whole chicken, a rabbit, or game you've eaten or keep a few pieces from each different type of animal you consume. Place the bones in borax or salt for a week or more to dry them out.

Creating the Casting Cloth

The casting cloth is the surface on which you will toss your bones when consulting your oracle. It can also double as a storage bag for your bones: place them in the middle, gather the edges, and tie them up with string to make a pouch.

Get a circle of black cloth about a foot and a half in diameter. Divide it into four equal parts by painting a cross in the middle with the lines extending to its edges. Each section represents one of the cardinal directions: north, east, south, and west. You can paint a symbol or letter on each section to mark this. Each cardinal direction governs a different aspect of our lives and can add information to the reading when you cast your bones, depending on which of the sections they land in on your cloth. When doing a reading, lay your cloth on a table or the floor with the letters corresponding with the actual directions in your space. For example, the N corner of your cloth should physically face north. Having the cloth aligned with the directions is important, as the bones will be pulled by the spirit of that direction or element when you throw them, especially if you've cast a circle and called upon the elements to assist you. The significance of the directions in a bone oracle is as follows:

North: Earth, family, stability, money concerns, survival, home, work, career

East: Air, communication, friendships, other people, wisdom, lessons

South: Fire, passion, sex, anger, war, creativity, rebirth

West: Water, emotion, intuition, love and relationships, moods, inner feelings

If you cast your bones and most of them fall in the northern quadrant, this denotes issues about family and finance. In the east, communication and outside influence have bearing on your situation. Bones in the southern quadrant indicate intense drama, and the west implies deep emotions are involved. If at first it seems the cardinal direction in which your bones land doesn't apply to the question, look for a connection. For example, if you've asked about your career, yet all the bones land in west for water (love and emotion), it means your job is somehow directly affected by a relationship and your inner emotions. Your bones may fall into several different cardinal directions at a time. Your query and how the bones land together will indicate what bearing the elements have on your reading.

Bonding with the Bones

It's necessary to create a connection between yourself and the spirits inside the bone oracle. You can accomplish this by sleeping with them under your pillow or spending some time each day handling them with your fingers and just feeling their power. You can try meditating with them to figure out what sort of energy already resides in them. Try not to let other people handle your oracle bones, as they're very personal. Those who read for others often have two sets, one for public use by clients and one just for themselves alone. The rapport between yourself and the spirit of the bones is crucial for doing meaningful readings.

Feeding the Bones

Some people feed their bone oracle regularly. This can be done by adding a drop of blood to them and shaking the bag around gently to spread the blood's energy, sprinkling some herbs on them (such as mugwort, which is associated with blessing divination tools), or dropping some moon water from your fingertips onto them. The idea behind feeding the oracle is to keep its energy active, show respect to the spirit, and maintain the bond.

Cleansing the Bones

It's imperative to cleanse your bones in between readings. Your thoughts and questions can cling to the bones and affect future readings, even if you're the only one who uses them. Cleanse them by laying them in the sunlight or moonlight for a few hours or by placing them carefully in a glass of moon water or rainwater. Let them sit in the water overnight, and then lay them out to dry completely. Pour the water on the ground or down the drain. Cleanse the bones after each reading.

When not using the bones, store them in their cloth or bag.

Reading the Bones

Spread your cloth in front of you, aligned with the cardinal directions. Gather all the bones in both your hands and close your eyes. Contemplate your question while gently breathing onto the bones. The breath communicates your underlying concerns that you can't put into words. When you're ready, gently drop them onto your cloth.

Look at the bones and loosen your gaze, like you would do when reading tea leaves or scrying. Together the bones will form shapes and pictures. Take note of the shapes, what they mean to you, and which cardinal direction they have fallen within.

The largest bone represents the actual object of your question. If your concern is family, the largest bone represents family. Examine how the bones lie around it. Are there vertebrae touching it and supporting it? Is it isolated and alone? Is there a broken bone near it? Wing bones represent swift change, whereas vertebrae connote stability. The bones may fall together touching each other, forming a shape that resembles something else, such as a cross, a square, or even a star formation. These symbols are just for you, and only you can say what they mean. For example, a cross for me means the meeting of two different people or ideas, whereas to many people a cross signifies religion. Your bones will speak directly to you.

The bones around the largest "question" bone will tell you the state of your family. If many ribs point sharply at the large bone, it means your family is under some kind of attack, whereas if there is a sturdy triangle shape around it, it is secure. If they land over the top of one another in a toppling fashion, it means the situation is not stable and likely to fall apart, or the relationship is in a precarious position.

It can become very complex and personalized, but with practice, you will develop a rapport with your oracle and be able to understand what it is telling you.

Additional Objects

Some people like to add other objects besides bones to their oracle for clarity. A shell, for example, can represent a shield, and where it falls in a reading, it denotes protection. A piece of wood from a tree can signify growth, and if it falls near the big main bone of a question, it means an increase. If it falls far away, it could mean a decrease. A coin can be added to indicate work, so if it falls near your main bones, it means you will have to work hard to solve your problem. A pair of dice can be used to show timing based on what numbers turn up, and a stone can represent yourself or a key person.

Here is an example reading of my own bird bone oracle that I'll share with you so that you can see the different elements that go into interpreting it.

Bone Oracle Sample Reading

For this reading, my friend asked me, "What can I expect in my social life?" Here is a diagram of how the bones landed and an explanation of how I interpreted them.

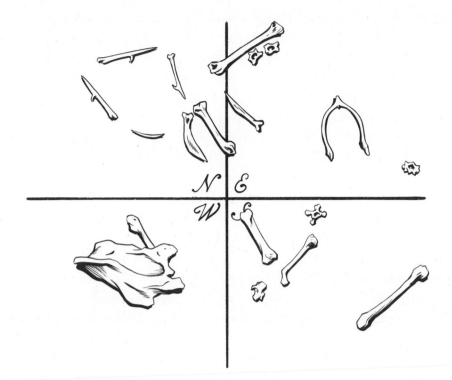

The largest bone is in the west. This big flat bone is covering a smaller one, as if shielding or protecting it (A). Since they fell in the western quadrant, these bones pertain to emotions. They indicate the querent is hiding or shielding their feelings, perhaps to protect themselves socially. This could represent their fear of opening up to others about something that is important to them.

In the southern corner, the realm of fire and passion, we see a small vertebrae (B) with several larger bones bursting away from it like fireworks. This means the querent is a "small," quiet, and largely unknown individual who is bursting out of their shell and having a huge impact on those around them, perhaps without realizing it. Since this is in the realm of fire, it means this person is making serious, dramatic waves around them in terms of how they're affecting others. Their reason for doing this has to do with passionate, tumultuous feelings that they're unable to hold in.

In the east, the realm of air and communication, we find the wishbone (C). Where the wishbone falls is always especially important. In this case, it means the gift of communication right now, a run of good luck, and success in terms of being heard and making connections. The large bone in the upper corner (D), which is touching several smaller bones, is holding space for the querent. This represents a mentor or more experienced person who is there to support and aid them in their goals. This person is staying to the side out of the way and letting the querent take the stage, supporting them from the sidelines.

In the north, we can see a direct pattern in which the bones are facing away from the wishbone in the east as if propelled by it. In terms of social life, the north represents those who are in your immediate circle. Here we see quite a few flimsy bones being supported by larger, thicker ones (E). The querent may feel they are speaking for those who are weaker than them or less able to do so, holding them up, so to speak. Some of these small bones have scattered into other quadrants, indicating that there have already been people close to the querent who have been lost or negatively affected by social issues. However, their winning streak with communication in the east (the wishbone) is clearly showing that their actions will give stability to those they care about.

In conclusion, to answer the question "What can I expect in my social life?" the querent is someone who feels small and less important than others and has not been heard in the past due to shyness or other factors. The querent has something very important to convey, and emotions are running high because of it. There could be injustice involved and a desire to speak out against it. The querent is already having a big impact on those around them with their passion. Soon they will have time to shine, really get their message out, and be heard perhaps for the first time, with the aid of a more experienced, older person backing them up. This will lead to strengthening the querent in a social sense, allowing them to learn the value of their voice. They will be able to help those who need it and positively impact others, especially those nearest and dearest to them who are struggling.

SPELLS USING BONES AND SKULLS

The following spells all make use of bones or skulls in different ways.

Chicken Bone Breakup Spell

This spell is to end a relationship between two people. If you wish to break up a couple for your own reasons, please take a moment to reflect on how this will affect everyone around them, including their families and children, and decide if it really is in the best interest of all involved. This spell is potentially destructive, and you should proceed with caution.

MATERIALS

2 bones from a chicken or other small animal (substitution: 2 sticks
    from a lilac tree or rose bush)
Felt-tip pen
Various colors of paint
Hair of the 2 people involved, if possible
Rusty old nail
1 foot pure cotton thread (must be biodegradable)

Cast your circle. Decorate each bone to represent a person in the relationship. Write their name on it with the pen and paint it with their favorite colors. Spend time with each bone one at a time, pouring the essence of the individual into it. If possible, tie a piece of their hair to the bone that represents them. If you don't have hair, visualization will have to do.

Now hold the rusty nail in your hand, and notice its corroding, rotting state. Imagine how painful and destructive it would be to have a nail inserted into flesh, how it would oxidize and cause infection to all it touched. This nail represents a fight or problem that will come between the people and destroy their union.

Tie the chicken bones together with the cotton thread.

Now insert the nail right in the middle of them, at a 90-degree angle, wedging them apart. Say:

> Break apart, break apart.
> This nail will separate your hearts.

Close the circle.

Bury the charm deep in the ground. As the thread rots, so will their bond, until they fall away from each other.

Skull Spell to Guard a Secret

This spell uses a dog or other canine skull because they're known to be loyal and protective. If you have a secret that you wish to keep hidden, this is a spell to create a guardian amulet to protect it from being exposed.

⇥ MATERIALS

Canine skull, such as a dog's or coyote's (substitution: plastic, wood, or clay replica)

Bowl with 1 cup dark moon water (see page 43)

½ cup witch's salt (see page 49)

Turquoise crystal

Small open padlock and matching key

Place your materials on your altar and cast a circle.

Hold the skull in your hands and look into its face. Feel affection for it as you would for a beloved dog who was part of your family. Send the skull this love from your heart center to let the spirit know that you are a friend, kind of like how you'd allow a dog to sniff your hand before petting it.

Once you've developed an energetic connection, visualize what you'd like the spirit to do. In this case, their job is to guard a secret. Imagine a canine creature standing vigilantly in front of a locked gate on the lookout for intruders. Send this image into the skull. This lets the spirit know that its job is to guard and protect.

Set the skull down and dip your finger in the dark moon water. Place several drops of dark moon water on the skull. Say:

Loyal spirit, guard my secrets
Viciously with teeth and claws.
If anyone tries to see inside the circle,
Bite them and chase them away.

Pour the witch's salt in a circle on your altar, about 6 inches across.

Turquoise is said to absorb the feelings of those who handle it. Picture your secret exactly as it is and hold the crystal against your forehead. The secret is now inside the crystal. Place the crystal inside the salt circle.

Now take the open lock. Snap it shut. The clicking sound signals your secret is closed and locked up. Set it down inside the circle near the crystal.

Place the skull on top of the lock and stone so it is touching both.

The canine spirit is now guarding the secret, which is locked up tight inside the protective salt circle.

Release the magick circle. Put the key away until you're ready to release your secret.

Every day place several drops of dark moon water on the skull. This feeds its energy and acknowledges its spirit. You can also make an offering to the skull each day by placing a dog bone, toy, kibble, or meat before the skull. If it is meat, remove it and dispose of it each day. This tells the spirit that you appreciate it and the work it is doing.

To further protect your secret, it's best not to allow anyone to see the altar with this setup on it. You can drape cloth over it to keep it hidden during the process of the working if you like.

When you're ready to release the spell or the threat of your secret being told has passed, unlock the lock and cleanse it to use for something else. Throw away the salt circle and bury the turquoise stone.

Keep the skull for future spells or as a general protection amulet in your home.

The Hand of Glory

The hand of glory is a very old spell that originally was said to work the following way. The left hand was cut from a hanged man's corpse during the night, then dried and cured. The cured hand was slathered with the rendered fat of the hanged man to make it flammable like a candle. The hand was placed fingers up in a holder. It was believed that when this charm was placed next to the intended victim and each of the five fingertips lit like candles, it would render the targeted person completely immobile and motionless.

The following spell is meant to render someone's power immobile. This will not be a physical immobility, but rather the spell will stop their actions and power over you or others.

←─ǝ MATERIALS

Death candle (see page 51)

Thoroughly dried paw bones from any animal. This represents the "hand." It can be one bone or several; it doesn't need to be a whole intact paw. (substitution: a stick that has a shape similar to a hand or a cardboard cutout of a hand)

1 tablespoon death oil (see page 48)

Photo of the targeted person if necessary, any size

Lighter or matches
Charcoal disk
Fireproof dish

It's best to do this spell with the targeted person nearby but without their knowledge. If that's not possible, a photo of them will do.

During the dark moon, gather your materials on your altar. Cast a circle and invoke deity if you wish.

Light your death candle.

Hold the bones in your hand and breathe on them gently to bring them to life energetically. Imagine you are holding the hand of a hanged man. These bones contain the same death energy as the hand from a hanged man would, as they are both from a deceased being.

Put a dab of death oil on your fingers and gently massage it into each of the bones. This replicates the act of putting tallow or rendered fat on the hand. It also carries the essence of death itself, imbuing the bones with the absence of life and movement.

Place the photo of the person next to your fireproof vessel and light your charcoal disk. Put the disk in the fireproof dish. One by one, place the bones on the charcoal disk and watch them burn. Imagine the smoke is rising from them carrying the power of death and stillness, drifting through the air to find the intended person, stopping them cold in their actions. Do this with each bone. Imagine the person becoming powerless as the smoke surrounds them.

If you're using a bone that is too large to fit on the charcoal disk, you can light it on fire with the lighter and let it burn in the dish. You may have to relight it several times during the process depending on how dry it is.

When the bones are done burning, let the candle burn all the way out and extinguish the charcoal disk. Close the circle.

You can keep the ashes of this spell to add to protective witch's salt or for use in future curses.

Please keep in mind that bones smell bad when they burn, so you may want to do this spell outdoors or in a well-ventilated area.

Wing Bone Spell to Flee a Situation

While this spell won't actually induce physical flight, it is to provide an opportunity for you to fly out of a difficult situation and become "free as a bird."

This opportunity can come in the form of unexpected assistance from other people or simply a new way of thinking you hadn't explored before.

⤙ MATERIALS

    8½-by-11-inch piece of black construction paper

    Chalk or white crayon

    Sterile lancet

    Wing bone from a bird (substitution: a feather)

You can do this spell either at your altar or outdoors near a high cliff or overhang where there are no people.

Cast your circle and invoke deity if you wish.

Write your situation on the black paper exactly as it is. Describe precisely what it is you want to be free of, whether that is a person's name, a situation, or a feeling. Allow the pain and negative feelings that go with feeling trapped to pour over you while you write. Using the sterile lancet, prick your finger and add a drop of your blood to the paper, transferring the pain into it. Imagine the piece of paper is surrounded by an oppressive murky gray aura.

Set the paper aside and take the wing bone in your hand. See the bird in flight. Imagine the freedom of being a bird, feeling the wind all around you as if you were flying away. Envision your own freedom exactly how you wish it would be.

Fold the black paper all around the bone with the writing facing inward. The black paper mutes the energy of the bone, trapping it inside.

Close your circle if you're indoors.

Go to a place such as a high cliff or a bridge over water (avoid anywhere that has lots of people). Hold the charm out over the edge and see your situation as it is now. Unfold the bone from the paper, and feel the freedom and power bursting out of it. Throw the bone over the edge of the cliff as hard as you can and let it fly. As you do so, see yourself breaking free and flying too.

Now rip the paper to shreds, destroying the thing that trapped you, rendering it powerless. Burn or recycle the paper.

Goat Bone Chaos Spell

Goats are associated with the devil in all of his many guises and forms. The Christian devil represents lust, sin, and carnal desires. The devil is often imagined as being a lying trickster who enjoys causing trouble. Goats are unpredictable, clever, and devious and manage to get into all kinds of trouble too. You don't have to believe in the existence of the devil to perform this spell, but rather bear in mind the qualities of his animal representation, the goat.

Goat energy is lustful, fun, and playful, but it is also cunning, troublemaking, and destructive. Goats are famous for being able to manipulate and demolish almost any fence put around them and destroy any landscape by eating it. They're known to be very noisy and disruptive, and the males let off a terrible stink when in rut. It's these unpredictable qualities of the goat that this spell focuses on.

⤙ MATERIALS

Goat bone of any kind or piece of horn or hoof (substitution: a jagged piece of wood with splinters)

Marker or sharp object for inscribing the bone or hoof

Box with a lid of appropriate size to hold the bone

1 cup cayenne pepper powder, or enough to fill the box

3 prickly thistle leaves

13 thumbtacks

Cast your circle and call your deity.

Place the goat bone on your altar and fill your mind with images of destruction and chaos. This can look like an explosion or fight. It can sound like an alarm or siren. As you visualize this, draw or scrape the image of an asterisk symbol into the bone. The asterisk, with its converging lines, symbolizes the clash of many different energies, creating chaos. Instead of an asterisk, you can design your own sigil if you please.

Fill the box with the cayenne pepper, prickly thistle leaves, and thumbtacks. Together they make a burning, stinging, piercing, and irritating concoction that would be unbearable to have in the skin or eyes. This mixture encompasses all that is irritating, inflammatory, and unpleasant.

Place the bone in the box and cover it completely with the cayenne pepper mixture. Imagine the cayenne pepper saturating the bone with burning, irritating energy. Visualize the inflammatory qualities of the cayenne pepper soaking into every pore of the bone and into the chaos symbol. Put so much irritated energy into the box that it feels almost unbearable to open it or look inside.

Close the circle.

Let the bone sit in the mixture for 3 nights.

Remove the bone and wrap it up in paper so you don't have to touch it. Take it with you to the place you want to disrupt or release havoc upon. Remove it from the paper and place it discretely somewhere on the property or in the room you wish to affect. Walk away and allow it to fill the space with chaotic energy, shaking up every situation and interaction that takes place there.

Dispose of the ingredients. You can cleanse and reuse the thumbtacks for similar future spells.

Raccoon Penis Bone Breakup Spell

As you start digging into the topic of using bones in witchcraft, you're bound to discover that the penis bone of a raccoon is a coveted object. It can be salvaged, as explained earlier, or bought at many witchcraft stores.

A penis bone, or baculum, is generally used in magick to increase sexual attraction. However, in the spirit of shadow work, this spell is meant to banish sexual chemistry between two people by breaking the bone, thus breaking their attraction to each other.

⟶ MATERIALS

Death candle (see page 51)

Raccoon penis bone

Marker

Small dish containing ¼ cup witch's salt (see page 49)

Cast your circle and invoke deity if you wish.

Light the death candle. Write the names of the two people involved on the bone, leaving a space in between. You will break the bone in between their names, so make sure there is a gap in the middle of the writing.

As the death candle burns, hold the bone in your hands. Visualize the sexual chemistry between the two people as it is now. Their sexual chemistry is inside the bone. Now tightly grasp the ends of the bone in your fingers. Snap it cleanly in half, and then immediately stick the broken ends into the salt. Imagine the salt entering the broken parts of the bones, getting inside it, and breaking down its power. Imagine the salt burning into the bone, softening it and making it porous with its death energy. Envision the witch's salt weakening the bone and the tie between the two people until it dissipates into nothing.

Release your circle. Allow the candle to burn out.

Compost the remaining bones and salt.

the

FORBIDDEN

CRAFT

This section of the book brings us to the nitty-gritty of shadow work. Here you'll learn about the objects and ingredients used in dark magick as well as how and when to perform a curse. We're also going to delve into the misunderstood topic of sacrifice, how it applies to witchcraft today, and ways to integrate it into your own practice.

This section includes topics that make people squeamish, explaining magickal objects and practices that are avoided in public discussion or are used specifically in dark magick. It skips over the usual witchcraft supplies, assuming you already know what most of those are and what they're for. Instead we'll focus on things you may be curious about but were afraid to try. Some of these objects have been used in magick since the beginning of humankind. Others, such as brimstone or tombstone moss, are common in witchcraft but have a questionable reputation, which I will try to clear up. A few of these items deserve exactly the bad reputation they have.

In the dark witch's cabinet, there are some things that are repulsive, some things that smell yucky, some things that are frightening, and some things that society as a whole just wants to ignore. Grab your hand sanitizer and come on in.

CHAPTER 8
A WITCH'S CURIOS

The objects, recipes, and ingredients explained here are used at other times in this book. It's best to understand them and in some cases prepare them ahead of time, for many of the spells to come.

GRAVEYARD GOODIES

Graveyard materials are exactly that: materials collected from a graveyard. These things are used to connect the spirit of a deceased person to your working and utilize their abilities or attributes to boost the power of your spell.

When I was quite young, I was compelled to visit graveyards out of curiosity. When I felt drawn to a specific headstone, I would keep something from its base, like a stone or some dirt, and keep it as a talisman. I felt like by doing so that I had spirits of the dead guarding me.

When a grave is considered important or special in some way, it's a common practice for witches to collect moss from the headstone for luck or magick. Even nonwitchy people will often visit the graves of famous, powerful people to take a souvenir like a pebble or dead flower to act as good luck charms or for more intentional purposes.

Graveyard dirt in spells is mostly seen in African American conjuration practices. It's used by root workers and those who practice Voodoo, Hoodoo, and ancestor veneration. Conjurers and root workers have their own very old traditions handed down from their ancestors, a tradition all their own, which is far older than my own intuitive approach.

Collecting graveyard materials is not as simple as wandering into a cemetery and grabbing a handful of soil. There are many things to consider when
acquiring this special ingredient for your spells.

First of all, you must be fully aware of who is buried in the grave you take
an item from and what that person was like in their life. Their life story will
indicate what kind of spirit they are and what they can be called upon to assist
with. I personally would only ever take moss or a pebble from the grave of a
family member or friend who I know would support me in my life, but some
people go beyond that and collect items from many different graves based on
their needs.

Graveyard Rules

Be Respectful: When in a graveyard, it is important to show reverence for the
spirits of the deceased, as well as their living families. Do not disrupt any
monuments or floral displays that are set out. Be quiet and solemn. When
you do find the grave you wish to work with, take only a small amount of
dirt, a little twig, a pebble, or some other unremarkable thing. Never take
live flowers or gifts that someone else has placed there. If what you take
will be obviously visible, interpret that as a very clear message that the spirit
doesn't wish for you to have it.

Ask Permission: Not every spirit is willing to work with you. When you approach the grave, sit or stand near it and spend some time communicating
with the spirit. Explain to them what you wish to have their aid in. Enter a
quiet frame of mind and try to feel what they are telling you. Pay attention
to things such as birds, trees, the wind, and any signs these may carry. If the
spirit does not wish to help you, you may feel dizzy, nauseous, or frightened
or otherwise sense that the answer is no. If you feel happiness and positivity,
the answer is yes. If you are proficient in divination, such as with tarot cards,
you can use them to seek permission from a spirit as well. Here is a simple
tarot trick using the Moon card and the Sun card. After connecting with
the spirit through meditation, ask if you may have something from their
grave to assist in your working. Shuffle the cards and flip one up. The Sun
indicates "yes" and the Moon indicates "no." Respect the answer.

Bring an Offering: Always. This can be a drink to pour on the ground, flowers,
special coins, crystals, or jewelry. You must always repay a spirit for their at-

tentions. If you do not, it is stealing in a spiritual sense and you are bringing trouble upon yourself.

Choosing a Grave: As I said, the grave site of a loved one is the best choice if possible, in my opinion. A family member or friend will likely be willing to aid you in your workings, as long as it is in your best interest. A loved one will protect you and help you attract love, happiness, and success. They will also back you up in reversal or cursing spells. Steer clear of family members with whom you had a tumultuous or dysfunctional relationship. If you can find the grave of a public figure or historical person whose values in life mirror your own goals, they might be approachable too. Remember, pets are also loved ones! Moss or dirt from the grave from a beloved familiar can be used in all kinds of spells, including loyalty or even in finding a mate.

Legalities

Taking something from a graveyard without permission, even if it is just a leaf or bit of moss, is considered vandalism in some places. Many cemeteries are locked at night. Please do not go scaling walls in the darkness and wind up being fined or worse. If you cannot gain access to a cemetery, you can purchase graveyard dirt online. While it is unlikely that you would be penalized for planting a flower on the grave of your grandmother and privately keeping a small sample of the earth, anything from a stranger's grave may involve risks. However, if you are able to obtain permission from the owner of the cemetery to do some digging, go ahead. They may not understand why you want to take graveyard dirt, but they may still allow you to do so if they are open minded.

Since in most places entering a graveyard at night is likely to arouse suspicion and unwanted attention, you may have to do your cemetery journey in daylight. However, the phase of the moon is still in affect during daylight hours. The phases of the moon apply to collecting graveyard items in the same way as any spell work: dark moon for cursing or hexing, full moon for protection, waxing moon for gaining things and positive magick, and waning moon for banishing.

Other Kinds of Dirt

When it comes to using dirt in magick, you are certainly not restricted to the graveyard. It is believed that earth taken from any place will retain energies of whatever occurred there. Here are some alternatives if the idea of taking items from graves doesn't appeal to you:

Bank Property: The land upon which a bank or credit union is built can be added to prosperity and wealth spells.

Court Property: A bit of dirt from the lawn of the courthouse can be added to spells for justice and legal issues.

Banquet Hall: A building that hosts many wedding receptions may retain energy useful in love spells.

Hospital Grounds: This dirt can be used in healing spells or to cause illness. Intent matters here, as hospitals are a place of healing, but they are also a place of illness.

Schoolyard: Dirt from a school playground can be added to spells for protection of children, playfulness, and new beginnings.

University Campus: Spells for learning and intellect can include dirt from university grounds.

Murder Scene: A house or building where a murder occurred carries seriously dark energy. Dirt from this site can be used in your most vicious spells.

Woods: Soil from secluded natural spaces can be included in peace and serenity spells.

As you can see, you can get really creative with where and why you collect dirt from different places. Here are some ways to use dirt in magick:

- Use it to dress candles by rolling an oiled candle in it.
- Add the dirt to sachets, spell bottles, and powders.
- Put it inside poppets.
- Sprinkle it onto your own property (e.g., sprinkle bank dirt on your lawn to attract money).
- Place grave dirt from a loved one by the front door for protection.

RITUAL KNIVES

Weapons, specifically knives, have been viewed not only as tools but as symbols of great power. Swords are one of the oldest, revered for conquering and killing enemies. There is also a magickal side to these weapons, which is why they were often ceremoniously blessed prior to battle, and many cultures encrusted their weapons with jewels. The old story of the sword in the stone illustrates the power of the blade, for whoever could pull it from the stone was to be gifted with the power of a king. Great pits of buried weapons dating back to the Bronze Age have been uncovered, believed to be sacrifices to the gods and goddesses.[9] Knives weren't always just for physically killing things; they have been used as symbols in ritual for just as long.

The knife or sword carries heavy meaning. It's considered a phallic symbol, that of so-called masculine energy. When I say masculine, I don't mean the physical male sex. I'm referring to the way that many witchcraft traditions split the world into masculine/feminine, active/receptive, or solar/lunar terms. It represents aggression and the active pole in nature. I feel we all have both these energies inside us and that they have nothing to do with our physical anatomy or gender.

In ceremonies celebrating the great rite, a knife is plunged into a chalice or cauldron to represent the unity of male and female and how this union brings forth life. Many altars display a ritual knife, sometimes called an athame, which is used to cut through energetic ties or to direct energy like a wand.

Vanquishing enemies in the old days wasn't considered evil: it was a means of survival. Luckily, times have changed and most people don't have to fight for their lives every day, at least where I live. However, the sword is still a symbol of power, victory, and survival.

In terms of dark magick, a sword, knife, or blade is a useful tool to represent endings. In many myths, the gods and goddesses use a blade, sickle, or pair of scissors to snip the invisible life cord attached to humans to end their existence on this plane. The grim reaper holds a huge scythe for harvesting the souls of the living and taking them to the underworld. So while the blade is a battle symbol, it's also tied to death energy.

You can use your ritual knife in spells designed to end situations, to fight against enemies, and to instill fear. Some people do use ritual knives for bloodletting in a controlled ceremonial manner, but I don't. A knife can be difficult to control in terms of how deeply you cut and can lead to accidents, unlike a

---

9. Lewis, *Ritual Sacrifice*, 4.

lancet. Also remember that it is considered a weapon, so it's illegal to carry it with you.

In choosing what a ritual knife will look like, to me it's important that it appears powerful and even intimidating. I found a pair of oversized, brutal, rusty shears at an antique shop, and those are my favorite because they remind me of old things and decay, which is in keeping with banishing magick. I can picture a scary old ghost woman snipping souls away with those things. My other favorite ritual knife is a big curved sickle that has a rusted blade and a bone handle that looks like it's been through some battles. Neither of these is sharp enough to cut paper, mind you. While I prefer a scary-looking knife, you may feel more power from something fancy, jeweled, or artisan-made. Everyone's style is different, so whether you chose something sleek and modern or something rustic, all that matters is that it resonates with your intention.

Here are a few ways to integrate your ritual knife into spells and rituals:

- Stab it through a photo of your enemy in victory spells.
- Cut up a photo or the name of your rival in any situation to slay them in competition.
- Place near the entrance of the home where its energy will frighten intruders (be safe, of course—keep it out of the reach of children and pets).
- Have it present during all spells in which you overpower another person.
- Meditate with it for strength and courage.

You can get creative with what symbolic weapons you use in spells. All over the world and throughout history, various weapons have been regaled as symbols of power. The key thing to remember is that they are symbolic. They shouldn't actually put you or anyone else in physical danger.

DARK CRYSTALS

Crystals are undergoing resurgence in popularity nowadays, especially within the wellness and self-care industry. Where crystal collecting and healing used to be seemingly reserved for new agers only, they're now for sale at ordinary department stores, along with mass-produced salt lamps and sage bundles. Holistic health and beauty gurus definitely focus only on the positive side of crystals, touting their good vibes, healing energy, and cleansing properties. While some of this is valid, witches have been using crystals and stones for time out of mind in our practice. It's only recently that it became cool instead of nerdy!

The current crystal trend is heavy on the "good vibes," which is fine, but it's important to understand that like every other thing in life, crystals have a shadow side, some kinds more so than others.

Many crystals are actually a by-product of natural destruction such as volcanoes or pressure and heat inside the earth. Some are millions of years old. These stones, crystals, and minerals are products of great change, which often includes endings. We can use these crystals, some of which were birthed by destruction and disaster, in corresponding areas of life.

Just like all magickal tools, your intent or how you "program" your crystal has a huge bearing on how it will work. That doesn't mean you can charge rose quartz, known for love and gentleness, with hatred—that simply doesn't make any sense. It does mean, however, that you could charge a rose quartz with the extreme, distorted side of love and gentleness by using it to create a malleable, pliant character. There's a "dark" way to look at everything, even crystals.

When deciding on a crystal to use in shadow magick or cursing, think of them the same way you think of herbal medicine. A little bit can heal, but too much can cause illness or worse. This same theory can be applied to the energetic properties of many crystals. What is considered a good thing on one hand, such as warmth from carnelian, can be destructive on the other hand when exaggerated, such as angry fire energy in carnelian. A little fire energy is a happy spark. Too much fire energy is an impassioned rage. The list that follows briefly explains basic crystals that can be used in cursing. This list is quite small, as it's limited to my go-to gems, but if you know the metaphysical properties of other crystals, you can figure out their shadow qualities by exaggerating their traits.

Amazonite: Amazonite can cast confusion into the mind, creating barriers in thoughts. It acts as a filter to negativity, so when there's too much of it, it could create general blockages in the energy field.

Amethyst: Amethyst can promote apathy and laziness or can make someone so preoccupied with the spiritual realm they fail to notice the physical one.

Black Obsidian: Black obsidian has been used throughout the ages to fashion sharp deadly weapons, such as knives and arrowheads. It can be used in hexes to cut through something or someone or to hinder them in some way. Obsidian can be used to "freeze" someone in their tracks, turning their plans from active to static form.

Bloodstone: This type of jasper can be used to symbolically get into someone's blood, to crawl inside their very self and affect them from within.

Carnelian: A fire stone, carnelian can be used to cause outrage, anger, and impulsive, damaging actions.

Diamonds: Diamonds are as multifaceted in magick as they are in jewelry. They can be used for defense due to their ability to cut anything. They can beguile someone, blinding them with beauty and sparkle.

Emerald: While often associated with dispelling envy like other green stones, emerald can also be used to inflict jealousy upon someone so that it eats them up whole.

Flint: Flint was used to make weapons and other tools. A solid, strong stone, it can be used as blunt force in defensive spells, magickally knocking someone out, so to speak (not literally).

Garnet: Garnet was believed to ward off thieves and repel negative energy, and its dark red color is associated with blood. Charge a garnet with threatening bloody energy and wear it; the effect is like you are soaked in the blood of your enemies. Others near you will feel the threat and leave you alone.

Hematite: Real hematite will develop rust over time, and this can symbolize decay and rot in magick. Real hematite produces red or rusty streaks when rubbed onto a surface, like dried blood, and can be used to symbolically bleed someone.

Howlite: Howlite is associated with recalling past lives. It can be used to immerse someone in their past actions and bring regret.

Jet: Jet is believed to be able to absorb a person's soul. Therefore, it's said that you can capture someone's essence in jet and imprison them.

Malachite: Malachite is believed to dredge up hidden qualities in people, triggering life changes that they may or may not be ready to face. In terms of cursing, malachite can be used to give someone a taste of their own medicine or used in reversal spells that make someone see themselves in a new light.

Onyx: There's a myth that black onyx is a demon imprisoned in stone who causes breakups. Onyx is used to cool the desires between couples and potentially split them up.

Petrified Wood: "Petrified" in this case is another word for hardened or ossified. Petrified wood can be used to cause someone to become "atrophied" and unable to fight against you or a situation.

Pyrite: Often called fool's gold, pyrite can be used in spells to trick someone who is materialistic and easily distracted by earthly pleasures. It can be used in spells to expose someone as fraudulent, give them illusions of grandeur, and make them play the fool.

Quartz: Quartz amplifies all spells and rituals, including dark ones.

Rose Quartz: Use rose quartz to make someone more submissive and to subdue their defenses.

Sodalite: Sodalite is normally a stone of communication, but there is such thing as too much talking. Sodalite can be used to get someone to confess to something they normally wouldn't or cause them to spill secrets.

Tiger's Eye: Usually associated with bravery and courage, tiger's eye in both blue and golden form is a truth-seeking stone. It is believed to detect lies and warn us when someone is being dishonest. When you feel you're being deceived but can't quite prove it, carry a tiger's eye stone. You will be shown the truth, even if it is ugly, so be prepared. It can also be used to create conceit and egotism in someone.

Volcanic Rock: A porous substance, this can be employed to suck the energy out of someone.

BRIMSTONE

Brimstone, also called sulfur, is an infrequently discussed ingredient in some magickal workings. There are several reasons for this. First, it smells absolutely horrendous. Second, it can be difficult to obtain in its elemental form. Third, when burned, it can be poisonous, even though some people choose to burn it in ritual in small amounts.

Sulfur is a naturally occurring element in the earth and in our bodies. It's a by-product of mining petroleum products. This is called "elemental sulfur," the way it is presented on the periodic table. When mixed with other elements, chemicals such as sulfur dioxide or sulfuric acid are created, but those are not considered brimstone and not used in magick. Only pure elemental sulfur should be used.

Fire and Brimstone

You've probably heard of fire and brimstone. It's a popular biblical term referring to the wrath of God. When lightning strikes, the smell of burning sulfur can sometimes be detected, and since lightning was associated with God's rage, so was sulfur. *Fire and brimstone* is also used to describe a specific style of Christian preaching, in which the discussion focuses on threats of pain and terrible punishment bestowed upon nonbelievers and sinners. *Fire and brimstone* repeatedly appears in the Bible. It rained down upon and destroyed Sodom and Gomorrah, and Satan was cast into a lake of fire and brimstone. While being destructive, brimstone was also meant to cleanse and purge evil.

Magickal Uses of Brimstone

Sulfur is mostly used in spells for exorcism and banishing. It's especially useful in clearing the area after a situation involving extremely strong emotions or dramatic endings. Sulfur can be used to get rid of a person's influence, banish an enemy, and in protection spells. It is even said to ease heartache and break attachments to toxic people.

Sulfur is sometimes burned to fumigate an area of mold or insects. This tells you something of its toxicity but also how it can be applied to magick. It is used to get rid of some kind of parasitic influence in your life. The fumes from burning sulfur are poisonous and smell terrible, and if you're going to burn it for spells, I recommend doing so outdoors. Remember, sulfur isn't like sage, which can be burned regularly in your home or energy field. Save it for using only in extreme banishing situations, and don't breathe it in directly.

If you want to add the magick of sulfur to a spell but don't have any, you can simply add the head of a match to your spell as a dry ingredient (it contains sulfur) or burn a match with intent to emit the smell of sulfur in a nontoxic amount.

Other ways to use sulfur include the following:

- Add it to poppets that are used in banishing or restraint.
- Sprinkle a tiny amount (¼ teaspoon) onto the soil of your houseplants to add protective energy to them. (Don't do this if your pets like to hang out in or eat your plants.)
- Throw it into the footprints of your enemy to make them stay away.
- Add it to cursing herb mixes and charms.
- Add it to protection spells.

Safety Notes

Even though sulfur is naturally occurring, be sure not to inhale the dust or smoke from it, as it can irritate your lungs. When burned, sulfur becomes a chemical called sulfur dioxide, which is poisonous when inhaled. Inhaling the fumes from burning sulfur can cause sore throat and coughing. Touching sulfur with your bare hands can also cause irritation, so gloves are in order.

You can find elemental sulfur at some gardening specialty stores. It's a yellowish dry clump that can be broken into bits. If you decide to burn it, do so outdoors and use only a teaspoon. Burn it in a fireproof dish and light it with a long barbecue lighter. It will burn with bluish flames and turn into a dark liquid. Don't touch the liquid because it will burn you. When cooled, throw the remains of burned sulfur in the garbage.

Do not ingest the sulfur, and keep it away from pets, as it can be deadly to them.

HAIR AND FINGERNAILS

Many spells, especially those using poppets (which are discussed in detail in chapter 9), call for the hair or fingernails of the person involved to be added to the doll. This creates a physical link between the person and the poppet. While the idea of hair and nails is creepy to some, they do play an important role in magick. You'd be surprised how many people secretly hang on to a lock of hair from their beloved just in case they need it.

When you do any kind of spell, you make a link on the astral realm through visualization and imagery. Sometimes this is enough. Hair and fingernails contain the DNA of a person, which is unique to them and them only. Adding them to a spell creates a direct energetic bond to the individual involved.

Keeping the hair of someone you loved used to be an ordinary practice. In Victorian times, funeral jewelry was made with the hair of a deceased loved one. There were beautiful, intricate broaches, pendants, and rings made from the hair of the deceased, which the living would wear in their honor. These pieces still survive today, as hair can last for hundreds of years without decomposing. It was also customary to keep a lock of hair from your beloved with you, to keep a part of them close. Many cultures believe that all your personal power resides in the hair, and therefore it is never cut. Others say that the hair houses the soul. Even the Bible has the story of Samson and Delilah: Samson's power is represented by his hair and Delilah the seductress cuts it off, thus robbing him of his strength. Both men and women in different faiths have religious reasons for not cutting their hair and believe it symbolizes all kinds of things, from power and beauty to humility and modesty.

Fingernails don't have as rich a spiritual history as hair, but they're still important in witchcraft. If you can't get the hair of your beloved to use in a spell, fingernail clippings are an alternative. While they lack the spiritual reputation of hair, they are still a DNA link to a specific person and can be used in magick.

You're probably wondering how one goes about collecting hair or fingernails of a person without being thought of as a weird freak. Well, unless they know your witchy ways and give it to you willingly, it can be tricky or even impossible. Use your imagination. I'm not going to give instructions on stealing, even if it is just hair out of someone's brush.

The following are a few ways to use hair and fingernails in spells:

- Use a piece of your own hair in spells to bind something to you instead of string. If you wish to bind another person, you can use your hair to signify the "hold" you have over them, the hair symbolically keeping them tied in place.
- Weave a strand of your hair into your magickal crafts to create a bond to the physical plane. For example, when you make a protective amulet for your home in the shape of a wreath, include some of your hair. Add it to sachets and even to homemade candles and oils. Add nail clippings the same way. This ensures the energy of the spell is anchored to you.

- Add hair or fingernails to magickal oils or tinctures regarding a specific person, especially love spells.
- Burn the hair and fingernails of a person to banish them from your life.
- Tie a person's hair around your baby finger to keep them under control.
- Leave a lock of your hair as an offering to deity, to show personal devotion.

☉DDS AND ENDS FOR DARK MAGICK

The items listed in this section are used often as ingredients in spells, most often cursing or creating endings. They're mostly everyday items that are easily obtained and are used in magick to reflect their earthly qualities, such as being sharp to cause pain or acidic to "eat away" at things.

Binding Box: Just as you perform a binding spell with string, you can use a box to trap things. A wooden box that can be locked is best. Shut the thing you wish to restrain inside the box and bury or hide it. You can decorate the inside of the box with symbols or words to surround the object you've trapped, infusing it with the energy of the symbols.

Broken Glass: Broken glass is often used in curses. It's known for causing pain and maiming people. It can be added to poppets to symbolize the infliction of anguish, sprinkled around the base of candles, or added to spell bottles.

Broken Mirror: Mirrors are used in magick to deflect energy away from you in protection spells. They can also be used to reflect someone's actions back onto them. Bits of broken mirrors can be used in protection spells but also in revenge and to turn someone's ill intentions back onto them. Broken mirrors most popularly are associated with bad luck.

Bullet Casings: Bullet casings left over from successful hunting trips can be saved and later integrated into spells for their association with killing. The same can be said for arrows from bow hunting. An item that has actually killed a creature is very powerful. That's not to say it should be used in spells to kill people but rather for snuffing out life energy. Some people prefer to stay away from this entirely, as the energy left after an intentional killing can be very uncomfortable even when done for food.

Nails: Rusty old nails are oxidized and associated with tetanus and other diseases. If you step on a rusty nail, you can get blood poisoning or worse. While a rusty nail in a spell won't necessarily cause disease, it can symbolically spread negativity, pain, or other unfortunate circumstances. A rusty nail can be shoved into a photo of someone to destroy their happiness, pounded into the ground inside an outline of their body, or shoved into their footprint on the ground. Another type of nail you might encounter in magick is coffin nails. Genuine coffin nails that actually came from a casket in a graveyard can difficult to obtain. A piece of iron can be substituted for coffin nails.

Pins: Sharp and easily obtained, pins are used in sympathetic magick. Often seen piercing poppets, pins bring a stabbing, jabbing energy to one concentrated spot, such as the heart. They can poke holes in plans or create a piercing urge in someone that causes them to act.

Scissors: Scissors represent cutting the life cord and severing ties. Many banishing spells employ the cutting of ties with the past or with negative people. They can also be used to cause a rift between two people or to cut someone off energetically.

Thorns: Thorns are a plant's defense mechanism. Some plants, such as raspberry brambles, have small thorns, whereas some have huge spikes that can literally rip your flesh open, like the blackthorn. Whether small or large, thorns inflict a lot of pain! They can be used in defensive magick to keep threatening entities or people away from us. They can also be used to inflict pain upon others. Here is a brief list of some plants with thorns and what you can use them for.

> *Blackberries and Raspberries:* These shrubs are considered invasive and grow swiftly. Therefore, blackberry thorns can be added to spells that you wish to take over and spread fast. In several world myths, blackberries have been said to cause blindness to those who fall into the brambles, so blackberry thorns can be used to interfere with people's perception.

> *Black Locust Trees:* These trees have thorns covering them from the ground up in some cases. It's said that lightning strikes the locust more often than any other kind of tree.

> *Blackthorn:* Blackthorn has a history in cursing and dark witchcraft. Some witch-burning pyres were said to be made of blackthorn.

> *Firethorn:* This shrub has needle-sharp spikes on its branches and can survive in brutal conditions. Firethorn can be added to spells that require

extreme strength and tenacity. When grown, it creates an impenetrable barrier, making it good for protection magick.

Hawthorn: Hawthorn trees have thorns that are up to several inches long. Hawthorn has been associated with protection of children and babies. It's said that people in medieval times associated the smell of hawthorn blossoms with that of the great plague. Later, it was discovered that the blossoms contain the same chemical as that which is formed in decaying animal tissue. For this reason, hawthorn is associated with death and illness.

Holly: A hearty evergreen shrub, holly has tough spikes on its stems. It's said that throwing holly at a wild animal will cause it to lie down. You can apply this idea to spells aimed toward your enemies or those who threaten you by integrating holly thorns.

Rose: Use the rose in matters of the heart, including breakup spells and the dark side of love.

Vinegar: Vinegar is a cleansing agent with antibacterial and antifungal properties and can eat right through limescale, marble, and other hard objects. For this reason, vinegar can be used in spells meant to erode a situation and cause discord, as well as for cleansing and protection.

SPELLS USING COMMON DARK MAGICK INGREDIENTS

Death Oil Spell to End a Feud

This spell is to kill an ongoing fight or disagreement between two people or parties. Perhaps it is an old grievance that has dragged on for years or even generations. In this case, that disagreement has actually taken on a life all its own and is sitting between the opposing parties like a monster, stopping both sides from moving forward. This spell is for when it's time to kill that monster.

←◦ MATERIALS

Materials to represent the feud or grievance. Some suggestions are bits of broken glass, dirt from the scene of an argument, or a printout of a hurtful text or email. Hurt feelings can be represented by a spoonful of sour milk, rusty nails, or any object you find unpleasant.

Empty jar with lid

1 cup death oil (see page 48)

During the dark moon, cast your circle and place the items that represent the feud in the jar one by one. As you do so, visualize what each item means. The broken glass is the pain you have inflicted on each other. The rusty nails are resentment. The rotten milk is the soured feelings between you. When you have the items in the jar, spend some time reliving all the horrible feelings of the argument. If you feel shame, anger, or sadness, send it from your heart into the jar along with the objects by imagining brown muck coming out of your heart center. That brown muck is alive—it is all the energy you and your rival have put into this fight. Allow the jar to fill with that energy until it completely disgusts you.

Then pour death oil over the items, completely covering them. See the death oil stifle the energy in the jar the way that water kills a flame. As the oil completely saturates every pore and groove in the items, see it mute the sour, repulsive power you've put into it as well, and then shut it off completely. Seal the jar. Close the circle.

Place it somewhere you will not have to see it. Once the feud or argument ends, dispose of the contents and recycle the jar.

Brimstone Spell to Banish Toxic Relationships

There are many different types of toxic attachments when it comes to relationships. So-called love can turn you into a fool—or worse, make you an emotional servant to someone else's whims. This spell is for when you have tried absolutely everything to rid yourself of an attachment to a toxic person and just can't break free of them.

This could be a person who is very manipulative and keeps reeling you back into their sphere with guilt or intimidation. Other times we can believe we're so deeply attached to another person we just can't let them go no matter how hard we try. You may even feel like you are helpless against your love for them, even though deep down you know they don't have your best interests at heart. It could even be something more tangible, like believing you must stay with a person because they support you financially. These are all examples of toxic attachments that, if left unchecked, can spiral into abuse.

On the other hand, this spell can also be done to make someone stop being attached to you, if they've become unrelenting in pursuing you even though you're not interested. Not only is this disrespectful of them, but it can slide into the territory of stalking. Please talk to family, friends, and authorities to ensure your safety before turning to magick.

You can do this spell for yourself or for someone else who is hopelessly enmeshed in a destructive relationship.

~3 MATERIALS

> Access to an outdoor space
> 1 teaspoon elemental sulfur
> Fireproof dish
> Hair or fingernails of the person if possible or their name written on
>   a small piece of paper and rolled up small, the size of a pea
> Barbecue lighter

Outdoors under the dark moon, cast your circle.

Place the sulfur in the fireproof dish. Focus on the sulfur and see it as wrath. Lightning, fire, and utter destruction are represented in that yellow material. See it glowing with noxious yellow energy, stinky, repellent, and holding inside it the power to obliterate and purge.

Hold this image in your mind and add the personal effects or name to the pile of sulfur. See them become immersed in the sulfur and therefore the fury of fire and brimstone. Say:

> *Fire and brimstone,*
> *Purge and burn.*
> *(Name) is destroyed*
> *And cannot return.*

Light it on fire. As it burns, visualize yourself rising up above it all, free and clear of this person. As you linger above, see them burning down below in the sulfur fire. Hold this image until the fire puts itself out and they disappear. Dump the remains on the earth (don't burn yourself) and cover with dirt. Now, see yourself as clear and free of the person, independent and unattached. Once the remains have cooled completely, scoop them and the surrounding dirt up in a dish. Release the circle. Throw the dirt and burned sulfur in the garbage.

Go indoors and have a shower to wash away all the traces of the sulfur smell on your skin along with lingering attachments to the person.

Remember that detaching from this person may be painful or uncomfortable but is necessary. Be ready for some difficult but imperative changes with this spell.

Sulfur Spell to Break a Habit

Addictions and habits take many forms, not always involving drugs or substances. This spell is to help overcome addiction to a thing, person, or behavior by destroying it with brimstone. This should of course be done in conjunction with trying to curb your habits in daily life and with therapy and medical attention.

Select an object beforehand that represents your addiction or habit. If it's smoking, use a cigarette butt. If it's binge eating, use a tiny bit of food. If your habit is something like technology addiction, you can use a small piece of an old broken phone or device.

⚜ MATERIALS
Item representing addiction
Small dish
Jar with a tight-fitting lid, filled with sulfur
Small chunk of black obsidian or jet

On the last night of the waning moon, cast your circle. You may wish to call upon a deity of destruction to aid you.

Place the item on a small dish in front of you. This item holds within it all the power of your addiction. See yourself at your worst as a result of this item. For example, if it is smoking, think about all the times you've lost your breath trying to walk upstairs. If it's an isolating behavior, recall the times it has resulted in you missing out on important things. Picture how your habit has affected those around you. Bring to mind how you have been sickened physically by it. As you recall all these negative things, see the item start to glow in your mind's eye with murky gray and brown sludge. The longer you imagine the powers of the addiction, the darker and darker it becomes. Pour your feelings into it, from your heart into the object in a dirty stream.

Now stuff the item into the jar of sulfur, covering it completely. Imagine you hear an actual hissing sound, like when water is dumped on a fire, as the sulfur extinguishes its power. Now all the negative energy is absorbed by the sulfur. Seal the jar.

Close the circle.

Bury the jar outside and place the black onyx or jet on top of the burial site. When you recover, you can dig it back up, throw away the sulfur, and recycle the jar.

Brimstone Matches

Ordinary kitchen matches contain sulfur, so it smells like brimstone when you light one. Instead of purchasing large amounts of sulfur, or for situations that need a quick cleansing, empower a book of matches ahead of time with purification powers and carry them with you.

⊷⋅⋅3 MATERIALS

Marker

Book or box of kitchen matches

½ cup witch's salt (see page 49)

Create your own clearing and protection sigil if you're dealing with a specific situation, or simply use a pentacle. During the dark moon, draw or paint this on the book or box of matches, both inside and out.

Sprinkle the witch's salt in a circle and place your matches inside it.

Cast your circle and call upon your chosen deity if you wish. See the dark of the moon as a dark circle in the sky, connected directly with your salt circle. Create this connection with your mind. Release the circle. Leave the matches there overnight to be imbued with protection and cleansing energy.

Release the circle.

Carry the matches with you.

When you need a quick energetic reset for any reason, find a spot outside. Light a match, and as it burns, imagine the unwanted energy fizzling out of existence, leaving your energy field bright, strong, and healthy. Imagine the brimstone and fire destroying the unwanted feeling you're having. If you want to get more specific, you can write what you are banishing on the matchstick with pen or marker.

Don't do this indoors, as people may think a fire is starting.

CHAPTER 9
THE POPPET

One of the most popular and misunderstood images in witchcraft is that of the magickal doll. It brings to mind a creepy wax figure stuffed full of pins, used to torture and kill people. Despite its macabre reputation, the poppet is a staple item to witches worldwide in many different traditions.

I have always used the term *poppet* for these spell dolls, although they're most commonly known as *voodoo dolls*. Magickal dolls have appeared in spiritual practice as far back into history as ancient Egypt, with all kinds of uses: healing, protection, blessing, love, and, yes, cursing. The poppet is a human figure made of clay, wax, or cloth, often containing the hair or fingernails of the person it represents. What is done to the doll by the witch, be it filling the doll with healing energy or stabbing its heart with a stick, is said to affect the person it represents. While pop culture makes it look like you can use a poppet to spontaneously snap the bones of your enemies or make them burst into flames by throwing the doll in a fire, it's not quite like that. Poppets can be used to affect a person's behavior or energy.

CREATING A POPPET

Poppets have been whittled out of wood, fashioned from corn husks, and even carved out of potatoes! You can use almost anything you have on hand, as long as it represents a specific person and the intent is there. Here are the basics of creating one.

The Cloth Poppet

The most popular material for making poppets is cloth, stuffed with appropriate herbs and objects. What you put inside the poppet differs according to intent. I've included a few poppet spells later on, which all include different ingredients. Most often your poppet will be stuffed with herbs, plants, roots, and natural materials that match its purpose, along with a piece of hair or fingernails of the person it represents.

⟶ MATERIALS

Piece of cloth around 2 feet by 1 foot in size, preferably of a material that is thin and easily sewn, such as a bedsheet. It's even better if the person has touched or worn the cloth. If you're using a piece of the person's clothing, it can have patterns on it, but it is easier to decorate the doll's features if it is a solid color.

Different colored markers or paint for adding details to the doll

Scissors

Needle

Thread of appropriate color. I prefer red, like veins.

Stuffing such as herbs, roots, and other natural materials

Fingernails or hair of the person the poppet will represent

Fold your rectangle of cloth in half with the short ends together and draw the outline of a person on it. Give it the same general shape of the person it represents. Carefully cut along the lines, making sure you slice through both layers of fabric. This will give you a front and a back.

Using the needle and thread, start on one side of the head and sew all around the edge of the figure. Don't worry if you're not the best at sewing, the aesthetics of the doll aren't as important as the energy you put into it. While sewing, think about the person, see their face in your mind, and hear the words they've said to you. Imagine their smell. Recall your conversations. Focus on the person completely during the entire construction of the doll. Leave the top of the head open far enough for you to fit all the stuffing inside.

Through the hole in the head, start filling the doll with your chosen materials. Push it down into the legs and arms first, then the torso, then the head. The last ingredient to go in is their hair or fingernails. Then sew the head shut and tie it off. There is your basic poppet. Now, take your pens or paint and give the doll features like the person they represent. Give them the right eye color and hair style. Draw their clothing and any birthmarks or tattoos that define them. Last, you can write their name across the heart area if you please.

You should have spent this whole time holding an image of the individual in your mind, their mannerisms, and how they make you feel. Now lay the poppet on your altar and hold your hands a few inches above it. Imagine all those thoughts, sounds, and images condensing into your hands in a ball of energy, the essence of the person. Then send the energy from your hands into the doll. You're ready to use it now.

The Clay Poppet

If you prefer, you can make a poppet out of either store-bought or homemade clay. I prefer to stay away from polymer or plastic clay, as it does not biodegrade, but there are many natural, air-drying clays available in craft stores. You can also easily make your own, using this recipe:

⟶ SIMPLE CLAY RECIPE

½ cup to 1 cup of flour
1 cup to 1½ cup of salt
½ cup to 1 cup of water

Mix the dry ingredients first, and then add the water a bit at a time while stirring. You want a consistency that is not too wet and will hold its shape. Aim for the feel of Play-Doh.

This clay can air dry over a period of days, or you can slowly bake your finished poppet at 390 degrees Fahrenheit (200 degrees Celsius) for up to 4 hours in the oven or until hardened.

⟶ MATERIALS

Clay (homemade or store-bought)
Stuffing made of appropriate dried herbs for your intent. You will only be
    using about 1 tablespoon of it this time.
Hair or fingernails of the person the poppet represents
Simple molding tools, such as toothpicks and a butter knife
Paint

As you mold the clay into the shape of the person, remember to shape it like their physical body. Roll the stuffing into the clay while you work, including the hair or fingernails if you have them. Give it a belly button and accurate anatomy. Bake or air dry the clay. Then paint it with the person's features, with their eye and skin tone, clothing style, and personal effects. Follow the same charging instructions as with the cloth poppet, and it's ready to be used.

Jar Poppet

This is exactly like making a doll of a person without the arts and crafts. You will simply fill an ordinary jar with their qualities and effects. This includes hair and fingernails if you can get them. The jar will then act as the vessel that represents them. Fill the jar as if you are trying to encompass their personality. Add things they like, a symbol of their hobby or job, and a stone for their heart (depending on your intentions, it can be a beautiful crystal or an ugly chunk of cement). You can use earth elements such as sticks to represent their physical body and a large nut or seed for their head. Write their name on paper and put it in the jar. A piece of paper with their handwriting or their signature is even better.

Once you have all these items in the jar, you will put things representing your intentions inside the jar and seal it shut. For love and sweetness, you can put honey in it. For revenge, you can use cayenne pepper or a dead wasp. To make the person undesirable to others, you can add something that stinks, such as a bit of rotten food. The jar acts just the same way as a poppet that is shaped like a person, just in a simpler form with less craft work.

WHAT'S WITH THE PINS?

That iconic image of the witch's doll stuffed full of pins is loosely rooted in fact. Pins can be used in poppets in a variety of ways, for everything from love spells and healing to cursing and hexes. Each placement of the pin has dual meanings depending on your goal. A pin in the heart can bring love or pain. A pin in the forehead can open the mind or cause confusion. Intent is everything and can turn a healing spell into a terrible curse, depending on what is in your heart.

Below is a breakdown of where pins can be placed in a poppet and why. Once you have a working knowledge and understanding of how poppet magick works, you can incorporate some of these ideas into your image magick.

Arms and Legs: Pinning the arms and legs in a way that traps them from moving is a means of binding. Much like stilling their hands, it can stop their actions.

Eyes: To keep things hidden from someone, put pins in the eyes of the poppet which represents them. This will blind them to your actions and keep them in the dark. Sometimes this is a means of protecting someone from things that will hurt them, such as witnessing violence.

Feet: To make someone stay put or prevent them from running away from problems, insert pins into the feet of the poppet.

Groin: This is done to cause sexual dysfunction in someone, usually to get revenge on an ex. On the other hand, a pin can be placed into this area to poke it to life, so to speak, to encourage fertility, or perk up a lagging sex life.

Hands: Put pins in their hands to stop their actions and render them unproductive. If they're active in hurtful or dangerous doings, this can help stop them. If they are manipulating your life, you can still their hands so they can't pull your strings anymore.

Head: A pin to the head can spark ideas, intelligence, and intellect or awaken the creative processes. On the dark side, if you were willing to risk the consequences, you could employ this same method to get into someone else's head and wreak havoc, causing confusion, distraction, or a change of mindset.

Heart: This is the most popular place to stick a pin and you probably already know why: to make a person fall in love with you. You could also use this method in a spell to get the attention of a love interest, to spark the flame in an already-established relationship, or to otherwise awaken someone's affections to you. The flip side of this action is to inflict emotional agony and heartbreak on someone.

Neck: Putting a pin in the throat will stop communication. This can be used to halt gossip or harmful rumors or stop someone from using their words to hurt people.

Spine: Targeting the spine of your poppet can be done to stop someone in their tracks and render them unable to continue what they're currently undertaking. This can be to impede the progress of a rival or slow down the competition.

Pins for Healing

To use a poppet for healing, all the aforementioned steps would be taken for construction. The poppet would be stuffed with personal effects and healing herbs. The pins would then be inserted into the problem area of the body to "release" the illness, much like acupuncture in a way. If it is heartbreak, put the pin in the heart of the doll to release the sadness. If it is mental, the pin would go into the brain. If it is the stomach, kidneys, bladder, or another organ, insert the pin into the area of the doll where it would be and visualize the sickness leaking out as if you'd poked a hole in a water balloon.

POPPET SPELLS

Poppet and Blood Strength Spell

The following is a poppet spell to strengthen someone you care about, either due to ailing health or a need for emotional fortitude. This spell is meant to transfer some of your own strength and vitality into them via a poppet and a drop of your blood. Be sure to perform this spell at a time when you are in peak physical and emotional health.

←—₃ MATERIALS

Cloth or clay poppet

Poppet stuffing: dandelions for their fortitude and tenaciousness, 3 large nails without rust on them (you've heard the saying "tough as nails"), solid pebbles or stones, hardy twigs, and crushed bay leaves. Feel free to include any items you personally associate with strength and toughness. If you have access to crystals, garnet is an ideal stone for health and vitality.

Hair or fingernails of the person

Lighter or matches

Red candle to represent vital life energy

Sterile lancet

Create your poppet with clay or cloth as explained earlier. Add features similar to the person it represents, and carve or write their name on the torso.

Cast your circle and place the finished poppet on your altar. Light the red candle.

Imagine your poppet is the person they represent, as they are now. If they are ill, see their sickness in the poppet. This can appear as blackish-brown energy or fog in their body near the affected area.

Using the sterile lancet, poke the index finger of your right hand to draw blood. Drip your blood onto the poppet in the affected area. Recite:

> *Red with vigor, strong and well,*
> *My blood carries life and health.*
> *Come alive, your health renewed.*
> *I lend my strength and blood to you.*

If you are not sure what part of the body is appropriate for their ailment, placing your blood on the heart center is fine. Now, visualize the person filled with health, life, vitality, and the ability to heal. You have transferred some of your life's energy into them.

Close the circle.

Once a week, repeat the ritual with the blood and the chant. Once they recover, bury or dispose of the poppet.

Poppet for Smashing Enemies

This spell is to stop an individual from hurting you or someone else. The intention is to harness their negative conduct inside a poppet and then destroy it, thus disrupting their flow of hurtful behavior.

←⅜ MATERIALS

Lighter and matches
Death candle (see page 51)
Hair or fingernails of the person the doll represents if possible
Bowl for holding the "stuffing" of your poppet
Protective gloves for handling broken glass
Poppet stuffing: broken glass, a small, ugly stone, and dirt
3 drops death oil (see page 48)
Air-drying clay, enough to make the shape of a person

Place the items on your altar and cast your circle. Light the death candle while you work.

Put the hair or fingernails in the bowl first.

Put on the gloves to protect your hands, then pick up the broken glass and hold it up to the dark sky. Declare out loud:

This broken glass represents (name)'s hurtful attitude.

Place it in the bowl. Remove the gloves for now.

Hold the stone up to the sky. State:

This ugly stone is (name)'s misguided heart.

Add it to the bowl.

Hold the dirt up to the sky and say:

This is (name)'s low-down, filthy behavior.

Add the dirt to the bowl.

Hold your hands over the mixture and visualize the vibrations of your enemy. It will feel bad and offensive. Direct it through your hands and into the bowl of ingredients.

Add 3 drops of death oil to the bowl and set aside.

Now put on the gloves again to protect your hands from the glass, and make your doll out of clay. Mold the loose ingredients into it as you form a human shape. The more effort you put into making the doll like the person, the stronger the bond between your victim and the doll will be.

Close the circle when you're done.

Allow the clay to air dry, which takes several days. During this time, continue to empower the doll by every so often casting your anger at it, thus charging it with your vengeful energy. You can do this by holding your hands over it while you think about the person and allowing your emotions to flow through your hands and into the figure.

Once the doll is dry, it is time for the second part of the spell.

Take your poppet outside where no one can see you, preferably at night under a dark moon. Be still for a moment and tell the dark moon what you are doing and why. Cast a circle or call upon deity if you wish. Then, put the doll on the ground, stand over it, and *stomp the hell out of it*. With your heaviest boots or spikiest heels, stamp and crush the doll, grinding it into the dirt until it is pulp. Mash and smash it until it's an unrecognizable mess. As you do so, channel your anger and bad feelings into your actions. You can also use a hammer or whatever tools necessary if stomping is not possible. When you are done, kick some dirt over the top of the remains. Spit on its grave a couple times if you want to. Then walk away, knowing that you have just blasted your enemy with an energetic butt-kicking.

It is unwise to leave broken glass sitting around like this, so after you have cooled down, clean up the remains of the doll and dump them in the trash.

Poppet Binding Spell

Binding is a term used in magic to describe the act of symbolically restraining a person, energy, or action. It is most often used to stop someone from destructive or hurtful behavior, much like straight-jacketing a person to keep them from harming themselves or others. Often, people will behave in negative ways because of an underlying emotion, such as anger, jealousy, sadness, or hurt. This spell addresses this underlying issue in an effort to stop the problem completely.

⚬ MATERIALS

Match

Cast-iron pan or fireproof bowl

1 cup of dirt (best if it's from somewhere the person has spent time) in a container

Hair or fingernails of the person if possible

Cloth poppet. Have it ready to be stuffed, all sewn up except the head. You may also wish to draw the finishing touches and details on it prior to the spell to simplify things.

3 feet black ribbon or black string

In this case, the match and the fire it produces represent the offensive behavior that you are trying to "bind." The flash of fire that occurs when you light the match is the hot flare of underlying anger, jealousy, or rage that is causing the person to act out. You will be snuffing out the flame with the dirt and then binding the doll.

Gather your materials on your altar during the dark moon. Cast your circle or call deity.

Holding the match before you, imagine it is surrounded by a black grungy ball. This is the negative emotion that's causing the person to act in an undesirable way. See in your mind the precise actions that are a problem, and send these thoughts into the match. When your visualization is at its peak, strike the match and let it flare for a moment. Drop the lit match into your fireproof vessel, and then quickly dump the dirt over it, snuffing out the fire. Add the fingernails and hair to the dirt. Use this mixture to stuff your poppet, including what's left of the match.

Sew up the doll's head. Then, take the ribbon and start winding it around and around the doll. Start at the head, to stifle their words. Work your way down the whole body, restraining all that snuffed-out rage and unhappiness inside the doll. Cut off the energy coming from their cold heart. Bind their legs to stop them on their destructive path. Completely cover the doll in ribbon, rendering them silent and still.

Close your circle.

Then bury the doll in the ground or deposit it in a garbage can somewhere away from your home. Again, walk away and forget about it. Know that the fire of their hate has been snuffed out inside them and held back with reinforcements.

Killing Jar Spell

This spell is to help someone to stop bad habits, overcome addiction, or cease their unhealthy behavior.

⟶ MATERIALS

Hair or fingernails of the person if possible

Jar with a tight lid

Object representing the problem. For example, a cigarette if they're trying to quit smoking, a shot of booze for alcoholism, or a picture that encompasses the habit.

Dark moon water, enough to fill the jar (see page 43)

Lighter or matches

Death candle (see page 51)

Black cloth or paper

String

Cast your circle and call upon deity.

Place the hair or fingernails in the jar, visualizing the person clearly (if you can't get hair or fingernails, substitute with an item they have touched or a photo). Add the item that symbolizes the behavior that needs to end. Spend a moment seeing them indulge in this behavior, and let the feelings this ignites flourish. Rage, sadness, guilt—these are the feelings you must let loose in this spell. See the objects in the jar become imbued with this vibration.

Pour the dark moon water into the jar right to the top. Imagine a sizzling sound as it drowns the energy in the objects, snuffing them out with death current. Immediately put the lid on the jar tightly.

On a heatproof surface, light your death candle, and drip wax onto the lid. Use the hot wax to hold the candle upright in place, and then let it burn all the way down on the lid. You may close your circle during this time and let it burn at its own pace (do not leave it unattended). Black wax will drip down and streak over the jar, coating it in the power of the dark moon.

When it's done, wrap it in the black cloth or paper, tie it securely with string, and hide it out of sight until the problem passes.

CHAPTER 10
CURSING AND OTHER MAGICKAL MANIPULATIONS

Hate. Love. Revenge. Retribution. These are topics every witch comes up against sooner or later. When I was a baby witch in the 1990s, there was a heavy-handed emphasis on "an ye harm none" as well as the threefold law. The threefold law states that whatever magick you send out into the world will come directly back onto you with three times the strength. These rules are still followed by many witches today. The threefold law certainly forces a person to consider their intent very carefully before casting a spell, which is important. However, I could never find an explanation for how or why exactly the energy tripled and then came back, and as a person who likes to know the *why* of things, it just never sat right with me. That being said, of course curses aren't meant to be cast carelessly, and for that reason the threefold law is useful. You must carefully weigh your intentions and dig deeply into yourself about why you want to perform a curse and then only do so when it's truly necessary.

We can't pretend that shadow energies such as rage, vengeance, jealousy, and conflict don't exist. They are clearly visible in nature and within us. Anyone who claims to never experience a feeling of ill will toward another is straight-up lying. Despite this, cursing should always be a last resort because there are often surprising repercussions. If you harm other people, even when you think they deserve it, remember that it creates a ripple effect and will impact everyone around them, including you. This can take some very unpleasant forms, so please think long and hard prior to cursing and consider performing a binding spell instead.

BINDING VERSUS CURSING

Binding and cursing are two very different things, although they're sometimes confused.

Binding, in magick, is a means of stopping someone from an action or behavior by energetically restraining them. Cursing, on the other hand, is to actively send destruction or misfortune to someone.

Some people avoid cursing entirely and believe that binding someone is always a preferable solution, because it lacks the harmful intent of a curse. Binding spells are used to render someone ineffectual without actually hurting them. However, some people argue that binding is a form of harm all on its own because it is interfering with the will of another, hindering their actions. Where you stand on this is your own choice.

In a bad situation, consider performing a binding spell before heading straight for the curses. Binding is a gentler approach in that it involves much less negative thought and energy. When performing a binding, you don't have to feel hatred, rage, or sorrow as you do in cursing. However, with cursing, you do have to feel and express those emotions, which can be draining and painful for you and those around you.

Simple Binding Spell

This simple spell is to stop a person from engaging in behaviors that are hurting others or themselves. With binding, you do not decide how or why they stop, but rather squash out and mute the energy that is causing them to act destructively in the first place.

←─৪ MATERIALS

Object representing the problem (for example, a picture of lips for gossip)
Black thread, string, or ribbon, enough to cover the object completely
    when wound around it

Cast a circle, invoke deity, and imagine the object infused with the actions you wish to stop. This can appear as an erratic, spiky energy field surrounding it or as a heavy, oppressive vibration when you hold the item. Visualize the behavior you wish to stop. Wrap your black ribbon or string around the object tightly. As you do so, imagine it stifling the energy. Wrap the string around and around until none of the object is visible, thus trapping the energy. Tie 3 tight knots. Now their negative actions will be detained.

Close the circle. Hide the object until the problem passes and then recycle the materials.

If you perform a binding spell on an especially destructive person but it doesn't work, you can repeat it during the next moon cycle or turn to cursing.

This raises the question, why curse at all? Can't you just perform a binding spell when someone is a problem? Yes, you can. But if the person's will to commit hurtful actions is stronger than your binding spell, you may need to think about cursing.

What about Karma?

You may have heard that performing a curse will bring "bad karma."

The word *karma* has been overused and misunderstood in Western culture for a while now. People say things like "karma's a bitch" anytime they feel slighted, which is a way of dumping accountability onto an unseen force. They also erroneously link karma to good or bad luck. The word *karma* originated in India and actually means that your actions and intentions in this life and your past lives shape what your future lives will be. It's a belief in ethical retribution that spans lifetimes. For example, if you live a life of altruism and service, you will be rewarded in your future lives, whereas if you spend this life being materialistic or hateful, you will experience suffering when reborn. Hinduism, Buddhism, and Jainism all believe in karma as applied to the long-term spirit rather than immediate earthly experience. In other words, karma is not crouching in a corner, filing its nails and waiting for a chance to ruin someone's day for cheating on a test or cutting people off in traffic.

COMMON SENSE

Like attracts like. This isn't as cut and dry as literally getting back exactly the same thing you send out. It has more to do with common sense. If you spend all your time feeling angry and blaming your misfortune on others instead of looking inward to try and fix it, you will attract more negative situations. If you're searching for someone to blame your problems on instead of solving them, you will find that person. If you go looking for trouble, then trouble is exactly what you'll find. On the flip side, if you are kind to others and act intelligently and honorably, you'll find your life is much calmer and easier. People will be more inclined to help you or be kind back. Didn't we all learn this in kindergarten?

If you find that every spell you want to cast is a curse, or you feel like every person you meet has wronged you, maybe everyone else isn't the problem. If you spend your days angry and hateful, it's time to look inward and figure out what's causing it before just going out and throwing curses willy-nilly.

Before Cursing, Take a Look in the Mirror

If someone is actively abusing you or others, they deserve to be cursed and worse.

However, it's not always that simple.

When you feel the desire to curse someone who *isn't* an overtly harmful, destructive beast of an abuser, it is important to stop and really take a look at yourself first. If we're honest, the desire to curse is often all about us and has very little to do with the object of our intent.

Disliking a person is normal. Maybe someone flaunts their material possessions in a way that is galling. Maybe they're dating someone you like. Maybe they have the job you secretly want or are spoiled and ungrateful for what they have. Maybe they just have a really annoying personality. Irritating as these things are, none of them warrant throwing a curse.

Often people we dislike personify a quality of ourselves that we are ashamed of. They force us to see something in us we wish we didn't.

If in your shadow work you do not find the answer within yourself regarding bad blood between you and another person, and your reasons for wanting to curse them turn out to not be all about you, then—and only then—is cursing or hexing an appropriate action. Before going ahead and cursing someone, try doing the tarot reading on page 68 to gain insight into your true motives. If, underneath your dislike, the situation is all about your own insecurities, cursing isn't an option; those feelings are your own pattern that will come to you again and again in life until you face your shadow and deal with them.

Here is a brief meditation to do when deciding whether or not to curse someone.

1. Perform a relaxation technique like the one described on page 57.

2. Imagine your enemy standing or sitting in front of you. Really see them. Look at the color of their eyes, the texture of their skin. Feel the warmth coming off their body. See them as the human they are.

3. Allow yourself to feel whatever comes up. This will probably be negative feelings. Allow this feeling to wash over you as much as necessary, as you have to work through it to get to the next part. After the initial rush of emotion, you should be able to shift your focus away from your feelings.

4. Now, put yourself inside your enemy's body. Move your consciousness into their form. Imagine you are inside their body. Your arms and legs are now theirs. Your mouth and teeth are theirs. Feel their clothes on your body.

5. Look through their eyes at yourself. What do you see? Don't project your own feelings onto this—allow yourself to feel things naturally. How do you appear through their eyes? What part of your body do they focus on most? Are you talking or silent? Is there a certain feature or action the image of you is doing to draw your attention? How do you feel when looking at yourself from their perspective?

6. Write down your impressions. Be honest. What do they feel when they look at you?

This exercise is a way of creating empathy between yourself and your enemy. It may be uncomfortable to put yourself in the body of someone you dislike. However, if you can get past that and relax enough to see a different picture, you may just learn something important about yourself and realize that cursing isn't necessary at all. You may discover that you understand their behavior, damaging as it is. You may also recognize that they are living in their own self-imposed cursed state, which is often the case for harmful people.

This is why doing your shadow work is imperative before proceeding to cursing. The meditation and divination in part 1 of this book set you up to really know yourself and your motives. Skipping your inner work will result in carelessly casting curses with harmful consequences for you and others.

If you perform this exercise and it doesn't result in any form of empathy or understanding that can help you resolve the problem, consider binding and then cursing.

Remember, cursing is a last resort. It is only appropriate in extreme cases. What warrants an extreme case is your own decision. Cursing takes a formidable amount of energy and is best reserved for important situations where there is no other recourse. Sometimes a person simply can't be stopped without something brutal occurring to them directly. Some people will not stop hurting others until they get a taste of their own medicine or will not be swayed from their destructive path unless they stumble and fall. Sometimes your curse is the thing they trip over.

WHEN YOU'VE BEEN CURSED

We've all had those days or weeks where literally everything seems to go wrong, and we may jokingly say, "I think I'm cursed!" But what if you suspect you really are?

For this to happen, you must have had contact with someone who is inclined to perform witchcraft of some kind or at the very least is able to create very powerful thoughts. If you believe you're cursed and spend time worrying about it, your fear opens up your energy field for it to actually occur.

Sometimes you will know that someone has sent a curse your way simply because you're an experienced witch and you can feel it. Other times it's not quite that clear. Here are some typical signs that someone's sending bad magick your way.

- You experience random physical pain. Experiencing body pain that flares and then disappears with no underlying health condition could be a sign that someone is messing with your energy body and it's manifesting in your physical form. Of course, go to a doctor if you have serious pain.
- You feel lethargic, mental cloudiness, and fatigued seemingly for no real reason, and the feelings don't go away.
- You have vivid nightmares.
- Little accidents pile up. You stub your toe, your cat gets sick, you break your favorite mug, and then your car breaks down all in one day. Unusual levels of discord can be a sign that your energy is being tilted askew by someone on purpose.

- Pets act strange. Animals can sense low-energy forms and may be acting odd around you as a result, by cowering, barking, or acting like they see something you do not.

- Relationships breakdown. Small irritating fights keep springing up between you and your loved ones, often over nothing in particular yet you're annoyed at each other all the time.

- You keep losing things.

- Ongoing colds and minor health issues occur one after another and never abate.

- Communication breaks down. You may feel all of a sudden that other people are not hearing you as they normally would, or your influence over other people is altered in some way. Sometimes it's as if they can't even hear or see you.

- All the plants in your home or garden die for no apparent reason.

- There is obvious evidence. If you find a jar of nails and urine on your property, consider yourself cursed!

These are just some examples of ways a curse can affect you. Typically, it takes an unusually powerful person to create physical illness in your life, and if you think you're sick, of course go to a doctor as well as perform a ritual. For smaller curses, like those mentioned here, you can do several things:

- Create a protective barrier around yourself every morning. Before you begin your day, meditate on seeing a strong shield all around you that no one can permeate. Negative energy pings off this sphere like stones off a roof. At the same time that you are surrounded by the shield, make sure you see your inner self lit up from within, strong and healthy.

- Perform protection spells.

- Carry a mirror charged with deflective energy.

- Take cleansing ritual baths.

- Cut energetic ties to the person who has cursed you during your dark moon ritual.

- Write the name of the suspected curser on a bay leaf and burn it.

- Perform a home cleansing ceremony and then pour witch's salt all around the perimeter of your property.

Bear in mind that your mental powers are just as strong as any curse, and if you wish to blot out bad energy, you absolutely can with repeated visualization.

NEGATIVE EMOTIONS IN MAGICK

There's a general belief that feelings of anger, rage, and repulsion are "negative," and not only should we avoid talking about them, we should never express them. It follows that we should certainly never apply them to our magick. It's believed that involving these feelings in a spell or in daily life will bring upon us retribution and punishment. On a social level, shunning these bad feelings is considered polite. There is a heavy pressure on us from childhood to be nice, to play the peacemaker, to turn that frown upside down. We're told to stay positive at all costs, including the detriment of our own well-being or that of others. We're taught to "turn the other cheek" when someone treats us terribly or when we witness injustice. None of this actually helps anyone.

The thing is these darker feelings are a part of your whole experience in life. Just as you experience birth and death, you also experience all aspects of light and dark. This includes emotions. Anger and other so-called negative feelings can be used in magick just as love, joy, and gratitude can.

When you're casting any kind of spell, feeling and directing an emotion is the most important part of energy work. You visualize, you feel the emotion in all its purity, and then you direct it into the spell. If you lack emotion in your spells, they will simply have no power.

Anger

Anger can make powerful energy for use in protection spells, reversals, and curses. Allowing yourself to feel and express anger through magick, rather than trying to repress it, not only makes for very powerful workings but also helps you let go of these difficult emotions because you've given them an outlet.

Have you ever noticed that when you are in close proximity to an angry person, you can actually feel it? Even if they do not speak or express themselves, you just *know* they're angry. It comes off of them like a stink. Without even realizing it, you might tiptoe around them, avoid them, or try to placate them without them having to say a word. That's how tangible the energy of anger is. It affects the behavior of others just by existing.

When you're driven to curse someone, there is often some kind of anger spurring it on. Don't shy away from this; it is useful. When you are doing spells for vengeance, or even for protection, pouring your anger into it will make it work better. During spells of this kind, allow yourself to feel all your rage, dislike, and hate. Gather it up in a ball of terrible energy and release it into your curse. Believe me, it works!

Revulsion

Since there are quite a few spells in here using the carcasses of insects and a few other unsavory items, I thought I should talk about the power of disgust. For example, while making the fly ointment explained later in this chapter, it's natural to feel utterly grossed out while crushing flies and putting them in oil. Because that ointment is used to put a curse on someone and make them seem unappealing to others, the grosser you feel while making it, the better! That feeling of disgust will transfer into the oil, empowering it with exactly what you need.

That being said, feeling revulsion when trying to do a love spell isn't appropriate, so if you really are grossed out by certain ingredients and can't get over the feeling, perhaps switch to the plant-based alternative. Feeling like you want to gag during a love spell is never going to work out. You can channel disgust and revulsion into a curse just like you did with your anger, using the same visualization and energy-transference technique.

Sadness

Sadness can be transferred into spells, but it is a low-energy vibration. That means the impact it has on magick can be slower moving than other emotions. You can integrate it into a reversal spell when sending someone back the hurt they've caused you. Occasionally, sadness is like a punch in the stomach, and you can use the pangs of grief you're experiencing to send that feeling to another person who for some reason deserves it. Crying during ritual, even in meditation sometimes, is not uncommon. Sadness is just as much a part of life as happiness. Allowing yourself to feel sadness and direct it toward something in a spell can also be part of healing.

Jealousy

No one likes to admit it, but very often the root of dislike is jealousy. Jealousy is a hideous emotion. It consumes us inside like a disease. It makes us behave in ways that are hurtful to others, it ruins relationships, and it destroys us from the inside out, tainting everything we touch. It makes people behave so badly that if you indulge in it too much, you may just find yourself on the receiving end of a curse!

Jealousy is a completely internal emotion that is not about anyone but you. Cursing and binding others will do nothing to tame the green-eyed monster churning up your guts, and it will only keep coming back until you deal with it. That's why I'm putting a spell right here for it.

Spell for Transmuting Jealousy

While having ingrained jealousy issues tends to run more deeply than something that can be solved with a single spell, this working can aid you in your journey to overcoming it.

⚜ MATERIALS

Garden or pots of dirt
Flower seeds or bulbs
Dark moon water (see page 43)
Death candle (see page 51)

Sit at the place where you will plant the seed or in front of the pot of soil. Have the seeds or bulb in your hands. Breathe onto them while feeling the pain of your jealousy. Let your jealousy flood you in all its ugliness. See it as a sickly yellow glow flowing out of your energy body, into your breath, and into the seeds. Infuse the seeds completely with the feeling.

Hold the seeds up to the waning or dark moon. Say:

> *I give these seeds over to the darkness.*
> *Take my pain and absorb it into the great cauldron*
> *To be transformed.*
> *As these seeds grow and break out of their shells,*
> *Together we will grow and blossom into something beautiful instead.*

Plant the seeds in the earth according to directions. Pour a cup of dark moon water on top of them. Light the death candle nearby and let it burn. Spend some time allowing yourself to feel the jealousy raging through you. Send it into the candle flame to be burned until you are tired. You can let the candle burn out or place it in the earth (if outdoors) close to the seeds. Remember to water and tend to these seeds to ensure that they grow and flower. It may take a lot of work and attention, but so does changing your jealousy pattern. Allow nature to transform the energy into something new and better.

Curse Tablets for Vengeance against Thieves

Curse tablets, also known as *defixiones*, are historically a very common way to hinder one's enemies. Defixiones have been discovered by archeologists under temples in Europe and Greco-Roman areas quite recently.[10] A curse tablet is a sheet of metal, often lead, upon which pictures and words are carved detailing how, why, and when misfortune should fall upon someone. Invocations of deities and spirits of the dead were engraved on the tablet, along with drawings of said deity alongside the targeted person. Curse tablets contained surprisingly specific words of intent, outlining the exact punishments the maker wished to bestow upon their enemy. They often said, "May (name) suffer from the following ills," followed by a list of terrible things. Some request that if the thief doesn't return what they stole that they suffer and die as punishment. Sometimes the tablets were used in binding spells and had imagery of snakes or ropes tying the hands and feet of a person. The defixiones would be rolled up and nailed shut, then placed somewhere that the dead would be able to receive it, such as in graveyards, down deep wells, beneath temples, or in other places associated with the underworld.

In history, the majority of curse tablets seemed to focus on stolen items, so this spell will continue in that vein. The idea is to bind a person and make a statement to spirit that they must return what is yours or suffer the consequences of your choosing. They may have stolen material things from you or something intangible such as trust or recognition that is rightfully yours.

---

10. Daniel Ogden, "The Curse Tablets: An Overview," in *Witchcraft and Magic in Europe: Ancient Greece and Rome,* ed. Bengt Ankarloo and Stuart Clark (Philadelphia: University of Pennsylvania Press, 1999), 4.

⟜⟞ MATERIALS

Stylus or chisel for engraving

Thin sheet of metal. You can buy very thin tin or copper sheets at craft
stores. It must be thin enough to easily be rolled up by hand.

3 rusty nails

Hammer

3 coins

Death candle (see page 51)

Lighter or matches

Cast your circle during the dark moon in an area where you can see what
you are doing by the light of the death candle. Light the candle, and using your
tools, carve a rough picture of your enemy into the metal. You can engrave
their initials or name on it. Next to them draw your chosen deity. Then draw
snakes twining all around the image of your enemy.

All around the pictures write the following: "(Name), you have stolen from
me the following things," and make a list. Then write, "I bind you from taking
anything more from me and command you to return what is rightfully mine.
If you do not, you shall experience the following," and add what you think
is just as their punishment. Either they lose the same thing that you lost, get
arrested, or have some other similar experience you feel is fitting. On the next
page is a drawing of a curse tablet I made as an example.

When your engraving is complete, using a nail or other sharp tool, pierce
the forehead of your enemy's picture. Say aloud:

(Name), you will return what is rightfully mine or the equivalent.

Remove the nail.

Roll the tablet up and hammer in the rusty nails to shut the roll in three
places. As you hammer each nail, say:

Spirit, bring me justice.

Close the circle.

Go to a graveyard or other liminal place you feel connects you with spirits. Recite aloud what you have written on the tablet. Bury or hide the tablet. Scatter coins in thanks to the spirits of the area, and then walk away. What is rightfully yours, or something of equal or better value, will be returned to you.

SPELLS TO CAUSE IMPOTENCE

One of the things that witches have long been blamed for—along with crop failures, diseases in livestock, miscarriage, illness, and basically everything else —is impotence in men. Yep, they blamed that on us too!

I'm sure there were in fact spells cast many times to spurn the unwanted advances of men or to render a cheating lover unsatisfied; however, I also think that it was just a convenient way to blame yet another problem on women and our so-called evil.

In the spirit of cursing, here are two modern spells to cause impotence. Typically, they're used as revenge against someone who was unfaithful or to ruin their future sexual relations. Bear in mind that the results of this spell are not physical and won't necessarily impact their actual body but rather their sex life in general.

These spells traditionally make use of phallic imagery and are therefore aimed at men, but if you use your imagination, you can certainly tweak the spells to be aimed at a person of any gender.

Impotence Spell #1
⊷ᰶ MATERIALS

> Rotten cucumber or zucchini
>
> Black cloth, large enough to wrap the finished product
>
> Marker
>
> Knife
>
> Personal effects of the target such as hair, fingernails, a piece of their
>   handwriting, or a small object they've touched
>
> 3 tablespoons cayenne pepper
>
> 3 tablespoons witch's salt (see page 49)
>
> 3 tablespoons death oil (see page 48)
>
> Lighter or matches
>
> Death candle (see page 51)
>
> 3 feet black string

Lay the cucumber on the black cloth and cast your circle.

Using the marker, write the target's name on the cucumber. Use your visualization to transfer the image of the target's anatomy onto the cucumber. Try to get one of similar size and shape. Holding an image of their private parts in your mind, use your ritual knife to cut a line from one end of the cucumber to the other, creating an open lengthwise slit. Make the slit about halfway through the width the cucumber, but do not cut it completely in half. Imagine hearing an anguished scream in your head as you cut. Shove the hair, fingernails, or personal effects into the slit and say the target's name 3 times.

Feeling as much anger as you can, pour the cayenne pepper powder into the slit of the cucumber. Imagine it burning. In your mind, see your target unable to sexually perform. Imagine how they would feel when it happens, and pour that emotion into the charm.

Next add a generous helping of witch's salt all along the cut vegetable, and imagine it sizzling the life out of it the way salt kills a slug. Then take your death oil and saturate the cucumber completely. See the death oil snuffing out all the life, vitality, and fertile energy of the phallic symbol.

Place your death candle in the slit of the cucumber, making sure it is pressed in securely upright, and light it.

As it burns, spend time thinking about how angry you are, transferring it into the object before you. Again, imagine how you want them to feel when experiencing your curse, perhaps humiliation and dissatisfaction. Do this until you feel relieved of your feelings and the candle burns out.

Wrap the whole thing up securely in the black cloth and tie it up with string.

Release your magick circle. Throw what remains in the garbage.

Impotence Spell #2
MATERIALS
Black taper candle or penis-shaped candle, available at magickal shops

Black cloth measuring 1 square foot

Knife

Several drops of your own menstrual blood (optional)

1 tablespoon death oil (see page 48)

13 pins, or 1 pin for each month or year you spent with the person

13 small shards of broken glass

Small photo of the target

3 feet black string

Lay the candle on the black cloth. It is not for burning but is the phallic symbol in the spell.

Cast your circle.

Infuse the candle with the essence of your target, visualizing it as representing their anatomy. Carve their name into the candle with your knife.

If you choose to, anoint the candle with your own menstrual blood while focusing on the negative aspects of the blood, specifically the old belief that it kills everything it comes in contact with. See the death energy in that blood soaking into the person's anatomy.

Now break the candle in the middle and imagine the target's scream. Essentially, their penis is now "broken."

Lay the candle on the black cloth. Pour death oil into the broken part of the candle, and imagine it seeping into it and killing all the life energy it touches. Imagine the target experiencing impotence and all its associated emotions.

Heat up your first pin in the flame of a candle and then shove it through the black broken candle. See it searing through the target's anatomy and stopping the blood flow. Repeat this with all the pins.

Place the shards of broken glass around the black candle. As you wrap it in black cloth, gently press them into the exterior of the candle. Bind it all up with black string and release the circle.

You can keep this hidden somewhere or throw it away.

A MISCELLANY OF CURSES

Money Owed Dirt Spell

If someone owes you money or goods but isn't paying up, this spell is meant for them. The dirt included in the spell should be from the land of the actual bank their money resides in. If the bank doesn't have dirt or grass near it, like in many urban places, try to get pebbles or other natural debris from directly around the building.

←—⊰ MATERIALS

Piece of paper on which you wrote the amount owed

Coin with their name painted onto it

Hair or fingernails of the person if possible

½ cup bank dirt

2 feet black thread

Cast your circle and lay the paper in front of you. See the number amount you have written. Visualize yourself receiving the amount of money from the person and what you would do with it. See money going from their hand into yours.

Place the coin and personal effects of the person on the paper and cover them completely with the bank dirt. This connects your visualization to their bank account.

Fold the paper all around the contents so they don't fall out, and bind it tightly with black thread. This act of binding ties their money to you, ensuring that, one way or another, you will get what is owed to you.

Spend some time feeling the energy of the packet you've created. You've trapped the person, their finances, and the amount they owe you all together. They will not be free with their finances until they pay you.

While you don't get to decide how or where they get the money, just know that it will come to you.

Close the circle.

Hide the charm, and once you get what you are owed, untie it and dispose of it.

Bad Neighbor Curse

If you've ever had the misfortune of living in close proximity to toxic people, then you know how horrible it can be to have a bad neighbor. I don't mean someone who you can generally ignore and go about your business, but the kind of neighbor who actively seeks out ways to make your life unhappy. Maybe they disagree with your lifestyle or they simply have no other way to entertain themselves. The "why" isn't your problem—your problem is stopping them.

If you have a neighbor who is intentionally making your life a living hell and you genuinely don't deserve it, this spell is to get rid of them. This could take the form of them moving away or their life changing in such a manner that they can no longer be bothered with you. Again, how it happens isn't your problem, only that you stop them from causing you further harm.

The spell below uses dirt from your neighbor's yard. If you live in an apartment building or shared housing, replace this with some dust or debris taken from near their doorway or living space. Bits of dirt and dust get tracked in all the time, and all you need is a pinch.

MATERIALS

A pinch of dirt from the target's yard, gathered at night when they won't see you doing it

Jar with tight lid

13 pins

Several shards of broken glass

1 tablespoon cayenne pepper

Vinegar (enough to fill the jar)

Gather your materials on your altar during the dark moon. Have the dirt sitting in the jar. Cast your circle.

The dirt in the jar represents your neighbor. It is their home life and their existence within their house. You are essentially going to put things into the jar, which will symbolize putting various influences into their home, and then you're going to shake it up every day until they are compelled to move, or at the very least their attention will be diverted away from you so they'll leave you alone.

First, hold the pins in your hand and focus on their sharp points. Drop them in the jar.

Carefully hold the broken glass and see the tiny cutting edges, all the miniature ways it can slice. It was once whole but is now shattered and dangerous. Add this to the jar. Contemplate the cayenne pepper and its burning, irritating qualities, and add it to the jar.

Look at the vinegar. It kills germs and eats through matter like grease and lime. Pour it into the jar and fill it up.

Tighten the lid.

Give the jar a shake, and see how the contents are disturbed, sloshing around with the sharp pointy pins and broken glass, like they're slicing and stabbing through it. Every time you do this, imagine your neighbor's house being shaken up from the inside out, struck through with energy that makes living there unbearable.

Close the circle.

Keep the jar hidden, and every day give it a shake. Watch the sharp objects swirling around, and visualize your intention.

When your desire manifests, throw the ingredients away and recycle the jar.

This spell can be tweaked and changed for different intentions. If you wish your neighbor love and happiness in their home, instead of adding pins and glass to the dirt, add rose petals and seashells, and instead of vinegar, use sweet fruit juice. Sugar can replace the cayenne pepper.

Blood and Corn Curse

As mentioned, menstrual blood has been used in witchcraft in many ways. It has been deemed disgusting, filthy, and shameful for a long time. While this is a negative connotation that needs to be debunked, it's still a very old trope whose energy can be drawn upon in magick.

For this working, we will focus on the negative beliefs around menstrual blood, the same beliefs that made people in times past so utterly terrified of it. We can bring the spirit of that into hexing or cursing someone in a terrible way. Menstrual blood is, after all, dead cells that your body is expelling, and it does contain death energy.

This spell draws on the belief that menstrual blood could kill entire crops of grain. You're going to destroy a whole crop of bad behavior.

↠ MATERIALS

Knife

Fresh or dried ear of corn with the leaves peeled off

1 tablespoon or more menstrual blood in a container

Lighter or matches

Death candle (see page 51)

Cast your circle and invoke deity if you wish.

Using the knife, remove kernels of the corn from the cob in the shape of the person's initials. The more anger and wrath you feel, the better, as you violently cut their initials out of the vegetable. If you feel like calling them mean names and curse words while you work, by all means do so.

Hold the corn cob in your hands and think about exactly what they've done that makes you angry and vengeful. Imagine them doing the very thing that irks you most, calling up the feeling in your heart. Send the hateful feeling from your heart, down your arms, through your hands, and into the corn. The corn now holds the energy of their wrongdoing.

Now hold the container of blood in your hands and see it the way so many people in the past did: as diseased, dead cells carrying death, as a substance that can decimate entire fields of crops. See this substance as death, terror, and plague—a curse unto itself, for that is what it's often called.

Cover the corn with blood as much as possible, especially in the initials. Get it in between the kernels, destroying every single one, and see now the person becoming sickened to their very soul. Draw upon the repulsive reputation of the blood and imbue the person with that feeling. Pour illness, death and repugnance all over them and all they touch.

Now light your death candle and drip wax onto the corn cob, sealing it completely, encasing the noxious curse. As the wax hardens, the curse takes physical form.

Close the circle.

Wash your hands.

Bury, compost, or dispose of all the materials except the knife, which you can thoroughly wash and reuse.

The terror and repulsion you've released on your enemy will manifest in the person's life, not necessarily as a physical illness but in some other way that stops their behavior.

Fly in the Ointment Spell

There is an old idiom about "the fly in the ointment." The fly in the ointment describes someone or something that may appear minor but is tainting the whole. The whole can be a relationship, situation, family, or workplace. The fly in the ointment is a tiny annoyance that turns everything around it toxic, eventually ruining a good thing. It spreads problems throughout a group. If the problem is one particular person, putting fly ointment on their belongings will expose them for what they really are and stop their progress.

This spell can also be applied to a place or thing you feel has dangerous energy, such as a building that attracts bad luck and misfortune. If there is an object causing fights among family or friends, as can happen when people fight over inherited items or money, the fly in the ointment can be applied to the problematic object.

⊷⊰ MATERIALS

2 dead flies (substitution: 2 pieces rotting garlic)

Mortar and pestle

3 tablespoons oil, such as olive or jojoba

Small jar or bottle with a tight lid

Cast a circle.

Crush the flies in the mortar and pestle while focusing on how disgusting they are. See the diseases and germs carried by the flies, give yourself the shivers, and let yourself be horrified. The more repelled you are the better. After all, this is to be used to signify a rank and horrible person or thing. Add the oil 1 drop at a time and make a thick paste. You only need a very small amount of this ointment, and there is no need to make extra. When you have charged the mixture with all the nasty energy you can, seal it in a small jar or container. Release the circle.

This oil is meant to be put on a person or thing in order to send out an energetic marker or signal that will intuitively alert others to stay away. The gross energy of the ointment will send out a nasty warning vibration. This can prevent the offending person or thing from making any more headway on their destructive path. Naturally, it would be difficult to put this oil on an actual person, so instead you can put it on their belongings (just a tiny amount so they don't see it); near their home or property; near where they work, such as on their desk or their locker; or even on their vehicle. If none of this is possible, you can use a photo of them and put the oil on that instead.

Dispose of any leftover ointment and don't forget to wash your hands!

Mosquito Spell to Stop an Energy Vampire

This spell is to stop a human energy sucker. This person is someone who takes and takes and never seems to give anything in return. This can take the form of the classic "energy vampire," which is a person who seems to just suck the life force out of you, leaving you drained and irritable while they become more and more animated and powerful. It can also be used on someone who is draining any of your resources, such as money, sympathy, and time.

⊷⊰ MATERIALS

Dead mosquito (substitution: picture of mosquito)

Small paper bag

Sprig of mosquito-repellent herbs, such as 1 or more of the following: lavender, citronella, lemon balm, basil, peppermint, and rosemary

3 feet black ribbon or string

Mentally connect the bug with the image of the person who is leeching off you: their face, their voice, their smell. Then imagine their clingy, manipulative actions and unwanted behavior. Pour it into the mosquito. Now the mosquito represents their behavior.

Place the dead mosquito in the paper bag.

Charge the herbs to represent protection. Imbue them with repellent, protective qualities. Rub them lightly over your skin or in the air close to your body to symbolize your protection from the person, and then add them to the bag.

Roll the top of the bag down bit by bit, squeezing the air out of it, while imagining the person's influence getting smaller and smaller. As you squash the bag in your hands, imagine you have squashed their nasty intentions flat.

Now take the black ribbon or string and wrap it around and around the paper bag until it is completely covered and restrained. Tie a tight knot in the black ribbon.

Close the circle.

Get rid of the charm as far away from you as you can. A garbage bin off your property is a good place for something like this.

Firefly BS Curse

We've all met someone who puts stars in our eyes and blinds us to reality. Some people do this intentionally, while others are completely unaware of the effect they are having on us. This spell is to get rid of the power of someone who is stopping you from thinking straight. This can be an extremely charismatic person who is a liar and cheater but who continuously manages to suck you in again and again. It could be someone who is putting on what you suspect is false friendliness for you, making empty promises to keep you around, or otherwise blinding you with fake niceties in order to manipulate you. This spell is to strip away the glamour they're throwing at you so you can see the truth.

We so often see what we want to see, especially when we are blinded by love. When we love someone, we can teeter easily into being taken advantage of, lied to, or manipulated. Unfortunately, deep down you sense when this is happening, but the person keeps just enough of a pleasant veneer over things to keep you hooked and fooled.

When you find a dead firefly whose light is extinguished, use it to take the stars out of your eyes.

⤚ᵌ MATERIALS
Small photo of the person, no larger than 5 by 7 inches
Dead firefly (substitution: remains of a burned-out match)
Lighter or matches
Cauldron or fireproof vessel

Fold or roll the photo of the person around the dead firefly. Imagine them surrounded by their lies and falsehoods. These can appear around their face in your mind as stars, lights, or sparkles that obscure their true nature. Little by little, remove the stars in your mind, until all that is left is their true image without the dazzle.

Burn the photo and firefly in the cauldron and say:

> *The light is out,*
> *The glamour stripped*
> *Off of your act,*
> *Illusions ripped*
> *Away from what*
> *Has kept me blind.*
> *I see the truth*
> *That lies behind.*

Bury the ashes afterward.

Wasp Spell to Disarm a Harmful Person
Ever heard the saying "kill them with kindness"? This spell is meant to stifle the hateful influence of an enemy with pure sweetness. Their poisonous behavior is represented by a wasp or hornet.

For the purpose of this spell, we are focusing on the stinger, the poison and the pain a wasp can cause. A wasp can relentlessly sting again and again, just like a toxic person can cause harm repeatedly without consequence. It is this association, and the fear many people feel when near a wasp, that we are using in this spell. Regardless of the big ecological picture, emotions elicited by wasps are strong and therefore powerful in magick. As always, use a wasp that you find already dead in this spell.

An interesting wasp fact is that when they sting, they release a pheromone that alerts other wasps to their distress and causes them to join the attack. This is a lot like how a negative person can sometimes have themselves a team of like-minded followers who support them.

←◦ MATERIALS

3-inch square of paper

Pencil

Empty jar or bottle with an airtight lid

Dead wasp

Something to represent the person, such as an item of theirs that they have touched or worn, their hair or fingernails, or, if all else fails, a picture or their name

1 cup honey, maple syrup, agave nectar, or even sugar dissolved in water to make a very sweet liquid

You're going to suffocate the negative behavior out of the person with sweetness. Cast a circle and see the individual in your mind. Write out a list on your paper of what they have done to you that is wrong. This can be a personalized letter to the person (don't worry—no one ever has to read it) or just your angry thoughts. The more you put into it the better. Rant it all out onto the paper. Fold it with the writing facing out and put it in the jar.

Hold the dead wasp in your hand. Reflect on its sting. Think of how the person has stung you. Think of the others they have drawn in to also sting and torment you. Think about their toxic, poisonous behavior and send it into the wasp. Place the wasp and the photo or personal effects of the person into the jar.

Now take your honey or syrup and hold it up to the light. See how golden and warm it is. See its sweet energy and, in it, the power of goodness. Fill it with positive, sunny thoughts until it is glowing with them.

Then pour the syrup over the wasp and paper and picture. Feel the honey literally drowning all the energies attached to them, stifling them down to nothing. See the honey invade every pore and fiber of those items, taking them over and nullifying them completely, drowning and killing them. Cover the objects entirely and close the lid.

Spend some time looking at the saturated wasp and paper. Sweetness has voided all their power, and their poisons are wiped out.

Close your circle.

Keep this jar in a safe place until the person has stopped bothering you. When the situation has passed or they have moved on, pour the honey out somewhere off your property and recycle the jar.

CHAPTER 11
SACRIFICE

The origin of sacrifice is drenched in bloodshed. There's simply no way to sugarcoat that, and I will not attempt to do so. That being said, I will preface this section of the book by saying that I do not personally perform animal or human sacrifice in my practice.

Sacrifice is perhaps one of the most widely misunderstood and feared of all rituals. Just the word brings to mind barbaric torture, cannibalism, and evil "devil-worshiping" rites. However, the true meaning of sacrifice is none of those things.

Sacrifice has a rich history in almost every society across the globe, throughout the ages and right up to modern-day religion. It bridges cultures completely unconnected with each other, which tells us it's perhaps instinctive to humans.

To fully understand the nature of sacrifice, it's important to look back through the past and examine how this practice has been a part of existence and spirituality since before calendar time. Looking at how and why different civilizations went about performing sacrifice helps us understand how it can be applied to our lives and workings today.

So what, exactly, is sacrifice? Sacrifice is to offer a life, act, or object to a deity in worship.

The act of sacrifice is far more complex and ingrained in the human psyche than many people realize. It is *ancient*. Like everything, the force behind this instinct is cyclical like the seasons and the moon. It's a give and take. It's the thinking behind bargaining with higher powers. It's the idea that we can offer something of value to a more powerful force and get good treatment in return.

REASONS FOR SACRIFICE

When we look back at history, it appears there were several reasons for sacrifice. One was a funerary action, in that it was performed when a leader died and people and animals were killed to accompany them to the afterlife. Another was to gain favor with the gods to ensure survival and ward off natural disasters. The third reason was for divination.

In most modern religions, sacrifice has evolved into the peaceful dedication of food, drink, and libations to a deity without harm. Animal sacrifice today is not very common and is only carried out by practiced spiritual leaders within specific communities. The animals are usually then included in a feast eaten by the group.

The gory roots of sacrifice display how vital it was in times past to show respect to higher forces, something lost on many of us today. Understanding this can add depth and meaning to our own practice when we make symbolic offerings in ritual.

Funerary Sacrifice

The most well-known funerary sacrifice was that of the ancient Egyptians. When a king died, whole communities of people and animals were sacrificed to be buried alongside him. This ensured that the king would have soldiers, laborers, servants, and family members to accompany him to the afterlife.[11] Similar mass graves were found in Mesopotamia, presumably with the same end in mind, and in Borneo, when a chief died, his servants were nailed to his coffin to accompany him in his next life.[12]

Over time, many of these mass sacrifices were eventually replaced with wooden or clay figures instead of real humans.

Sacrifice for Favor

Another kind of sacrifice was to appease or placate gods and goddesses. Natural phenomena such as storms, drought, floods, and earthquakes were believed to be caused by deity. Offering the life of a person or animal to this unpredictable deity (nature) was believed to ensure good crops, a fruitful hunt, or favor-

---

11. Lewis, *Ritual Sacrifice*, 41.

12. Lewis, *Ritual Sacrifice*, 149.

able conditions. Giving a sacrifice as thanks falls into this category, as showing gratitude would also presumably gain favor.

Just as in funeral rites, it was usually considered an honor to serve as a sacrifice.

The Aztecs believed offerings of blood and human organs were necessary to keep the sun in the sky. One of the most important traditions was the festival of Tezcatlipoca, the god of creation. A teenage boy was chosen to represent Tezcatlipoca, and for one year prior to the festival, he would live a life of luxury, bedecked with flowers, gold, and jewels while attendants waited on his every whim. On the day of the festival, the young man walked to the temple, where his heart was ripped out and given to the sun.[13]

A sacrifice being pampered and treated like royalty leading up to their death was common. People wanted to offer the absolute best specimen to the gods they could. The general belief seemed to be that the more "special" the offering, the happier the gods would be and the better experiences they would bestow upon people.

Sacrifice for Divination

The third type of sacrifice was for divination, in which the entrails, blood, and body parts of the human or animal would be interpreted to gain information and guidance.

In ancient Greece, animal sacrifice of this kind was a frequent occurrence. The Greeks sacrificed a bull, sheep, or goats in a place called an "oracle." A priestess would enter a trance, and divinity would speak through her after appropriate offerings were made. The most well known was the Oracle of Delphi, dedicated to the god Apollo. The Oracle of Delphi was consulted for everything from weddings to wars to building colonies. Animal sacrifice was so commonplace during this time that armies marching to war used to take flocks of sheep and goats with them. For every move the army made, whether crossing into new territory or planning an invasion, an animal was sacrificed in exchange for guidance and portents.[14]

It is said that the Celts performed human sacrifice for the purpose of divination too. The Celts would stab a human to death and then observe the

---

13. Lewis, *Ritual Sacrifice,* 86.
14. Lewis, *Ritual Sacrifice,* 55.

twitches and death throes of the victim to gain information. Other things that contained the answers they sought were the position of the fallen body and how their blood splattered.[15]

A common type of divination was haruspicy, the reading of entrails for divinatory purposes. An animal would be sacrificed, and then the way that its organs were placed inside the body or on the ground would be read for omens. Abnormalities such as lumps or lesions all had meaning, as did the shapes and pictures formed by the entrails.[16]

Vestiges of Bloodshed

All the situations regarding human sacrifice I've referenced here took place in ancient history, when people believed they were literally at the mercy of the gods (nature) and would do anything, including kill, to appease them. They believed their very survival depended on this. There have been cases documented by law enforcement of human sacrifice in recent times all around the world, but many of those are left unproven, and it can't be said for absolute certain if they were indeed religious killings or not.

Modern animal sacrifice still occurs nowadays around the world, albeit infrequently. The truth is that many sacrifices made by these groups are done respectfully and consumed in a ceremonial meal afterward. Keep in mind that in America, slaughtering livestock to feed families and communities was traditionally an ordinary part of life and still is in some cases. Most people see nothing wrong with this. It's only when you add the "ceremonial" aspect of it that people become upset. But if you think about it, is it really that different from saying prayers of gratitude before digging into a Thanksgiving turkey?

WITCHCRAFT AND SACRIFICE: MISCONCEPTIONS

Witches have been wrongfully linked to cold-blooded murder for centuries. Just look at classic fairy tales. In "Hansel and Gretel," the witch lures children into her clutches to fatten them up and eat them. In "Snow White," the witch commands the huntsman to bring her the bloody heart of her rival. In "Sleeping Beauty," the witch imposes eternal sleep on her hapless victim. These may

---

15. Lewis, *Ritual Sacrifice*, 69.
16. Lewis, *Ritual Sacrifice*, 59.

not be sacrifice per se, but they certainly put witches alongside the murder of innocent creatures.

The truth is witches didn't perform sacrifice. *Humans* performed sacrifice. All over the world, people of all persuasions, races, religions, and so forth can find this act in their history in some way

However, the stories about witches specifically being Satan worshipers who eat babies still haven't disappeared, casting the witch as a child-killing, blood-thirsty ghoul even now.

Witches have been linked to sacrifice and ritual killing for centuries, probably starting with the burning times.

The Witches' Sabbath

While the burning times seem long ago, in reality much of what was recorded has stained history and modern perception alike. The witch hunters forced false confessions out of their victims with unthinkable torture, demanding wild stories out of them about what went on at a "Witches' Sabbath." Some of the outlandish accusations they made were that witches would fly through the air to a sabbath, where they'd feast on human flesh, have sex with the devil or large goats, participate in orgies, sacrifice babies to Satan, and drink blood. These "confessions" were recorded as fact, and the association between witches and murder was made.

By the nineteenth century, the witch burnings stopped. However, the stories live on and cast shade over the word *witchcraft* to this day.

Ritualized Murders in the 1960s and '70s

The fear created during the burning times stuck, and the resulting hysteria has continued to pop up in several ways quite recently. In the 1960s and '70s, multiple creepy murder sprees took place in the United States, which together incited another round of witch hysteria in the country. Murders committed by the Manson family, the Zodiac Killer, and the Alphabet Murderer all included ritualistic elements that people automatically linked to devil worship and therefore witches. It didn't help matters that *The Satanic Bible* by Anton LaVey hit the shelves around the same time, so the collective mind couldn't help but link the ritualized killings to Satan and witches. In fact, it made people feel like cults of baby-killing, devil-worshiping "witches" were hiding under every shadow in every town.

It's only by coincidence that Anton LaVey's *Satanic Bible* came out around this era and got thrown into the fray. LaVey's Satanism in fact had nothing to do with sacrifice or violence toward children and animals, as the masses would have known had they taken the time to read it. Regardless, these things aligned witchcraft once again with murder.

Satanic Panic

Things hardly had a chance to settle down after the murders in the '70s before being slammed with what has been dubbed the "Satanic Panic" of the 1980s. Headlines suddenly blared the blood-chilling news that multiple day-care centers in the United States had subjected children to satanic rituals and abuse. Again, mass hysteria swept the country. Satanic cults were in the papers, on your television, and in your own backyard.

Just like the fabricated stories told by the witch hunters in the burning times, many people latched onto the satanic witch trend and ran with it while money poured into the bank. The media blew up with these stories, each headline more disgusting than the one before. The more horrifying the allegations were the more they captivated people. Law enforcement created a special unit dedicated solely to occult crime. Psychologists and therapists got involved, becoming self-proclaimed experts on satanic abuse. Popular memoirs were penned, and later debunked, by alleged survivors of satanic abuse.

In 1992, the Department of Justice rejected the myth of the satanic sex abuse cults once and for all. However, it was too late. The media had fueled a public wave of fear that took entire groups of rational, thinking adults to the same dark collective place that caused the witch hunts so long ago, and it was compounded once again in the general public's psyche that witches and blood sacrifice go hand in hand.

Modern Sacrifice

Despite human and most animal sacrifices going out of fashion in modern days, the act of sacrifice is still alive and well. It's also much less bloody. In many modern religions and spiritual paths, sacrifices are performed as fasts and giving up an action or thing. People offer flowers, fruit, food, and wine to their deities regularly in thanks, to gain favor and blessings, and to worship. During the season of Samhain, Pagan people build ancestral altars and place objects upon them as offerings to their ancestors.

In many Pagan festivities, wine, drinks, cakes, and breads are offered to deity and shared by the participants. Food, flowers, libations, and actions have taken the place of human and animal sacrifice when it comes to gaining favor with gods or giving thanks.

In the past, the sacrifice of an animal was usually followed by feasting, which included eating said animal. In a community where farming was part of life, slaughtering livestock doesn't seem as strange as it may to modern city dwellers. When used in sacrifice, the livestock was especially honored before it was eaten. Nowadays, preparing food in such a way is not considered a sacrifice or offering but a show of respect for a higher power. In some religions, animals must be prepared and blessed a very specific way prior to slaughter by an appointed person. Much like saying a prayer before a meal, this is more a dedication than a sacrifice, a way of ritualizing the act of eating and making it sacred, which, when you think about it, it should be.

These are a few examples of how sacrifice is practiced today:

Cakes and Ale: In modern Paganism, food and feasting feature highly in our holidays. The ritual of cakes and ale, the bread celebrations of Lammas/Lughnasadh, and even leaving food offerings of milk, honey, and bread for fae are common among us. Consuming cakes and ale after offering them to the gods and goddesses are a way of taking them into us, offering thanks, and communing with them.

Communion: Some Christians practice communion, which is the symbolic ingestion of Christ. His body is represented by bread and his blood by wine, and both are ritually consumed in a church ceremony. Partaking in communion signifies that the participants remember, respect, and recognize what their god Jesus has done for them by dying upon the cross for them and how he sacrificed his own life for their good.

Lent: A popular modern sacrifice is the Christian practice of Lent, which takes place for roughly forty days prior to Easter celebrations in spring. Christians will give up certain vices, habits, foods, or activities for that time in order to focus on their relationship with their god. Sometimes they volunteer their time to charitable causes as a way of giving something of themselves to the greater good.

Puja: Puja is a Hindu practice in which incense is lit and offerings of food are made to a deity in thanks. Puja is an offering of light to the Divine and can be done in the home or in a temple.

Ramadan: In Islamic culture, Ramadan is the month of fasting, abstaining from pleasures, spending time with loved ones, and praying. It's a joyous time that unites Muslim people and strengthens their connection with the Divine.

Yom Kippur: Yom Kippur is known as the Day of Atonement in the Jewish faith. It's a day for cleansing of mistakes, seeking forgiveness and new beginnings. On this day it's common for people to fast from food and drink, washing, and marital relations in order to focus on divinity.

While these are only a few examples of modern-day sacrifice, when we look at them all together, we can see a common thread: food is being dedicated to the greater good, given in thanks, or otherwise connected with divine favor. We can see that the practice of sacrifice has not left our lives but has merely changed over time.

FASTING AS A SACRIFICE

Fasting is one of the most common rites of sacrifice. It's the simple act of abstaining from food, indulgences, technology, sex, or inebriants for a specified length of time. Fasting from a pleasure or luxury is like giving it as a gift to spirit. It can be an act of gratitude, a means of receiving spiritual guidance, or a way of removing one thing in order to make room for another. Some people may include fasting prior to spells or rituals as a means of purifying themselves, while others do it to ensure receipt of something they need or want, almost like an exchange.

Before You Begin

When giving up food, activities, or items in exchange for something of spiritual value, it is important to set your intent when you commence the fast. This may take some thought and time to decide on. Fasting is usually performed in exchange for intangible things. It can purify your body and spirit after a rough time, welcome a new fresh start, or show dedication to deity in exchange for information in the form of omens or visions.

After you decide on the intent of your fast, you must choose a time frame. It is best to fast during a peaceful time when you are not under extreme pressure from work, physical demands, or other stress. This allows you to focus on your inner experience. You must also determine the length of your fast. This can be anywhere from one day to up to a full lunar cycle or longer (with the exception of water fasting). When it comes to something like water fasting, which has a dramatic and potentially dangerous physical impact on your health, the length of your fast doesn't determine the outcome; just because you fast longer doesn't mean you'll be more noticeable to deity. Putting your health at risk will not bring you any closer to your spiritual goals, so stick with what is healthy for you. As for fasting from inebriants or other vices, you may do so for as long as you wish.

Water Fasting

Water fasting is the act of abstaining from all food and drink except for water. Should you choose to include water fasting in your spiritual practice, there are some very important factors to consider. Do not fast if you have health issues or are on medication without first asking your doctor. Even going one day without eating can cause dizziness in some people, and this can be worsened or dangerous for those whose health is already compromised. Some other symptoms are nausea, fatigue, lack of concentration, and moodiness.

Theories abound regarding the health benefits of water fasting; however, I can't say whether or not these claims are true. I'll leave that up to medical professionals. The fasting I'm speaking of in this book is for spiritual ends.

Choose your time to water fast on a day or days when you know you will be able to have plenty of rest. It's unwise to undertake a water fast during a hectic time when you must perform a lot of physical or even mental tasks. It should be a time of repose, looking inward, meditation, and deep thought.

Consume nothing but water during your fast. For most people, this means no morning coffee, tea, juice, or other drinks, and more importantly, no food. However, some people do include carefully chosen herbal teas throughout the day, drunk without sweeteners or dairy. It's important to remember to drink much more water than normal while fasting. At least eight cups are required, but even more is better. It helps stave off hunger pangs, cleanses your system, and prevents dehydration. You are more susceptible to dehydration during a fast, so please do not neglect this step.

The longest water fast I've ever completed was fourteen days. I have read about people who can make it as long as twenty-eight days, but you must use common sense and pay attention to how you are feeling. I had to reluctantly end my fast because I felt like I was floating on the edge of reality, so deeply inside myself that I was not fully aware of the world around me, which made it dangerous to drive a car. That gives you some insight into how water fasting can make you feel. Removing myself from the needs of my physical body, aside from some initial discomfort, was incredibly transformative. Removing those needs opened the floodgates for other sensory, emotional, and spiritual energy to take up space instead. During a water fast, you may find your meditation experience is heightened and your divination abilities are enhanced.

Water fasting can be physically and mentally uncomfortable, especially for beginners. Some common effects are irritability, fatigue, hunger pangs, cravings, mood swings, weakness, and dizziness. These are just some of the reasons that quiet, rest, and solitude are important during your fast. Spend as much time as possible resting, meditating, and allowing spirit to send you messages. Go on calm walks in nature or take a cleansing bath. Pay close attention to your dreams, images that present themselves in meditation, and any omens you see.

If you're new to water fasting, I suggest a short one to begin, no longer than three days for a healthy adult.

There are modifications that can be made to soften the harsh experience of water fasting and make it a little more comfortable, such as cutting out only food but still drinking healthy liquids, such as fruit and vegetable juice, or consuming a small amount of plain rice each day. You have to do what is right for you and your physicality.

When it comes time to break a water fast, be sure to ease yourself gently back into normal eating habits. Consuming a large, heavy meal to break a fast can result in stomach pain and intestinal discomfort. It's best to eat small portions of fruits and vegetables at first, and slowly add more food groups over the course of a few days or weeks, depending on the length of your fast.

Technology Fasting

This is just what it sounds like: abstaining from all technology for a set period of time. Why? Well, our minds, our energy fields, and our very beings are constantly inundated with images, data, electronic frequencies, and constant diversion. We live in a state of unrelenting distraction. Just look around you in any public place and you'll see that people cannot tear themselves away from their devices for even a moment. It is an addiction, and it takes up every empty space in our brain until we are almost never sitting quietly and thinking to ourselves, about ourselves or the world around us. In fact, I think a technology fast would be more difficult than a water fast for many people!

A technology fast requires cutting yourself off from others to a certain degree. You will not use a phone, tablet, computer, or even a television during this time. If it has a screen and connects to Wi-Fi, it counts as technology. Ideally, this type of fast could be paired with camping for a weekend in nature or some other natural situation that's not conducive to your usual habit of checking your phone every few minutes. I think every single person could benefit from a technology fast. The purpose of it is to clear up all that noise and distraction and leave your senses open to what nature, spirit, and life force are trying to tell you. This can be cleansing and can open your inner eye to truths you have not been able to see in everyday life. A technology fast can be great when you're seeking clarity of mind, making a hard decision, or asking for divine direction.

Beforehand, tell people that you will be unavailable via text or social media. Your phone should only be used for actual emergencies. I have been alive long enough to remember a time very clearly when we didn't have anything but a landline and one television station. I survived, so it is possible!

After a week of technology fasting, you may be surprised by what you uncover about yourself and how you feel about other people and situations. Spend time reading books (the old-fashioned way, not on a screen), meditating, journaling, walking in nature, and just being with yourself. It will allow you to look inward and really see how you feel about something deep inside, without social media and other influences impacting your thoughts. A technology fast allows you to step back and get grounded, reconnecting with the earth and with the self. It can even be good for relationships when done with a partner.

Inebriant Fasting

Inebriant fasting means to stop intake of drugs, alcohol, caffeine, or nicotine. Depending on your lifestyle, this can be very simple or downright torturous. For those who do not imbibe very often, it's easy to abstain, but for those who are moderate-to-heavy drinkers or recreational drug users, it's a whole different story. Just like the other types of fasts, inebriant fasting forces your mind to work a little differently than normal, opening it up to unexplored energies and ideas. It will allow you to have a very clear and unedited view of your situation and your needs without the filter of alcohol or drugs. That on its own is a valuable clarifying experience, but in a broader view, combined with meditation and rest, it can open your mind to ideas and realizations you would have not had otherwise.

Fasting from alcohol or drugs tends to open up time you didn't have before, leaving an opportunity to try something new. Sometimes people discover that they'd rather exchange getting drunk for a hobby and give it up permanently.

If you suffer from what you suspect is an addiction to alcohol or drugs, please seek help from a counselor or doctor.

Other Options for Fasting

When deciding what, exactly, to sacrifice for a period of time, it's important to choose something that will make an actual difference in your daily experience. Offering a fast of junk food to deity when you only eat it once a month is not much of a sacrifice. It has to be something meaningful, but also something that will change or altar your perspective. Below are some other options to consider. These are all things that can create a shift in consciousness and general experience, making room for new ideas, perception, and insight.

Makeup: This may sound strange, but many people feel protected by wearing makeup. Removing it and facing the world can be cathartic but also scary and help you learn a lot about yourself. This could be integrated into a self-love type of working.

Meat and Animal Products in Your Diet: Some people associate consuming meat, eggs, and other animal products with having death energy in their body. Eating only fresh raw plants for several days may create changes in your body and mind that are beneficial.

Sex or Orgasm: In Chinese medicine, it is believed that keeping semen inside the body will feed the mind and soul in more productive ways than expelling it would.

Sugar: If your favorite thing in the world is sugary treats and you want to fast but not go completely hungry, offering up this one indulgence can make a big difference.

Dark Moon Fasting Ceremony

This is a simple ceremony to perform at the beginning and end of your fast in order to let spirit know what you are doing and what you hope to achieve.

This example is a short fast, done over the three days that the new or dark moon rules the sky. It is to be performed in exchange for clarity during a difficult time or when you need guidance in your life. The idea is that you're giving your sacrifice of food, technology, or inebriants to the dark moon or Crone in exchange for direction. Personally, I feel fasting from technology for this purpose is best, but do what feels right.

⊷ MATERIALS

Dark moon bath items (see page 47)

Candle specifically dedicated to your chosen deity or to the dark moon, anointed with dark moon water (see page 43)

Symbol of the thing you're sacrificing. If you're water fasting, a bit of bread or fruit. For technology fasting, your favorite device. For smoking, a cigarette. For drinking, a glass of alcohol.

Black offering plate. This flat black circle represents the dark moon.

Your fast begins as soon as you wake up in the morning of the day prior to the dark moon. Make sure you've done all your indulging the night before, as it is now off limits. If you're water fasting, this means no morning coffee or other food. For technology, no checking your phone. This ritual begins as soon as you open your eyes, no exceptions.

Have a dark moon bath as described on pages 46 to 48, and then go to your altar and cast a circle. Enter a meditative state. Light the candle and welcome your deity or the dark moon phase. In your own words, explain to spirit what you are sacrificing and why. For example:

Dark of the moon,
Black void in the sky,
For the next three days I will sacrifice my _____ to you.
Receive my offering
And fill the space with your knowledge and direction.
Guide me as I find the answer to my problem:
(State your problem in your own words).

Place your symbol as an offering on the black plate. Feel it being received by the dark moon energy.

Receive my respect and accept this sacrifice
That I leave to you with love and trust.
I welcome now your wisdom.

Release the circle.

Leave your offering on the black plate for 3 days.

For the duration of the 3 days of sacrifice, meditate often and spend time in nature as discussed earlier. Be open to seeing signs and learning lessons. Remain as open as you can. Don't socialize more than you absolutely must, for the answers are likely to come from within, not without. Write down any important things you see, think, feel, or experience. During this time, light the candle whenever you wish until by the end of the third day, it is burned out completely.

At the end of the third day after the sun has set, return to your altar. Thank the dark moon for the lessons you have received. A magic circle isn't necessary at this time.

This concludes the sacrifice.

If you had food or drink as a sacrifice, dispose of them. If you left your device on the offering plate, you can now use it again.

PLANT SACRIFICE

Plants are living, breathing things with life force that can be offered up in much the same way you imagine an animal would. You may feel a desire to offer a living thing as a sacrifice to deity, and a cruelty-free means of doing this is to use a plant. Here are some tips for choosing the right plant for your sacrifice:

- Choose a plant that you have personally tended and grown just for this purpose. The plant should be special to you and one you have spent a significant amount of time personally tending. A sacrificial offering should always be something that is treasured and special. Sacrificial animals and people were always pampered and treated with reverence prior to sacrifice, and a plant sacrifice is no different.

- Select a plant that matches the intention of your spell. For sacrifices to gods and goddesses of love, consider orchids, roses, or other highly scented and beautiful flowers. For money, choose a fruitful, abundant plant, perhaps with berries. For a curse, consider a thorny, poisonous plant. You could also look up the magickal associations of herbs and grow them accordingly from seed in pots specifically to be used as a sacrifice to the deities who rule over your desire.

- Always use a living plant when you perform the sacrifice. Purchase or grow one in a pot or find one growing outdoors. Cut flowers or clippings, while they may still be fresh, will not include the act of severing the life cord that is integral to a "live" sacrifice. Cut flowers are fine as offerings, but making an offering and a sacrifice are two different things.

- Consider the life of the plant as a gift to your deity. You want to give them the nicest gift you can, especially when requesting something in return or showing devotion. You may wish to decorate the pot it is in, tie ribbons or bells on it, and paint symbols or the deity's name on the leaves.

You can add a plant sacrifice to any spell or ritual at the time that you would invoke deity.

◆⋯⋄ MATERIALS

Items representing your chosen deity

Plant of your choice

Cloth on which to cut the plant in half. Make sure it is big enough to hold the plant remains after they've been cut. Choose a color that corresponds with your intentions.

Knife or scissors sharp enough to cut through the stem of the plant. If you used a woody plant, you may need a small hatchet. If this seems daunting, choose a plant that is easily severed from its roots without needing an axe.

After invoking deity as outlined in chapter 2, place the plant on the altar along with the items that represent the deity.

Visualize the aura of the plant. See how full of life it is, the living, breathing energy that is inside and all around it. Imagine the water in the veins of the plant, much like what an animal or person has, only filled with blood. The plant is plump and juicy with live energy.

Say:

> *(Name of deity), I offer this life to you.*
> *I acknowledge your power*
> *And feel your presence.*
> *In gratitude, I offer you this gift.*
> *See me. Hear me. Know me.*

If you are asking the deity for assistance with a specific task, now is the time to simply state your request in one sentence, such as "Please protect me from those who wish me harm" or "Please help me get money I need."

Lay the plant on its side on the cloth. Slice through the stem, completely severing the root from the blooms. Cut it completely in half. Imagine the life force streaming out of the severed stem and flowing into the heart center of your deity.

Note how the plant is now void of life energy and is just a husk. Wrap it in the cloth and set it aside until you've done your working. Afterward, put the plant in the compost or leave its remains outdoors to decompose naturally. Keep the cloth for another use.

SPELLS WITH SACRIFICE

The following are sacrifice-style spells that anyone can do. One is to ask for healing, one involves divination, and one is a funerary sacrifice to accompany a dying loved one to the afterlife.

A Healing Sacrifice

Sometimes a sacrifice is given for healing. A ritually killed animal would be offered to the gods in exchange for the health of the ailing person. First, the illness would be transferred from the person into the animal. Then the animal would be killed, along with the disease. The idea is that the gods would be appeased by the death of the animal, therefore choosing not to take the life of the ill person. While killing an animal is not typically an option, you can perform a similar healing sacrifice using a plant instead.

I recommend selecting a juicy plant that will release a lot of moisture when cut, to symbolize blood. Aloe vera and other thick, fat succulents are good if this is what speaks to you. Plants with a woody stem, like yucca, also work well, as severing the wooden stem is similar to cutting open the veins (even though there will not be as much moisture in plants as to mimic bloodshed, the idea is there).

This ritual is meant to heal spiritual ailments, such as emotional pain, overcoming inner turmoil, or healing inside from a traumatic experience. It is also for when someone feels they are being plagued by evil energy or beings.

This ritual can be performed from a distance on someone who needs healing, although it makes it more complicated. It's important that they participate in the meditation part of the ritual at the same time that you're performing the spell, so synchronizing the timing is important. Also, you will have to omit the bloodletting step if they're not present.

Perform this outdoors during the dark moon.

MATERIALS

> 1 cup witch's salt (see page 49)
> 6 black candles (preferably hurricane candles or candles placed in
>   glass jars to prevent being blown out by wind)
> Potted plant
> 1 cup clean water in a bowl
> Blanket to lie or sit on
> Sterile lancet (optional)
> Sharp knife for cutting or an axe if using a woody plant
> Trowel or shovel for digging

Cast your circle. Sprinkle a physical ring of witch's salt all around yourself and the person you're healing, large enough for them to lie down in if they wish, with you sitting next to them. If the person cannot be present, a photograph of them and a personal belonging such as a piece of their clothing can be used instead.

Inside the circle, place the 6 black candles in a smaller circle, the right size to put the plant inside. If you're sacrificing to a specific deity, place some of their sacred items here. If you're working with the dark moon or Crone, see the circle as a reflection or double of the dark moon in the sky, like a portal between the physical and astral plane.

First, it's important to thank and honor the plant for its use in your ritual. This is what the small bowl of water is for. Hold the bowl of water toward the sky and say:

> *With this water,*
> *We give our thanks*
> *To the spirit of the earth,*
> *Which gave us this plant for healing.*

Pour the water over the plant, and imagine it is spreading healing light all over the leaves, stem, and roots.

Now the visualization between the recipient and the plant must occur. While you will use your own visualization to help the transfer along, they must participate in order for it to work. This ritual may require that you guide the recipient through their visualization if they're unfamiliar with spells. Below is an outline of what you can say while talking them through transferring their energy into the plant.

Have them lie down or sit inside the salt circle, holding the plant near their body in such a way that they can touch its leaves and stem. Do some relaxing breathing exercises before you begin. Read this passage to them or make up your own.

> *As you hold your hand against the plant, breathe in deeply. Imagine yourself surrounded with soft white light. Imagine the plant is also surrounded with this same light. As you place your hand on the plant, your energy merges together into one, as you both are filled with the same life force. Feel this life force going back and forth between your fingers and the leaves, like a vibration. It surrounds you both like a cocoon.*
>
> *You and the plant are one and the same. Your body is composed of capillaries and veins like tiny rivers. Inside the plant, there are the same veins and rivers that keep it alive. Your veins are filled with blood. The plant's veins hold*

life-giving water. Your bones hold your body upright. The plant has wood and strong stems to keep it standing. You and the plant are of the earth; you are made of the same energy as the rest of the cosmos. As you take your next few breaths, visualize all these ways you and the plant are one.

At this point, prick their finger with the lancet and place the drops of blood onto the plant if they wish to include blood in the ritual. This blood bonds them to the plant so the plant may act as the vessel for them (saliva can be substituted).

Now, pay attention to your body and energy field. Where is your pain? Emotional and spiritual pain will show up on your energy body. Imagine this as a brownish gray cloud sitting where your heart is. Inside this stormy ball is gathered all the sickness that plagues you. It may appear to be spinning and filled with sharp debris, causing pain where it touches. As it spins, it gathers up all the loose bits of the negative energy from your body. See this dark shadowy ball spinning in front of your chest, filled with all your pain and sickness.

Pause to allow time for their visualization to clear out their energy body.

Now see the cloud moving out of you. It shifts into your arms and through your elbows. It rolls down your forearms and into your wrists. Feel it enter your hands, and then push through your hands into the plant. Feel it leave your hands and fingers and enter the plant. Now see the plant filled with the cloud and yourself glowing stronger with light. See the sickness all around the plant's aura. Remove your hands and shake them off, severing the tie between you.

Now that they have transferred their pain into the plant, have them rest while you complete the ritual.

Place the plant on its side in the circle of candles. Hold your knife or axe in your hands and say:

> *Deities of darkness,*
> *Dark of the moon,*
> *Pit of transformation,*
> *Receive this illness.*
> *Remove it from (name) forever.*
> *We release this illness back into the earth,*

Where it will become neutralized,
Inert, and grounded.
So mote it be.

Cut the plant in half. Either chop the stem in two, severing the roots from the leaves, or if it has many stems, cut them all with the knife. As you cut, see its life force snuff out and disappear, including the cloud of illness. What is left is only a skeleton of a plant, with no glow.

Bury the remains within the circle of candles.

Release the circle.

Sacrifice for Divination

This is a very simple sacrifice ritual based on haruspicy, or reading entrails. A similar plant-based practice can be performed using a very ripe pumpkin, gourd, pomegranate, tomato, or any fruit or vegetable that has lots of seeds and a somewhat firm shell. This is going to be messy, so doing it outdoors is definitely preferable. However, it must be on your own property so as not to be misunderstood as vandalism.

⇢ MATERIALS

Fruit or vegetable of choice, very ripe
Several drops dark moon water (see page 43)
Black or purple candle
Chalk for drawing on a hard floor or stick for drawing in dirt
Lighter or matches

Place your chosen vegetable or fruit on your altar and anoint it with dark moon water. As you rub water over its skin, charge it with psychic energy.

Light the black or purple candle. Hold it sideways and drip wax onto the skin or rind. Imagine the hot wax is imbuing the vegetable with psychic energy, marking it as ceremonial. Leave it overnight.

Draw or trace a circle on the ground after dark. Stand in front of it with the fruit or vegetable in your hands. Invoke the dark moon or your deity. Ask your question and drop your vegetable onto the circle. It's important that it is very ripe so it breaks open easily. If the vegetable you choose is too hard, it will not break open.

Now, sit down and scry the remains that are in the circle. Take note of shapes and patterns and any forms that look like pictures. Write down all your impressions and consider how they apply to your question.

When you're finished, be sure to clean up.

Dark Moon Blood Sacrifice

If you don't wish to fast or give up anything for three days, you can instead sacrifice your blood to the dark moon in exchange for knowledge, wisdom, or aid in your general working.

◆—◦ MATERIALS
Round black bowl of water
Sterile lancet

Cast your circle and gaze into the black bowl of water. It's absent of light like the dark moon. However, it is full of the shifting, moving power of water, filled with death and life at the same time. Water can kill and it can give life, as can the dark moon.

Contemplating this, prick your finger with the lancet and drop your blood into the water.

Say:

> *Dark moon, I offer my life energy to you*
> *In acknowledgment of your deep power.*
> *Let us be joined for this night*
> *Through blood and water and darkness.*
> *Grant me _____ in exchange for my blood*
> *So mote it be.*

Pour the water outside under the dark moon. Close the circle.

For the duration of the dark moon, remain receptive and meditate often. Be open to signs and symbols and pay attention to your dreams. If you've asked for guidance in your cursing, be mindful of the extra power being lent to you during this time.

Guide for the Deceased

Egyptian tombs contained evidence that when a leader died, their whole kingdom, including their family, servants, workers, and even animals, were killed and buried with them so they could accompany them to the afterlife. This practice was eventually replaced by the use of a Shabti, or funeral doll, instead of actual people. A Shabti was a small carved figure that was meant to perform a certain job in the afterlife, usually that of laborer or servant to their leader. Many Shabti were buried at a time, each with a very specific job to perform in the afterlife. The Shabti was carved from limestone or clay and engraved with a name and a purpose prior to burial.[17]

Many people are terrified of death and what comes after. If you have lost someone and want their spirit to experience a peaceful transition from this life to the next, you can create a modern version of a Shabti to act as a guide and bringer of peace. Create a figure that houses your feelings of comfort and well wishes for someone you care for and place it near them after they pass or during their transition. You should ask permission beforehand if you think they or their loved ones might be against the idea.

Shabti were usually human forms, but you can use the shape of a beloved or protective animal if you want. You can sculpt or carve the image out of clay, sew it yourself, or purchase a figure and paint it.

On the figure, carve or paint what you wish the figure to do. You may want them to protect someone, guide them, hold their hand, and lend them strength during their transition between lives. Spend a moment telling the figure its purpose while you paint or carve it. When it feels right, place the figure near the person who is dying to guide them from this life and the next.

Your funeral doll can also be placed near the grave or urn of someone who has already passed who you want to send peace and love to. If placing the figure near them is inappropriate or impossible, just keep it hidden in your own space somewhere, knowing that its spirit is accompanying your loved one to the afterlife. This may sound morbid. No one wants to even think about their loved ones dying. However, if this would bring you, and them, comfort, there's nothing wrong with following through with it.

---

17. Richard P. Taylor, *Death and the Afterlife: A Cultural Encyclopedia* (Santa Barbara, CA: ABC-CLIO, 2000), 320.

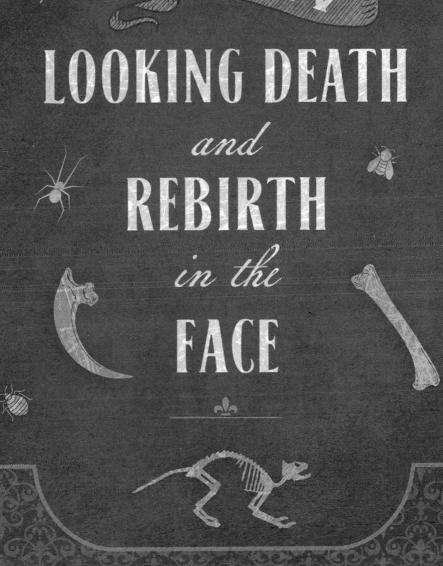

PART IV

LOOKING DEATH
and
REBIRTH
in the
FACE

If you ask almost anyone what their biggest fear is, you'll get some predictable answers: spiders, snakes, heights, fire. Why spiders and snakes? They're poisonous and kill people. Why heights? You can fall and die. Fire? You can burn to death. All these different fears are a symbol for the same thing: death.

Death is ever-present in our lives, a shadow hovering over every moment of our existence. We all know it's coming for us. It's a fact of life. Yet many people spend their entire lives fearing death. Why is that?

If we believe there is more to life than just this earthly experience, and that our soul is bigger or separate from our egos, then what are we afraid of? Many fears are rooted in the notion that there is literally nothing after death and we're just snuffed out and gone. Death is treated very clinically nowadays in Western culture—indeed, it is kept hidden, considered a distasteful subject and spoken of mostly in metaphors. This makes death seem very mysterious and therefore frightening. A person typically dies in a nursing home or hospice facility, rather than in their home, surrounded by staff instead of family. Their body is taken to a morgue, and the remaining family barely sees them again, if at all. The funeral home takes over. This entire process, from the illness to burial or cremation, is done by outsiders and therefore keeps us very removed from death and prevents us from understanding it. Being near someone who is dying and keeping them company while they transition is very difficult but also healing for both people involved. Accepting death, looking it right in the face and spending time with it (natural cycles of darkness), is part of being healthy and happy.

Physical death falls under the umbrella of the dark moon current because it is a journey into the unknown. It's the ending of this life and the beginning of another.

CHAPTER 12
DEATH AND DEATH RITES

Because the subject of death is often hushed up in the Western world, many people never develop a relationship with death, particularly those who don't practice religion or spirituality. Due to this silence and the hiding away of death, so to speak, when it comes calling—and it always will—not everyone is emotionally equipped for it.

What if we were to think of death as a celebration? To believe our loved one has completed their earthly tasks in this life and is now free, at peace, and being reborn into their spirit self? Knowing our loved ones have moved on to the next stage of their spiritual development and are still accessible to us is very comforting.

The afterlife is generally thought to be a place of reward and happiness. It's a metaphor for the soul breaking free of its human form and moving on to something presumably less painful and limiting.

Death of a loved one is a huge life event on par with the birth of a baby. I like to compare birth and death a lot because both are inevitable, both are catalytic in our lives, and both are unavoidable. Birth and death are law. Death is the shadow of birth. They're connected, and while someone dies on this plane, I believe they're simultaneously being born into something else on another. The laws of nature indicate this. Everything that ends begins again, including our spirit.

DEATH AS PART OF THE CYCLE

Death and birth are two sides of the same coin.

You cannot have birth without death, and therefore, you cannot have death without rebirth. The moon dies in the sky every twenty-eight days, only to reemerge as a brand-new, bright, white slice of potential. It doesn't end or disappear; it only changes form. We can see that in everything around us. In nature, of which we are part, everything is cyclical. There is no end, only transition.

When a flower dies, it spreads its own seeds and then composts into fertilizer for the future seeds to grow. That flower never "dies" in the permanent sense of the word. It simply keeps changing and shedding its form: flower, to seed, to earth, to flower, to seed, to earth. Our bodies do this when we die, as in we drop seeds (our children, creations, or whatever we have contributed during our life), and then we become earth as our body decomposes, which creates food to feed our future life. Our souls, I believe, embark on a similar journey when our body dies. That is to say, our soul is part of something much bigger, just as our physical body is part of the larger functions of the earth's cycle. Our soul dissipates into a larger energy body or "the cosmos," which we're all part of, and continues to fill its role in the everlasting cycle. Where the cycle is leading no one knows. That's not for humans to understand, and we don't know until we die. This final understanding is part of the notion of "paradise" after death. We all are made of the same spirit and stardust, and when we die, I believe we return to it.

Death in Everyday Life

Death enters your life every day in big and small ways as you cycle through existence, just like the dark moon current. Every ending in your life is considered a small "death." Different aspects of your life end and change all the time. With every passing day, you are growing and shedding your past self the way a snake outgrows its skin. It's not a bad thing. Not all endings are sad: for example, the end of pain, hardship, and difficulty are all endings that should be celebrated.

If you are seeing omens or signs around you that seem to denote death, don't automatically assume that this means a physical death or that something terrible is coming your way. Take note of it, because spirit is showing it to you for a reason, and accept it with an open mind. It could be pointing to a transformation that is going to take place in your life. All transformation involves a death or ending of something, often for our own good.

Some examples of the death current passing through our everyday lives in mundane ways are changing jobs, ending a relationship, moving residences, and graduation from school. You'll notice none of those sounds like bad things. Perception is everything. Sure, losing a job can be bad, but many times it can be the best thing that has happened to a person, forcing them to broaden their prospects and experience new things. Perceived "endings" are not always negative and can in fact be celebrated in many cases. We should approach endings in our lives as precursors to growth. This can be intimidating, especially when it is a painful ending. But what if instead of focusing on the door closing, you chose to see the one that was opening? This isn't to say that ending relationships and jobs isn't painful or scary—of course it is. Worse, sometimes it seems like literally everything "goes wrong" at once. I'm reminded of the Tower card in the tarot deck, which represents huge, inexorable life changes that shake your whole existence down to the foundation, essentially making your life fall apart, but in the end are absolutely necessary for you to fulfill your destiny.

Remember that when you have an ending in your life, it is a stepping-stone to your true life's purpose, even if at the time you don't understand it. Change is still difficult and there will be hardship, but you will come out better and stronger because of it. This is the Crone or dark moon current cycling through your life.

Accepting the endings or "little deaths" in our lives creates a natural flow as old as the cosmos. Understanding that you cannot control everything and letting go is one of the healthiest things you can do.

Spell to Help an Ill Person Cross Over

This spell is intended to help a suffering person cross peacefully into their next life. I wrote this working for someone who was on their deathbed and very afraid to let go and as a result was suffering greatly. Those who have not watched death happen firsthand may not be able to comprehend the need for a spell like this, but those of you who have witnessed terminal disease will understand. There comes a point in a person's suffering when there is no turning back, a time when death is right there in the room with them, just waiting for them to join it. This lingering between life and death can go on for weeks or even months. This is understandable, as many people have been taught that death is a bad thing, and therefore they fight it. The dying person also knows that their death is sad for their loved ones and therefore may try to hang on for the sake of everyone else. Other times they are simply lingering in their earthly body out of fear of the unknown. Perhaps all those things are true. Part of having a dying loved one is wishing for them to cross over, not because you don't love them but because you know there is no choice but for them to go, and you wish to end their suffering. This is a perfectly natural feeling and comes from a place of love.

This spell is to let your loved one's spirit know that it is okay for them to go. It's meant to communicate to a dying person on a deep energetic level that they don't need to be afraid to leave the earthly plane. If possible, ask the person for permission before performing this spell.

You can use either a plant or a deceased animal for this spell. Whether you use an animal or vegetation, for the sake of simplicity I will call the object the "vessel."

⊷⊶ MATERIALS

Vessel

Biodegradable box in which the vessel can fit

Photo of the person. You will be wrapping it around your chosen vessel, so choose the size accordingly.

1 foot black yarn or string

1 foot black ribbon

Flowers

Piece of black cloth, large enough to wrap around the vessel

Pen or marker

Item of their clothing, a letter they've written, or some other thing they've touched. If this isn't possible, you may use something that represents their interests. For example, if they loved music, include a sheet of music, or if they liked gambling, include a playing card.

Put the vessel, box, photo, string, ribbon, flowers, and cloth on your altar. Cast a circle and call upon deity if you wish. A psychopomp may be helpful for this spell.

Write the person's name inside the box. Around their name, write some things you wish for them to experience, such as peace, freedom, and release. Write that you love them but that you let them go. If they are afraid of dying, you can add words of courage and strength. This can be very personal, and once you get started, you may find you fill up all the blank space on the box with text, both inside and outside. Think of it like you are surrounding them with loving words and encouragement to find release from their pain. It is also okay to cry during this, and adding your tears to the box can symbolize the love you're sending with them.

Lay the black cloth out flat and lay the vessel on top. Using the black string, tie the photo of the person to the vessel. If the vessel is small, you can roll it up inside the picture. Empower the vessel to represent the person and see them as one and the same. Surround it with the personal items. Spend time visualizing them, filling them with love, and picturing them being released and free from their bodily life. When you are ready, wrap the cloth around the items and use the ribbon to tie the bundle up. Tuck the flowers into the ribbon as a blessing. Place the vessel in the box. Close the circle.

Now you must bury the box outside where it will never be found or disturbed.

As you place the box in the hole and then cover it in earth, think of it as gently tucking the person into bed. They're headed to a place of sweet dreams and well wishes.

Remember to bury it deep enough that it will not be dug up, and cover the spot with a heavy stone or block.

DEATH OF A FAMILIAR

A familiar (or pet, as nonwitches call them) is a spirit in animal form who has chosen to spend their earthly life with you. Some live longer than others, of course, but no matter what, they're with you for a reason. As witches, our bond with animals, especially those who share our homes, is very strong. The death of a familiar is a sad time, but when you understand the great cycle, it's also accepted with peace and understanding. The familiar has completed their task here on earth, and it's time for them to go on to their next incarnation. To help accept this concept, especially while grieving, you can make a list of lessons you learned from your animal during their time with you and how these lessons can be applied to the rest of your life. These can be little things. For example, if your dog was always chewing up your shoes, you will have learned that this particular material thing isn't that important after all. If your cat insisted on sitting on you all the time, you may have discovered your softer, snugly side whether you wanted to or not.

Having an animal live with us changes our relationship with nature. Animals are earth, air, fire, and water spirits, depending on habitat, and being close to one teaches us that we are all connected and made of the same energy. That's why sometimes it feels like our animals understand us and know our moods despite not speaking the same language.

Keeping a Familiar's Remains

You may wish to preserve the remains of your familiar in the same way you have with other animals you've found. You can follow the instructions for cleaning bones in chapter 6 if you wish. The skull and bones of your special familiar can be excellent altar pieces or included in spells and amulets. If you don't wish to keep your familiar this way, you can instead hang on to a bit of fur, a claw, or personal effects to keep their energy close.

Sometimes the process of burying, digging up, and cleaning the bones of a beloved animal is difficult, even disturbing. If you feel this way, then by all means, leave them buried. Their spirit will still be accessible to you whether you keep their remains or not. I personally have left many of my familiars' bones to rest in peace in nature. Even though I may be, shall we say, pragmatic in terms of handling death, bones, and flesh, I still felt compelled to leave their bodies in the earth.

Whether you keep the bones of your familiar or not, their personality, strengths, and traits will live on in their spirit, which will stay with you. If your animal was loyal and protective in life, its spirit will have the same qualities after its body is gone. The spirit of a cuddly, affectionate animal will bring comfort when you ask it to. If your familiar guarded your home while living and kept intruders at bay, its spirit can be asked to do the same task.

Making a Casket for a Familiar

When your familiar passes away, your vet may offer afterlife services such as cremation and burial. In this case, they will have professionally made caskets and urns to choose from, and sometimes even a cemetery plot for pets, so you can visit your friend any time. Just as with people, memorial jewelry and other keepsakes can be made with their ashes, fur, and photographs.

But professional pet memorial services can be expensive and aren't always an option for everyone. An alternative is to bury your pet yourself, on your own property. Check the bylaws in your area to ensure this is allowed beforehand.

This casket can be made to hold the physical remains of your animal when buried or as a memorial box of their favorite items. If you're unable to keep the remains of your pet for burial, you can still hold a ceremony for your animal to honor it and achieve closure. Inside the casket or memorial box, instead of their body, you will put some of their fur, toys, and other small things that hold their energy. This is also an option if your animal is too large to bury yourself.

Select a box made of natural materials, such as wood or biodegradable cardboard. When it comes to a family pet, involving children in decorating the box can ease their pain a little, as it allows them to send love to the animal. When my cat died, I drew a picture of the Egyptian goddess Bastet on the box, along with an ankh for eternal life (this particular cat really resembled pictures of Bastet, so I felt it only fitting). You can write your pet's name on the box and add words, symbols, or pictures that seem appropriate. Here are some symbols of eternal life:

Ankh: This looped cross is shown in a lot of ancient Egyptian art and is the symbol for life itself.

Infinity Symbol: An 8 on its side. You can trace this shape and it will never end, symbolizing the ongoing nature of existence.

Meander or Greek Key: These interlocking right-angle spirals represent the unending flow of life.

Moon Phases: All the moon phases together encompass birth, death, and rebirth.

Ouroboros: The snake eating its own tail represents birth coming from destruction. In other words, life from death.

Simple Circle or Knotted Circle: A circle has no ending and no beginning, just like our soul's journey.

Spiral: All life moves in the circular motion of the spiral, always moving and changing, never ending.

These are only a few options. If you look into your own ancestry and family history, you may find symbols that speak to you as well.

FUNERAL RITE

This is a generic funeral rite that can be performed for a person or familiar.

When you perform a funeral rite for a person, there are some outside factors to consider. For example, their family and relatives may have their own traditions already that they will be performing according to their own beliefs. Respect this. You can always do this funeral rite later on, or even from a distance, in a way that will not cause them any more distress than they're already experiencing.

Remember that cemeteries are public. Whatever you are doing to honor the dead will be visible to passersby. I think most people would be respectful when they see someone honoring the dead, but be warned there is the odd nosy grouch who might report you if you light a candle in the graveyard (I wish I was kidding).

Also, the rite mentions burying a box of the deceased's favorite items. If you do this ritual in a public cemetery, skip the burial part and simply put a lid on a box and take it home with you, as digging in cemeteries is frowned upon. If the act of burying the box is an important part of achieving closure for you, consider performing the ritual on your own property so you can dig a hole without attracting trouble.

The ceremony can be performed at the gravesite of the deceased after the traditional funeral has already happened. It can even be performed for someone who died in years past. You can visit a person's grave any time and perform this rite as a means of honoring them and finding closure. If you're unable to visit the grave or feel it is too public, as I mentioned, you can perform this ritual at home.

If you're doing this ritual for an animal, it can be performed wherever you choose to lay your familiar to rest, whether in a commercial pet cemetery or at home. In this case, the box mentioned may contain the remains of your familiar, and the gifts can be placed inside the box as well. The box should be buried afterward. If you are unable to keep the remains of your pet, you can place some of their special items in a box to bury instead.

This ceremony involves a small temporary altar, a box of remains or objects, a burial spot and some ritual items.

⟿ MATERIALS FOR THE ALTAR

Small table to build the altar on or another flat surface

Photo of the deceased

Bowl of their favorite food or drink

Item belonging to them

White candle in a jar to protect it from wind. It's important to choose a chime candle or other small, fast-burning candle, as you will be letting it burn out during the ritual. A candle that burns for hours and hours is not ideal.

Flowers

Place these items on the altar in a way that is aesthetically pleasing and honorable to your loved one. Surrounding their picture with flowers is a great place to start.

⟿ MATERIALS FOR THE CIRCLE CASTING

Stick of incense

Yellow candle in a jar

Bowl of rainwater

Bowl of earth or salt

⟿ MATERIALS FOR THE OFFERING

Bottle of milk, juice, wine, or beer

Small glass for each attendant

⟿ MATERIALS FOR THE CEREMONY

Appointed person to act as orator, or speaker. This person doesn't have to be ordained in any way and can even be a loved one of the deceased if they're able. If not, they can be a trusted friend or family member.

Gifts for the deceased to see them through transition peacefully, such as coins, a guardian doll, lucky items, or well wishes written on paper. Allow people to choose their own gifts if they wish, as they may have something personal to add. If not, use the suggestions on page 261.

Box containing items that were important to the deceased, representing things they enjoyed.

Straw or long grass about 3 feet long, braided and tied into a circle shape. You can do this yourself or purchase one already woven. This will be left on the gravesite to decompose, symbolizing the impermanence of life.

Gather together by the gravesite of the deceased if possible. Place the altar and box of important items in the center of the circle. If you are burying the box, dig the hole for it ahead of time. Light the white candle.

Cast the Circle

The orator can cast the circle themselves, or you may appoint one person for each of the directions.

Standing in the east, hold the lit stick of incense up. Walking clockwise around the assembled people, say:

> *Spirits of east,*
> *Powers of air,*
> *We honor and invoke thee*
> *To help carry the soul of (name)*
> *On their journey into the afterlife.*

Place the incense in the eastern corner.

Light the yellow candle and face the south. As you walk around the circle, say:

> *Spirits of the south,*
> *Powers of fire,*
> *We honor and invoke thee*
> *To transform the spirit of (name)*
> *On their journey into the afterlife.*

Place the candle in the south.

Hold the bowl of rainwater in your hands, facing the west. Walk around the circle clockwise, sprinkling the water from your fingertips. Say:

> *Spirits of the west,*
> *Powers of water,*
> *We honor and invoke thee*
> *To cleanse and comfort the soul of (name)*
> *On their journey to the afterlife.*

Place the bowl of water in the western corner.

Face the north. Walk around the circle, sprinkling earth or salt from the bowl. Say:

> *Spirits of the north,*
> *Powers of earth,*
> *We honor and invoke thee*
> *To accept and comfort the soul of (name)*
> *On their journey into the afterlife.*

Place the bowl of earth in the north corner.

Now, everyone joins hands, holding them high above their heads in a circle. Everyone says:

> *Great spirit,*
> *Kings and queens of death and rebirth,*
> *Ancient power that lives within us,*
> *We honor and invoke thee.*
> *Receive (name) back into the whole*
> *In perfect love and perfect trust*
> *In a perfect circle that never ends.*
> *The circle is cast.*

Make the Offering

In this ritual you're asking nature, the universe, and spirit to reclaim the earthly remains as well as the soul of the deceased. First, you'll make an offering to the land on which this is being done. Have a large bottle of wine, milk, juice, or beer and enough glasses for everyone present (use a nonalcoholic beverage if participants are underage). Everyone assembles in a circle around the area where the burial will take place. If you are at a cemetery, stand around the existing grave. Give each participant a glass with some of the drink in it, including the orator.

Everyone holds their glass up to the sky.
The orator says:

> *Sun and moon, star and sky,*
> *Wind filled with spirits,*
> *Whispers of the dead,*
> *Accept our offering as we return (name) to nature.*

Now everyone holds their glasses near the ground.
The orator says:

> *Earth and roots, stones and bones,*
> *Home of death and rebirth,*
> *Peaceful resting place of the dead,*
> *Nurturing place of birth,*
> *Accept our offering as we return (name) to the earth.*

Everyone says in unison:

> *As above,*
> *So below.*

All participants take a sip from their glass. Then everyone pours the remaining drink onto the earth at their feet. Set the glasses aside.

Perform the Ceremony

The orator takes the white candle from the altar and places it into the grave or on the ground. Have everyone gather the gifts they would like to bury with the box.

While placing the candle, the orator says:

> *This is for safe passage, to light your way in the darkness.*

Go around the circle clockwise, with participants each placing their gift into the grave or box, stating what they are for. Here are some examples of suitable gifts and wording to accompany them:

Bit of Food: "This is to sustain your spirit on its journey."

Crystal: "This is to reconnect you to spirit."

Doll or Poppet: "This is so you will never be lonely and will carry us with you."

Paper Heart: "This is my love which, will be with you."

Thorn: "This is to protect you."

If people have chosen their own personal items, they can add them as well, briefly explaining their significance.

After the gifts have all been placed in the grave or box, pass out one flower to each person.

Allow the candle to burn out while sustaining a moment of silence to contemplate the deceased. When the candle goes out, place the flowers in the grave or box one by one.

If you're burying the box, place it in the hole now. Everyone takes turns shoveling earth onto the box and refilling the hole. If you're in a cemetery and are not going to bury the box, simply put the items inside it and close the lid.

Everyone stands around the grave, holding the grass wreath. Make sure everyone has one hand on the wreath. Chant all together:

> *As above, so below*
> *As within, so without.*
> *Death and birth, birth and death.*
> *We honor the great cycle*
> *And release (name) back into spirit*
> *Until we meet again.*

Place the wreath on the ground.

Release the circle by having all participants walk widdershins around it, while the orator says:

> *We release the circle into the universe*
> *The circle is open but never broken.*

You may wish to leave the altar items outdoors for some time if weather allows. Leave the grass wreath on the ground and allow it to naturally decompose.

If you don't want to bury the keepsake box, you can keep it in a special place in your home instead.

If you perform this rite for a familiar, you may want to have their remains in the box as well for burial.

TEARS IN MAGICK

Crying is universal. Every single human being in the world does it to release sadness. Tears can be contagious too: some people can't help tearing up if they see someone else doing it first.

Like blood, tears are a powerful fluid packed with meaningful energy. There are all different kinds of tears: tears of anger, tears of loss, tears of compassion, and even tears of joy. Very rarely are tears—real ones—ever meaningless or frivolous. When you look at it this way, tears are very powerful little drops of energy!

Some researchers think that tears evolved as a means of signaling distress to other humans, and there's no denying that when someone cries, they send out a big cloud of emotional energy that we react to whether we like it or not, sometimes with extreme discomfort. These days it is sometimes considered shameful to cry and people become very embarrassed by it. However, Dr. William Frey of Ramsey Medical Center in Minneapolis found that emotional tears release stress hormones and increase endorphins in our brain, which explains why you feel better after a good cry.[18] So I say, let the tears flow. It's healthy.

Here are some ways that tears can be used in magick:

- Collect some tears during a crying spell (no pun intended) in a jar or on a leaf. Pour the tears (or drop the leaf) into a river or fast-moving body of water. Ask the water to dispel your sadness and neutralize it.

- Put some of your tears on top of the grave or urn of someone who has died. When you cry over the loss of a person, the tears you shed are because you love them, when you get right down to it. Let your tears carry that message to their spirit.

- Wipe the tears from your face with your fingers and hold them over a candle flame. As they evaporate in the heat of the fire, ask that your sadness also evaporate. Like the tears transform from water into vapor, ask fire to turn your sadness into a new form.

---

18. Judith Orloff, "The Health Benefits of Tears," *Psychology Today,* July 17, 2010, https://www.psychologytoday.com/ca/blog/emotional-freedom/201007/the-health-benefits-tears.

- Add a few tears to a poppet you are making out of clay. If the poppet is part of a reversal spell toward someone else, adding your tears to it will make them know the same level of anguish as you. The same can be done with a photo of a person who has made you cry.

- Gather your tears in a jar. Meditate on it, stare at it, and will the energy you see in it to change from sadness into happiness. You can do this by imagining it first surrounded by muddy gray light and then turning it into bright white pure light. Then drink it, letting your body transform it into something new and positive.

- Keep your tissues from a crying jag and then burn them all in a fire to banish a situation or influence.

FUNERAL CRAFTS

Memorial Witch Ball

This type of customized ornamental craft has been done for many things, typically for decorations on a holiday tree. You can make a memorial ornament honoring your loved one to add to the tree or, if you prefer, display as a Samhain decoration.

To make this, all you need is a transparent, empty Christmas ornament, the kind you can open and place things inside. What you choose to put in it depends on what items you have that belonged to the deceased and how well you knew them. Here are some suggestions:

- Ribbons of their favorite color
- Strip of their handwriting
- Dried bits of their favorite flower
- Symbols of their hobby or profession, such as a musical note for a musician or yarn for a knitter
- Lyrics from their favorite song written down
- Piece of their jewelry
- Coins for good luck
- Crystals in their favorite colors
- Stones or sticks from a place they loved or from where they grew up

Hang this ball somewhere you do spirit work, on your holiday tree, or as a Samhain decoration. These can be as varied and have as much personality as the people they're dedicated to.

Funeral Flowers

Most funerals have elaborate arrangements of carefully selected flowers on display. Guests of the funeral bring flowers to honor the dead and offer sympathy to the living. Flowers are a means of communicating the complicated feelings that surround death when you don't have the words. It's a tradition that people give bouquets and wreaths to be displayed at the funeral or celebration of life when someone dies. Leaving flowers on gravestones as an offering to a deceased loved one is also still done often today.

The lifespan of a flower is fleeting, just like ours. In the olden days, the people who laid the flower arrangements on the grave at a funeral were chosen with as much care as pallbearers. Usually women, these flower tenders were typically the nearest and dearest to the deceased, and laying the flowers was an honor.

You can keep some flowers from the funeral of a loved one to dry and use for various purposes.

Hang the flowers upside down in a dim, dry place before they start to wilt. This will help them retain their color and shape. When they're dry, you can display them in an arrangement or keep them for future use.

You can burn some of the flowers and add the ashes to your witch's salt mixture, especially if you use it for blessing a space.

If you manage to keep a flower mostly intact, you can place it on your altar during workings in which you want to include your loved one. You can also press the flowers when they're fresh, using a large heavy book or a flower presser. This will flatten and dry the leaves and petals, which retain their color and can be integrated into many crafts. You can use them to decorate the outside of candles for devotional work by painting melted paraffin or soy wax over them as glue.

Healing Flower Powder

Flowers are offered at funerals as a sign of respect, sympathy, love, and peace. Once the flowers you've selected are dried, crush them with a mortar and pestle into the finest powder you can and store it in an airtight jar. This is a healing powder that can be used during grief, as the flowers hold on to the spirit in which they were given—that of love, sympathy, and support. Add this powder to healing sachets and incense or sprinkle under your bed to bring healing while you sleep.

Dried Flower Beads

You can make dried flower jewelry by integrating pieces of flowers into simple beads.

⤙ MATERIALS

Oven-bake clay in your choice of color. Transparent clay makes for an interesting look. Lighter-colored clay will show the dried bits of flower better than a dark color.

1 tablespoon of crushed dried flowers

2 feet sturdy wire

Oven

Break off a small piece of clay about the size of the bead you'd like to make. Work it in your hands until it is pliable. Add a pinch of dried flowers and knead them in with your fingers. The result will be a sprinkling of dried flowers in the clay. You only need a pinch, because if you add too much, the clay will crumble apart. Mold the clay into the shape of bead you'd like, and then press the wire though the center to make a hole. Leave it on the wire and bake the clay in the oven according to the package directions. You can place as many beads onto the wire as you can fit, as long as they don't touch each other.

Once cooled, remove the wire. Your beads are complete and ready to be strung. You can make jewelry, mobiles, ornaments, or even wall hangings. The jewelry will be specifically dedicated to your loved one because of the flowers in it. There are many artisans out there who craft incredible jewelry using polymer clay. Look online for inspiration.

You can also have a variety of jewelry custom made from the flowers using resin and other methods.

Dried Bloom Garland

Dry the funeral flowers upside down as described. This will leave them with the petals and heads intact on the stem. Carefully cut the crowns from the stems. Using a needle and thread, gently string the dried flower heads together into a long strand. This creates a garland of dried flowers. You can put this on your ancestral altar or use it as a Samhain decoration.

Ancestor Incense

You can mix some bits of the dried flowers with other ingredients to create incense specifically for honoring the deceased. Mix equal parts dried funeral flowers, frankincense, and dry mugwort.

Burn this incense mixture on your ancestor altar or any time you are inviting the person to join in your rituals and spells.

Ancestor Amulet

Your own family members, as long as you had a good relationship with them in real life, are your best spirit allies. They are rooting for you and always there to help you. This spell is to ask one or more of your family members or friends who have passed to protect you in general when going into any situation where you feel vulnerable. It can be carried in your bag or hung on your car mirror for protection.

⊶ MATERIALS

Flower from the funeral of a loved one. You can include more than one person if you wish. If there are no flowers, try some moss from their gravestone or a pinch of dirt from above their grave.
Small piece of mirror, to reflect harm away from you
Tiny bottle with a tight-fitting cork, available at most crafts stores
Glue

Place the flower and mirror in the bottle. At your altar, ask the spirit of your loved one to guard you, watch over you and deflect harm and negativity away from you. Tell them specifically in what area you need to feel protected (e.g., while driving, out walking, or on public transit). Glue the cork in place and keep the charm with you to carry their protective intentions everywhere you go.

CHAPTER 13

WORKING WITH THE DEAD

While I don't consider myself a necromancer, there is most certainly a place in my practice for my ancestors and loved ones who have gone on to their next life. Sometimes this is simply having something of theirs present on the altar to invite their blessing, while other times they make themselves impossible to ignore when they want to be included. This has happened to me more than once by surprise.

Including ancestors in your practice can bring depth and meaningful energy to spells and rituals that otherwise aren't there. However, before inviting them into your magick, you have to be comfortable with how it feels to have contact with them. This is best learned by working with someone you had a good relationship with or who was at least a benevolent force in your life. You don't want to call upon those who inflicted pain or violence, unless you're experienced and ready to confront the issue and transform it into healing. This is a huge process all on its own.

METHODS FOR CONTACTING THE DEAD

While some people prefer to use tools for a very clear response from spirit, one that they can see with their physical eyes, it's my experience that it helps to allow for more subtle contact than that, which means meditative practice. Achieving this open, calm state is a stumbling block for many people, but it is essential for doing work with spirits. Spirits are on a completely different plane than us and can't always move or impact physical objects here on earth. However, these tools can be useful for those just getting started.

A popular way to contact the dead is with a Ouija board. This is a board with the alphabet and numbers zero to nine painted on it, along with a spade-shaped object called a planchette, which is supposed to move around on the board and point to letters, spelling out messages. Some say that a Ouija board is a gateway for all kinds of negative entities to enter into our world, and that using one is dangerous. I tend to disagree with this. If you are curious about using a Ouija board but are frightened, consider creating a protected safe space within which to work. You can cast a circle beforehand, visualizing a sphere of white protective light around you while you work. You can request that your ancestors shelter you, or burn a candle dedicated to protection. To use a Ouija board, you place your fingers on the planchette and ask a question of spirit. The planchette is supposed to move of its own accord, pointing to letters and spelling out messages, but in my experience, it is not so simple nor passive. A spirit rarely reaches invisible fingers into our world to shove objects around and spell things (although it can happen). It's far more likely that the spirit will come through your own subconscious and use your fingers to push the planchette. This may feel at first like you're just doing it yourself, but, again, it requires a meditative and open state. Allow the planchette to move and see where it lands, even if you feel like it's your own doing. A spirit is far more likely to come through your subconscious mind than through a plastic planchette.

The same can be said for pendulums. A pendulum is a weighted object on a chain or thread, often made of crystal or stone. It's suspended from the fingers, questions are asked, and its movements are interpreted. While it would be great to just ask questions of the dead and get yes and no answers as clearly as a nod or a shake of the head, it's usually not that straightforward. With a pendulum, a meditative state is also absolutely necessary, and you may feel like you're moving it yourself. It could be that your arm was pushed by your subconscious mind to move the pendulum back and forth, and that spirit was nudging your mind in the first place. Establish before you begin what the movements of the pendulum mean. Back and forth typically means no and side to side means yes. Also give a specific meaning to circles and figure eights before establishing contact.

Automatic writing is an effective technique that asks spirit to come to you through the written word or pictures done in your own hand. Have a pencil and large piece of paper ready. Ask the spirit to communicate with you. Start by just closing your eyes and drawing figure eights or circles, until you feel compelled to move the pencil in a different direction. On one hand, you may just scribble during the interaction and afterward examine the markings to see if there are symbols, letters, or words in it. You might also feel compelled to write actual words down while making contact, which is an interesting exercise.

Other techniques are gazing at a candle flame and ask spirit to communicate through the movements of the fire, inviting them to come to your dreams while you sleep, or simply asking for a sign.

A Word on Mediums

A medium is a person who believes they can connect with the dead on behalf of others, typically for a fee. While some mediums are very convincing and really do seem to be connected with your loved ones (for example, they identify very specific things they couldn't possibly have known about you), it's my belief that you must be very selective in who you give your money to. When you lose someone you care about, it can seem like all you want is some closure, and you can feel a desperate need to connect to them, but this is when you're most vulnerable to being taken advantage of. Some so-called psychics are simply really good at what is called cold reading. They ask a few leading questions and then, based on subtle cues like body language, clothing, age, language, and education, come up with a very vague, broad statement that the querent will then give meaning to all on their own, agreeing with the reader and supplying them with more information to work with. Next thing you know, the half-hour time slot that cost a hundred dollars is over, and while the psychic did most of the talking, you yourself gave their generic words personal meaning all on your own. I'm not saying all readers are like this—many are intuitive counselors who really do provide insight and guidance and are not out to scam anyone.

There are no hard and fast rules to finding a reliable medium that is the real deal, but going on word of mouth helps. If someone you respect has recommended a medium and believes in them, that's better than just choosing a stranger on the internet and sending them money. It's also said that you will find the perfect medium when the universe wants you to, and it will happen naturally. I must confess, I think that any contact a medium can make with

your loved one is contact you could also make yourself with practice. However, working with a medium can open the door to your own spirit connections and set you on the path.

RECONNECTING WITH YOUR LOVED ONES

You don't have to be casting a spell to ask your loved ones to pay you a visit so
you can feel their presence or receive a message from them. This is a simple
meditation to connect with someone who has passed. While this isn't a means
of gaining anything from them or asking for help, it is a way of coming to
terms with their death and gaining insight into what comes after. It also makes
it very clear, when done correctly, that there is in fact something after this life.

When I did this, I was surprised at how practical the messages from my
loved ones were. It was very much the sort of advice they'd give in real life,
about my work, finances, and my relationships. There were no astounding
revelations for me, but maybe that's because I've had the privilege of easy relationships with my family both living and dead. If someone has unfinished
business or regrets over their relationship with you, they may convey that. This
can be cathartic for those still living as well as for the spirit, who may be restless due to the pain you're carrying. However, this can also open old wounds,
so like I said, it is maybe best left for when you are ready.

Do this ritual in a quiet time when you will not be disturbed or distracted.

Have on hand an object that belonged to the deceased. It can be a piece of
their clothing or jewelry, a beloved trinket, a bit of their handwriting, or (in the
case of my grandma) some of their knitting. Choose an object that reminds
you of them, preferably one that you remember them using, wearing, or handling. This creates a strong energetic reaction of memory and triggers visual
images of the person, which is helpful in connecting with them. If you don't
have anything of theirs, try using a photograph instead.

If you know of music they preferred, you may wish to play some. If you're
unsure and are calling on your ancestors in general and not a specific person,
select music that is from their heritage to the best of your knowledge. As you
play the song for them, enter into a meditative state using the technique on
page 57. Hold on to the object and welcome their presence. It will seem like
memories at first, but as you relax into your practice, you may discover that
you can smell their scent or just sense their company. Their energy will feel

the same way it did in life. There's nothing to be afraid of if you had a positive relationship with this person. If they loved you in life, they will love you still, sometimes in a way that is clearer than ever before now that they are free of their human complications and problems.

In my experience, I know my family member is present because I can actually feel them near me in the form of heat or pressure nearby. Some people can see auras and energy of the departed, while others hear their voice. For me, the feeling of having them near is the same as having them with me in their earthly life, a sense of having someone physically beside me or in front of me.

Allow yourself to be completely open, and don't worry about judgment. You may feel an urge to talk to them out loud, and that's fine. Say hello and be receptive. Notice what immediately starts to float around your mind. Did you suddenly think of your marriage? Your children? Your phone bill? Those are what your loved one is also concerned about and is communicating to you. Seems mundane, I know, but in my experience that is how it goes! You may be expecting a ceremonious hello, but the spirits of your loved ones have been with you all this time and often will just jump into what they want to tell you, now that you've finally opened up to them. My mother was always worried about whether or not I was keeping my house clean, and she still is! Seems like a strange, random thing for a person in the afterlife to be thinking about, but it's her signature of sorts, and by slamming me with cleaning instructions, she's making herself known. Your loved one may be letting you know they're present by mentioning a thing they often did or talked about in their life, even if it's something as mundane as housekeeping, because it will help you recognize them.

It's important to be patient in this exercise, as it may take several tries to get comfortable and establish contact. From there, it takes time to get accustomed to receiving images, sounds, and feelings from spirits. Be relaxed, open, and unafraid. Let it unfold in its own way. Let go of expectations or how you think it's "supposed" to be. Let sounds, pictures, or words come in. If you feel prompted to talk back either with your mind or out loud, go for it. When you're done, write everything down to analyze later.

Everyone's experience is different based on the relationship with the deceased, but once you've gotten comfortable with having them present, communication will come easier. Your loved ones never just disappear. You don't have to make a big ritual of saying goodbye after each contact, as they're with you always. You'll find they send you help in daily life all the time once you learn to see it.

CONNECTING WITH ANCESTORS

We have discussed connecting with a loved one who has passed, but what about your lineage and all those people connected to you, by blood or in spirit, whom you never met? If you're lucky, you have seen photographs of your ancestors, but many people don't even have that. There may be tidbits of information passed down about your great-great-grandparents, but you have no idea what they looked like or what kind of personalities they had.

I myself have always felt a very close link to my paternal grandfather, although he died before I was born. I always felt deep down that he was somehow especially important to me and over the years I have seen again and again how I have the same traits and dreams that he had while on earth. He was a free thinker and a musician, a dreamer and a creator. However, he lived in a time when this kind of attitude was discouraged and all that mattered was putting food on the table, so he never got to fully realize his potential. He passed these traits on my father, who taught me also to be unique and to pursue my love of the arts for the sheer joy of it, even while he too was a laborer who had to keep his passions on the side. And here I am now, the first person in our family to have been able to turn my artistic and creative abilities into a career, despite having spent most of my life up until recently working in various low-paying manual labor jobs. I was faced with the same paradigm my forefathers faced and managed to break the cycle of endless work and lost dreams. This artistic strain began before my grandfather, and it will continue in my own bloodline until it has served its purpose here on earth. Many things take multiple lifetimes to come to fruition.

Ancestors pass their goals and ambitions down to you. It makes it seem like there's something bigger going on, doesn't it? Often, the people you are closest to in this life are part of that same task or goal. You are born to create change in your soul and those around you, to end a cycle in your ancestry or to bring something specific to the earthly plane. Sometimes you have to finish the work they started in their life. Sometimes you're a bit player in bringing change, as your actions in your daily life make small and steady impact on the collective unconscious. In the grand scheme of things, our lives are actually quite short, considering how old the earth is, and it can take several lifetimes for a large catalyst to manifest in a person.

Someone who is doing big things, whether it's being a central figure in social change or making any kind of historical imprint, is a culmination of their ancestors' experiences, feelings, and collective goals. Not everyone is the ultimate end goal of our ancestors, like a highly influential public figure, but they are part of creating that voice in the future. You are important. What you do here matters, even if it doesn't feel like it. You are part of something bigger. We all are.

You can invite your ancestors into your space, even if you don't know much about them, and ask them to guide you on your life's purpose. You may already have some ideas of what your life's purpose is but aren't sure. Working with ancestors is an excellent way to figure it out.

There are other spirits out there who may not have been blood related to you but are still an important part of your ancestry, history, or background in some way. You can call upon these people in exactly the same way you would a blood ancestor, as explained further on.

Ancestral Hand-Me-Downs

Just as you inherit passions and talents from your ancestors, you can inherit their pain as well. There are entire generations of people who live with the repercussions of traumatic events that happened to their family and ancestors before they were born. Those whose parents, grandparents, great-grandparents, and so on experienced genocide, violence, war, oppression, and slavery are just some examples of people who may have inherited trauma. Large-scale trauma like this reverberates through time like the echo of a gunshot, impacting generations to come. Typically, ancestral trauma is found in people descended from a group that has been marginalized based on race, ethnicity, or religion.

Inherited trauma can be seen on the earthly plane in many ways: how our current society still operates in a way that oppresses people of color and benefits white people is just one example. Even if humans were to somehow overcome and heal this imbalance, there is still going to be collective pain passed down generationally.

The same can be said of all the strong energetic forces that were alive in your ancestors. Their values, joys, pain, passions, beliefs, and life force are alive in you. These things don't just disappear when a generation dies; they stay in the energy fields of their children, grandchildren, and so on until they fulfill their purpose in the bigger picture. There are links to ancestors in folklore, mythology, and religion, as well as in more tangible forms, such as artifacts, traditions, art, and objects from their lives that have been preserved as antiques. Your ancestors are in your dreams and aspirations, the things you feel the strongest about. They're inside you and standing behind everything you do. When you think about it, every single person is an amalgamation of their ancestors physically, mentally, and spiritually. In this way, no one is ever truly alone.

If there is a recurring issue that seems to constantly repeat in your life no matter where you go or how you change, this could be the energy passed down from an ancestor.

Inviting Ancestors In

When working with ancestors you don't know anything about, make sure to sufficiently protect yourself energetically just in case, by casting a circle, asking a deity to shield you, or creating a physical barrier with a salt or chalk circle drawn on the ground around you. If you don't have a deity in mind, you can simply ask that the energy of the earth protect you and keep you grounded.

If you have some inkling of who your ancestors were, you can envision them and what they looked like, such as what clothing they would have worn during their time period. If you've heard any stories about them, use that to fuel your visualization. If you have an object that is a piece of your ancestry, keep it with you in your circle.

Enter a meditative state as described on page 57 and say either out loud or in your mind:

> *I welcome my ancestors to this circle.*
> *We share our blood,*
> *We share our souls,*
> *We share our mission.*
> *Be here with me now.*

Pay attention to what feelings come over you. You may feel positive, nurturing energy, as many of your passed relatives do love you and want you to achieve your life's purpose. Allow the feeling to wash over you and pay attention to images or sounds. Let your mind wander and see what they show you. You may feel one spirit or the presence of several different entities rising up around the circle. Spend some time focusing on each one, paying attention to their features, the emotions they send you, and what they're doing. The more often you do this, the more you'll notice personalities coming through or several distinct spirits returning repeatedly. Just like people, they will have different vibes.

Once you've established contact, you may recognize their influence in your day-to-day life in ways that have been there all along but you never noticed.

If you get a negative feeling from your ancestors, it could be that they were a chaotic force when living and left unresolved business behind. They may very well have been negative or worse, abusers of some kind, who have carried that energy into the other realm, not having overcome it. This is why you've protected yourself before making contact. You can maintain an energy barrier between yourself and them, while still gleaning information on who and what they were. Don't feel that just because you have an ancestor with negativity that you yourself are negative: you are part of changing it here on earth. If they're taking over your whole ritual and interfering with connecting to their spirits, you can tell them to leave.

Telling a spirit to leave is not an act of disrespect but one that is necessary for you to realize your own purpose. Firmly state that they are not welcome in your circle, and afterward cleanse the area with smoke from burning herbs of your choice. You may have to repeat this several times. If they still have not left, perform the cleansing ceremony on page 277.

You can perform this simple ritual to connect with your ancestors as often as you please to get to know them. After a while you might begin to feel them with you always and no longer need the ritual to connect to them at all.

Making an Ancestor Anchor

Once you have established a rapport with one or more spirits, you may wish to include them in your spell work just as you include the elements or deity.

Simply place an object that represents them in your circle and invite them in by feeling their presence. This object is what I call an "anchor," as it is a physical object that connects to their spirit directly.

Ideally, your anchor would be a photograph of the person at the height of their life, something they've worn or something they've touched, but this is not always possible. In that case, you can create your own anchor.

You can use a small object that reminds you of the person. This can be a figurine of a person or animal, or you can select a special stone just for this purpose. Go to a place where there are many rocks and stones, such as train tracks, a gravel road, rocky beach or path. Close your eyes, breathe deeply, and feel the presence of the spirit. Ask them to select a stone they would like to represent them, and open your eyes. The right rock will stand out and pull your attention to it. Take it home.

Cleanse the stone's energy by passing it through incense or leaving it out in the sun for a few hours. Then at your altar, place it in front of you. Envision your loved one sitting across from you. See their face, the lines or smoothness of it. Feel their energy and their love. See them reach out their hand and place it over the stone. Is their hand smooth? Wrinkled? Dirty from work or manicured? Place your own hand on the stone as well, and spend some time imagining the connection you are making with them, your combined energy going into the stone.

When this is established, prick your finger with a sterile lancet and add a drop of blood to the stone. (An alternative to blood is a few drops of wine or other drink.) You can allow it to dry on the stone, or wipe it off at the end of the ritual if you prefer.

It is done.

From time to time, such as every dark moon, repeat this ritual as an offering and to maintain contact.

When you wish to include ancestors in your spells and rituals, keep the stone or object in the circle with you to guide their presence in.

When you no longer need the ancestor anchor, you can cleanse and reuse it or bury it.

GETTING RID OF UNWANTED SPIRITS

Almost everyone has had at least one experience with ghosts or restless spirits. Typically, they're harmless, but sometimes they can take frightening forms that interfere with your daily life. Occasionally a presence can be felt that leaves you cold and filled with dread. They might even be able to move things about the home (such as shutting doors), flicker the lights, or make unexplained sounds. People can live quite happily alongside ghosts of the gentle variety; however, when you get a malevolent one, it can wreak havoc on your peace of mind.

Where does a ghost come from? My theory is that when a person experiences extremely strong emotion in a place, either from trauma, sickness, or another powerful event, they emit such a strong energy that even after they pass away, that emotion lives on in that location like an energetic stain. Whether this is due to a wish to be acknowledged or just because their will was very strong, you can feel it. Some people take a very literal approach to ghosts, believing that they are the actual soul of the person walking invisibly around a place, either reenacting their demise or expressing unhappiness with the current inhabitants. There are varying levels of awareness to spirits and ghosts, and everyone is different. Just as some people are very sensitive to lights or sounds, some people are receptive to spirit activity or energies from other beings.

We can all agree, however, that a malevolent ghost in the home can be disruptive to you, your family, and animals and needs to be removed. Here is a simple ritual to cleanse your home of unwanted spirits, ghosts, or malevolent forms. I suggest also doing a physical cleaning of the house first. Dust everything, throw out or donate any clutter, vacuum the floors, scrub the bathrooms, and wash the windows. As you do this, you're stating to the physical plane that you are cleansing the area.

This ritual is an aggressive cleansing, and the incense smoke involved will not smell very nice. That's why it needs to be done in weather when you can open all your doors and windows.

This ritual is designed in such a way as to ward off a spirit who is disruptive and mean, hence the commanding language. Like a stubborn person causing loud trouble, this kind of spirit needs to be told clearly to leave. However, if you sense the spirit in your house is sad or perhaps would be more likely to respond to gentler words, you can rephrase it however you wish.

This ritual is also good for cleansing the house in general after a big change or shift in your life.

⇠⇢ MATERIALS

Loud bell

Lighter or matches

Charcoal disk

Heatproof dish

Dried garlic mixed with bay leaves

Spritz bottle filled with lemon juice or brewed sage water. Mix the juice of
    1 lemon with enough water to fill the bottle, or boil a handful of sage
    in water, strain it after it cools, and fill the bottle with it.

Witch's salt (see page 49)

Open all your windows and doors as wide as they'll go. Make sure all closets and cupboards are open, even in the kitchen and bathrooms. Start at the uppermost part of your home if more than one story, in the easternmost room. Stand in the center of the room and ring the bell loudly. Notice how the sound vibrates in your ears for some time. Imagine that you can see the sound reverberating outward like a ripple in a pond, disrupting the air and energy in the room in a circle shape. This loud noise is meant to shake up the energy in the room, leaving clean white light in its wake. After the sound of the bell dies out, recite:

> *All unwanted beings must exit this space.*
> *You are not welcome here.*
> *I drive you out with light.*
> *Move on and don't return.*

You may have to ring the bell a few times in rooms that feel especially oppressive. Move around your home clockwise, ringing the bell in each room and stating your intention. Don't forget stairways or hallways. Do each level of your house, starting in the eastern room of each floor, including the cellar.

Return to the room you started in. Light your charcoal disk, place it on the heatproof dish, and set some of the garlic and bay leaves on it. Walk clockwise around the room with the smoke, being sure to waft it into every corner, inside each closet and inside cupboards. A fan is helpful for this, or you can blow the smoke with your own breath. As you walk the perimeter of the room, this smoke is now cleaning the energy that was loosened by the bell. As the smoke permeates every corner, nook, and cranny, imagine you are fumigating the area. See the negative energy running away, fleeing from the smoke like scared insects. Repeat this in each room in the same order as before. Take your time and visualize everything patiently. If a room doesn't feel cleansed, you need to burn more incense in there until it feels right.

Now begin again, this time making the rounds of your rooms with the spritz bottle of sage or lemon water. As you spray this around, see clouds of peace filling up every corner of every room.

When you are done, sprinkle witch's salt in all your windowsills and doorways that lead outside, visualizing the barrier it creates between your now cleansed, blessed home and outside energy, sealing the ghost out.

CHAPTER 14
REBIRTH

The dark moon current has come into your life, and now you know how to use it. But what next?

Perhaps you've now traversed the darkness and come out the other side. You've contemplated your inner fears, negative emotions, and your shadows. You've learned about death, rebirth, blood, dark magick, and all the mysteries of the night. You may be a little bumped and bruised, but you're definitely wiser and stronger.

Even if you are lost in the midst of your own dark moon phase at this moment, know that with every ending, there is a new beginning. After the dark moon current has taught you its lessons, the new moon will come, full of dreams, growth, and potential. It may not seem like it, but it's on its way to you right now.

Below are some rituals and spells to encourage growth and new beginnings, appropriate for when you've gone through a harrowing or dark time in your life but can see the light beginning to return. When you've fully worked through whatever darkness the Crone sent your way, it's time to let the light back in.

The things you have learned on the dark side will help you in your future tasks, whatever they are. Like I promised, morning always comes. Embrace the bright part of the cycle and grow!

SIGNS OF A NEW BEGINNING

In part 1, we discussed the symbols that pop up when you're entering into a dark moon phase in your life. Now that you're on the other side, you may notice a whole new type of symbol: that of new beginnings. This includes things like rabbits, flowers, sprouting plants, blossoms, songbirds, imagery of baby animals and people, eggs, and other growth imagery. You may not know exactly what they denote at this point, but just know that they're signs of new life coming your way. In the darkness, things have been growing and germinating in you. The end of your shadow work may feel as warm and relieving as the arrival of spring after a hard winter. What will you grow into?

Meditation for Welcoming Growth

Sit or lie comfortably.

Close your eyes. Take five deep, slow breaths, allowing your body to relax muscle by muscle.

Imagine your entire energy body is a black void, like the dark moon.

Become aware of your physical body. Imagine that it is made of deep, dark earth where worms turn and roots burrow.

Notice your breath. Imagine it is the very blackness of the night sky as it flows in and out of you.

Note your heartbeat and feel how it pushes the blood through your body. Your blood represents water, the deepest most hidden parts of the oceans where no human eyes have ever seen.

Feel the warmth of your body, how it generates its own heat. You are your own fire, constantly destroying and creating, burning with life force, incubating new growth.

Feel all the elements combined in you together for several breaths.

Now visualize a sun above you. You can feel its heat beating down onto your body. This warmth is benevolent and welcoming.

As you lie beneath the sun, notice how the night sky that is your breath turns it into bright blue daylight instead. Breathe in the bright, cheerful light deeply. Bring the sun power into yourself with your breath.

As you keep breathing in the sky-blue air, notice that the dark earth of your body is beginning to shift. Sprouts are emerging, nosing hopeful green tendrils to the surface, small and tentative at first but gaining strength. Leaves and stems push up through your entire body and start to grow. Your blood, warmed by the sun, keeps the new plant roots moist, while the heat of your body creates a warm, fertile bed for them to grow in.

Notice the little details of what is growing from you. What starts as a small green stub may become a tall blade of grass or unfurl into a brightly blooming flower. Maybe you are a whole field of flowers.

Fill yourself with greenery, blooms, and life. Your lush growth draws butterflies, bees, rabbits, and wildlife, while the roots of the blooms burrow through your body and become sturdily anchored there.

Spend some time lying there enjoying your own blooming growth. You are transformed from the darkness into a bright new beginning.

Open your eyes and welcome the light.

SPELLS FOR REBIRTH AND GROWTH

Road Opener Oil Recipe

Below is my own recipe for road opener oil. I use it to attract new beginnings by anointing candles with it, adding it to a bath, or sprinkling it around my property. You can also put a small dab on windows and doors to open the way for opportunities and fresh starts. You can even rub some on your pulse points each day. Some of my most meaningful, life-changing projects have begun with a bottle of road opener oil.

⭠⭢ MATERIALS

Key that has been used to actually open locks or doors before—not just an ornament

Witch's salt (see page 49)

Fresh flowers or herbs that are alive, not dried, preferably at the stage when they are just about to bloom

Pinch of rosemary or pine needles, or a drop of tea tree oil for cleansing properties

Olive or jojoba oil

Jar with a tight-fitting lid

Place all the ingredients in the jar.

You can empower this oil during the waxing moon phase; however, unlike the rest of the workings in this book, I recommend doing this in the morning sunshine or at dawn if possible. Draw a circle on the ground with a stick or chalk and place the jar inside it. Envision the purpose of each of the ingredients in turn, linking them to a life situation, like this:

Key: Visualize the key fitting into a lock and opening a door. Imagine doors of opportunity opening all around you in life.

Witch's Salt: This is cleansing, protective, and unique to your own energy. Imagine it acts as a layer of protection around you. This can be replaced with a drop of your blood if you wish.

Fresh Flower Buds: These flowers are on the cusp of bursting open with life, potential, and glory. Visualize how your own glory and accomplishment will take place in your life.

Pinch of Cleansing Herb or Oil: These materials have energy that cleanses away blockages and negativity. Imagine that which stands in your way being wiped away.

The olive or jojoba oil is just carrier oil, so there's no need to give it a specific job beyond holding everything together.

Shake the jar and observe all the different energies mingling together to create a potion of new beginnings. As day breaks, hold the jar of oil over your heart and spend some time visualizing your short- and long-term goals. Allow the jar to be filled with sun. Leave it in a sunny place for a day.

You can strain the oil if you wish or leave the ingredients sitting in it.

Earthing Spell

Sometimes when emerging from a dark period, it can take a moment to get your bearings. When in the midst of crisis or a dark moon current, you may have been distracted from life around you, even though it has been moving on this whole time. Now you need to realign yourself with waking life. This spell uses the grounding power of the earth to rebalance yourself as you emerge.

⊷ MATERIALS

Outdoor spot to sit

Foot bone or bit of hoof that fits in your hand or pocket. This should preferably be from a cow or other steady four-legged creature that embodies the stable, grounded earth spirit. Try to avoid fiery, unpredictable animals like a weasel or cat if possible. (substitution: a brown rock)

Find a place outdoors where you can place your feet or hands directly on the ground. This needs to be a place of actual earth or sand rather than cement or other man-made surface, as you will be digging a small hole with your fingers.

Cast a circle if you wish and invoke your deity. If you're in a public place and would rather omit the circle, that is fine.

Sit on the ground if you can or in a chair with your bare feet on the ground. Dig a hole in the earth before you that is just big enough to place the bone or hoof piece in.

Hold the bone in your hand and imagine that it feels heavy, almost like a magnet drawing it toward the earth. This is the grounded energy inside it. Place it in the hole and cover it with dirt.

Press your hand on top of the buried bone and concentrate on feeling the dirt beneath your palms. If you want, you can instead place your feet on top of it to feel the grounding sensation directly in your body as well. As the bone absorbs the grounding energy of the earth, say:

> *Element of earth,*
> *Stable and true,*
> *Ground me, steady me,*
> *See me through.*

Visualize the earth soaking the bone with heavy, steady vibrations.

Dig the bone out of the ground. Close your circle.

Carry the bone as an amulet, and any time you feel unsure or insecure, rub it between your fingers to ground and center yourself.

Filling the Void Spell

After doing shadow work, you may be left with a feeling like something is missing, because you've banished old habits and relationships. This leaves behind a hole to be filled with new positive things. This spell is to attract good energy into the space you have emptied of that which you no longer need.

You may not know exactly what you'd like to enter your life, but there's a good chance it involves some basic generic things, such as love, prosperity, spiritual energy, and good health. You can tweak this spell to be more specific if you like.

←•❸ MATERIALS

Jar with a lid

Items representing what you want to attract, such as one or all of these:
coin for money, heart charm or rose petals for love, pinch of ginger
root for health, or a quartz crystal for spirituality

Sterile lancet (optional)

Honey to fill the jar with sweetness (substitution: any sweet, sticky syrup)

Yellow chime candle to burn on top of jar

Gather your items at your altar and cast your circle.

Each item will be empowered one at a time and placed in the jar. The jar is empty and represents the hole of potential that is currently inside you waiting for new beginnings. Hold the jar against your heart and feel the nothingness inside it, how much space there is for new things in it. Put the jar down and pick up the coin.

Hold the coin in your hand and visualize yourself living with financial stability, with your bills paid and more. See it glow with green light. Place it in the jar.

Hold the heart charm or rose petals in your hand and imagine the type of love you'd like to attract into your life. This can be romantic, familial, friendship, or even self-love. See it glow with pink light. Place it in the jar.

Hold the ginger root and envision your physical self as full of energy, free of illness, and feeling great. See it glow with orange light. Place it in the jar.

Hold the quartz crystal and imagine yourself practicing spirituality in your chosen way. This can be a vision of meditation, spellcasting, or just an altar. See the crystal glow with white light. Place it in the jar.

Using the sterile lancet, add a drop of your blood to the jar (optional).

Visualize the green, pink, orange, and white light mixing together.

Take the container of honey or syrup and think about how sweet and sticky it is. Everything it touches is enrobed in sweetness and held in place by the stickiness. The stickiness is what binds the items and their intentions to you, drawing them into your life.

Pour the honey over the items and fill the jar completely. Put the lid on tightly.

Light the yellow candle and melt some wax onto the lid of the jar. Use this wax to stick the candle to the top of the jar like a holder.

As the yellow candle burns all the way down, dripping its wax all over the jar, visualize yourself with all these goals, living your best life. Allow the candle to burn out.

Close the circle.

Keep the jar somewhere you will see it each day, as a reminder of what good things can come your way.

Fire Visualization to Inspire Growth

The dark moon current corresponds with wintertime, when all is cold and dormant. After your own dark experience, you may be feeling frozen and unsure of how to move forward. Toward the end of winter, even while there's still snow on the ground, sap begins to run through the trees due to a slight increase in temperature. Even while the branches remain leafless, inside the tree is coming back to life as sap starts to move through its veins initiating the very first part of rebirth. This simple fire meditation is to get your spiritual blood flowing, so to speak, after a period of dormancy, just like sap running through a tree.

Ideally, you would do this sitting at a fire outdoors, but if that's not possible, a single green candle will do.

Sit in front of the fire or candle flame and pay attention to the warmth coming from it. Feel it on your skin and soaking into your body. Even with just a candle, when you hold your hands near it, the heat is very powerful.

Picture the veins in your body, which are just like the veins in a leaf or stem.

Hold your palms toward the heat of the fire and imagine it entering your hands, flowing up your arms and into your heart center. From there, it slowly creeps through your veins, filling them up with vibrant yellow light. Slowly at first, the light starts to move around your circulatory system. As the energy gains speed and brightness, it becomes warmer. Soon the energy should be flowing through your veins as freely as warm sap through a tree. Lower your hands and enjoy this feeling of your energy coming back to life. Continue until your mind begins to wander. Repeat as needed to welcome new growth and opportunities.

CONCLUSION

As you emerge from your shadow work, you may find that everything around you seems different. This is because *you* are different. Your perspective has deepened and expanded, balancing the light and the dark. Here are some things you may be experiencing as you cycle back into the light as your new self:

Emotional Stability: When you've looked long and hard at yourself, as you do in shadow work, you accept some difficult truths. This forces you to change yourself from within, and with this comes a calm acceptance of your own emotions. Understanding your own emotions and responses to life's events allows you to think objectively about situations. Next time you encounter hardship, you will have a far more level and reasonable reaction.

Inner Strength: Things you used to think you couldn't do, risks you wouldn't take, hardships you thought you'd never be able to endure … you've done some of those things now. Just as when you exercise a muscle in your body, it becomes more resilient, the same can be said for your spirit. Standing up to your own inner beasts has made you stronger on the inside, like you have the deep roots of a tree holding you in place. This will come through anytime you face adversity or negativity.

A Forgiving Heart: In the past you may have regarded certain people with anger or disdain based on their behavior or circumstances. You may discover that now you see their side of the story instead, and rather than pushing them away with dislike and avoidance, you can identify with their situation, sensing the core of what is really driving them. This transforms them from a monster into a frightened child, in your perspective.

Less Desire to Cause Harm: You will have gained a fuller understanding of curses, which can lead to the realization that you very rarely actually need them. When you first picked up this book, the idea of cursing your enemies may have sounded like a good solution to certain problems, but if you've done the inner work, there's a very good chance you've come to realize that most of those feelings can be conquered by looking inward at yourself.

An Acceptance of Endings: While grieving is an important part of loss, having done your shadow work, you'll now see the bigger cyclical picture. With a greater understanding of death and rebirth and being mindful of this endlessly repeating pattern in nature and the cosmos, you will be better equipped to handle change.

Understanding of Physical Death: In doing work with your ancestors, you may have realized just how much of them you have inside you. The same can be said for non-biologically related people who were special to you. You will understand that you are part of a bigger legacy, and that the people who came before you live inside you still, contributing to your life's purpose. We are all one and all working toward something much larger.

A Connection to Animal Life: Understanding and communing with the spirits of animals creates a strong bond between you and the natural world. For instance, you might realize you're not afraid of spiders anymore after you've done some spells with spider energy (this is what happened to me!). By working with the bones and therefore the collective spirit of creatures, you will appreciate and understand the living ones all that much more.

Cleaning House: Doing your shadow work means letting go of, or even banishing, toxic relationships and people in your life. This leaves so much room for positivity and growth. A new beginning means you can become and experience almost anything. It also means you are ready to welcome positive relationships and experiences into your life.

Knowing the Benefits of Sacrifice: Along with creating a bond with deity, sacrifice makes you stronger. During your sacrifice practices, you will have realized many things about your own needs and what is really important to your spirit. You will have gained an understanding of what techniques you employ to distract yourself from spiritual work or to numb yourself to life's difficulties, as well as discovered that you're strong enough to live without them.

Go forth into the darkness and do your work. Try not to get lost. Whether you exist in the dark or light right now, I wish you courage and insight as you cycle through this life and all the ones to come.

RECOMMENDED RESOURCES

BOOKS

These are just a few books that I found especially useful during my own shadow work for various reasons. You might want to read them too.

Dark Goddess Craft: A Journey through the Heart of Transformation by Stephanie Woodfield

This wonderful book is a collection of information about dark goddesses from around the world and includes detailed meditations and rituals to interact with each one.

The Pagan Book of Living and Dying: Practical Rituals, Prayers, Blessings and Meditations on Crossing Over by Starhawk, M. Macha Nightmare, and the Reclaiming Collective

This book examines all aspects of death, illness, and grief from a Pagan perspective. It goes into great depth on how to deal with the dying process of yourself and others.

Mysteries of the Dark Moon: The Healing Power of the Dark Goddess by Demetra George

This book very clearly explains the moon cycles, particularly the dark moon phase, and how they affect our lives and bodies. The author explores dark deity and the divine feminine.

Celtic Lore and Spellcraft of the Dark Goddess: Invoking the Morrigan by Stephanie Woodfield

This book has everything—literally everything—you could ever wish to know about the Morrigan and all her faces. It also includes rituals and rites to work with this triple goddess.

ONLINE SHOPS

Below are several places to purchase bones and preserved body parts of animals and humans.

The Bone Room
An American bone and curio seller with a good reputation.
www.boneroom.com

Skull Store
A Canadian bone and curio shop that is very clear about where and how their items were sourced.
www.skullstore.ca

Etsy
A worldwide crafter's website that sells all kinds of things, including animal remnants and bones sold as craft supplies. Use the search bar to find bone sellers around the world. If you're concerned about where the seller sources their parts, reach out and ask them prior to purchasing. Sometimes there are laws prohibiting the sale of animal parts between countries, so this website can be useful in finding a seller in your own area to avoid this problem.
www.etsy.com

BIBLIOGRAPHY

Ankarloo, Bengt, and Stuart Clark. *Witchcraft and Magic in Europe: Ancient Greece and Rome*. Philadelphia: University of Pennsylvania Press, 1999.

Baack, Gita Arian. *The Inheritors: Moving Forward from Generational Trauma*. Berkeley, CA: She Writes Press, 2016.

Beyer, Rebecca. "The Folkloric Uses of Wood Part VII: Black Locust." *Blood and Spicebush* (blog), July 9, 2016. http://www.bloodandspicebush.com/blog/the-folkloric-uses-of-wood-part-vii-black-locust.

Conway, D.J. *Maiden, Mother, Crone: The Myth and Reality of the Triple Goddess*. St. Paul, MN: Llewellyn Publications, 1994.

Cunningham, Scott. *Cunningham's Encyclopedia of Crystal, Gem & Metal Magic*. St. Paul, MN: Llewellyn Publications, 1988.

———. *Cunningham's Encyclopedia of Magical Herbs*. St. Paul, MN: Llewellyn Publications, 1985.

Day, Christian. *The Witches' Book of the Dead*. San Francisco, CA: Red Wheel/Weiser, 2011.

Digitalis, Raven. *Shadow Magick Compendium: Exploring Darker Aspects of Magickal Spirituality*. Woodbury, MN: Llewellyn Publications, 2008.

George, Demetra. *Mysteries of the Dark Moon: The Healing Power of the Dark Goddess*. New York: HarperCollins, 1992.

Hall, Judy. *The Crystal Bible*. London: Godsfield Press, 2003.

Kendall, Paul. "Hawthorn." Trees for Life. Accessed May 27, 2019. https://treesforlife.org.uk/forest/mythology-folklore/hawthorn/.

Lewis, Brenda Ralph. *Ritual Sacrifice: Blood and Redemption*. Stroud, Gloucestershire: Sutton Publishing, 2001.

Montanari, Shaena. "Hints of Skull Cult Found in World's Oldest Temple." *National Geographic*, June 28, 2017. https://www.nationalgeographic.com/news/2017/06/skulls-cult-turkey-archaeology-neolithic-gobekli.

Orloff, Judith. "The Health Benefits of Tears." *Psychology Today*, July 17, 2010. https://www.psychologytoday.com/ca/blog/emotional-freedom/201007/the-health-benefits-tears.

Piscinus, M. Horatius. "On Auguries." Societas Via Romana. Accessed July 8, 2019. http://www.societasviaromana.net/Collegium_Religionis/augury.php.

Polyphanes. "Writing a Defixio." *The Digital Ambler* (blog). Accessed May 27, 2019. https://digitalambler.wordpress.com/rituals/writing-a-defixio/.

Roderick, Timothy. *Dark Moon Mysteries: Wisdom, Power, and Magic of the Shadow World*. St. Paul, MN: Llewellyn Publications, 1996.

Romano, Aja. "The History of Satanic Panic in the US—and Why It's Not Over Yet." Vox, October 30, 2016. https://www.vox.com/2016/10/30/13413864/satanic-panic-ritual-abuse-history-explained.

Shreeve, Jimmy Lee. *Human Sacrifice: A Shocking Expose of Ritual Killings Worldwide*. New York: Skyhorse Publishing, 2008.

Stein, Elissa, and Susan Kim. *Flow: The Cultural Story of Menstruation*. New York: St. Martin's Press, 2009.

Taylor, Richard P. *Death and the Afterlife: A Cultural Encyclopedia*. Santa Barbara, CA: ABC-CLIO, 2000.

"The Sacrifice of Jesus Christ." United Church of God. Accessed May 27, 2019. https://www.ucg.org/bible-study-tools/booklets/fundamental-beliefs-of-the-united-church-of-god/the-sacrifice-of-jesus.

Van Beck, Todd. "The Value and Benefit of Funeral Flowers." In Lieu of Flowers. Accessed May 27, 2019. http://www.inlieuofflowers.info/index.php?s=4.

Woodfield, Stephanie. *Celtic Lore & Spellcraft of the Dark Goddess: Invoking the Morrigan*. Woodbury, MN: Llewellyn Publications, 2011.

———. *Dark Goddess Craft: A Journey through the Heart of Transformation*. Woodbury, MN: Llewellyn Publications, 2017.

SPELL INDEX